EARTHMIND

A Modern Adventure in Ancient Wisdom

EARTHMIND

A Modern Adventure in Ancient Wisdom

PAUL DEVEREUX

and

John Steele, David Kubrin

Foreword

Lyall Watson

HARPER & ROW, PUBLISHERS, NEW YORK
Cambridge, Hagerstown, Philadelphia, London
Mexico City, San Francisco, Sao Paulo, Singapore, Sydney

Published by Harper & Row Publishers Inc.

First US Edition

Created by Roxby Productions Limited
a division of Roxby Press Limited
126 Victoria Rise
London SW4 0NW

Editor: Gilly Abrahams
Design: Eric Drewery
Typesetting: Elite Typesetting Techniques, Southampton
Printed and bound in Yugoslavia

ISBN 0-06-015977-4

CONTENTS

FOREWORD

Everything changed in 1969.

That was the year in which, like a monkey in a mirror, we saw ourselves for the first time in those glorious photographs of the Whole Earth. We knew the world was round, of course, but seeing for ourselves was somehow different – and once we did, something astonishing happened. Something synaptic, that made us aware of our planet in a new and special way.

That was the year in which James Lovelock gave this awareness a focus and a name, drawing attention to Gaia, calling her the largest living creature in the solar system, making it necessary and possible to think about the world in more creative ways.

The Gaian point of view is turning out to be one of the most seminal of the century, forcing cosmologists, biologists, geologists and geographers to deal with the world in holistic terms, not in isolation, but as part of a complex galactic ecology.

We are, as a result, beginning to hear more about the planet's physiology, her nutrition and digestion. There are studies in progress on geometabolism and telluric healing. And, more cautiously, on the growth and maturation of a global nervous system. It is in this context that I find EARTHMIND so timely.

Paul Devereux and John Steele, as founder members of the Dragon Project, are well-placed to put the possibility of a planetary mind into scientific perspective. And they have, with David Kubrin's help on the historic side, put the whole question of a living, thinking world into its proper cultural niche. I welcome this collaboration as a bold step in the right direction – toward the creation and recognition of a world that is not only conscious, but also sentient and self-aware.

Lyall Watson

INTRODUCTION

It is a supreme irony that we had to leave our planet before we could really see it. When the astronauts showed us what our world looked like from space, it was as if a mirror had been held up for us to see our reflection. The image of Mother Earth, beautiful, fragile, dancing through space, was shuttled through the electronic communications systems around the globe and lodged indelibly in our minds.

This event was like a signal telling us that a particular time had arrived: the final moments of deciding how we are to regard our world and our relationship with it. The contemporary belief that the Earth is a dead structure that can be endlessly exploited simply did not match what we felt when we saw that media vision of the blue and white planet floating in the void. It was as if life recognized life.

It is, perhaps, a paradox that it was modern technology, and space technology in particular, that allowed this view of Earth to be obtained and to be transmitted to the minds of billions of people. But the triumph of that technology was not the putting of a machine into orbit, or men on the moon – it was the emotional and philosophical jolt made possible on a mass scale down on Earth. It was a crucial moment in planetary history that had to come; the technology was necessary to force us to look anew at our home.

The ghostly image of the Earth as seen from space has become an established media icon; we see it virtually every day on television, in newspapers, books, magazines and advertisements. This subliminal awareness of our planet has initiated an acceleration in ecological concern, in 'Green consciousness'. A process has been catalyzed. As a result, two philosophies are now locked in a struggle. There is the established, so-called 'economic' worldview that says we have to exploit the planet for the sake of 'progress', and that it is too expensive to change our procedures for doing so in any fundamental way. The opposing, emergent view says that it is too expensive *not* to change our ways, because the fine, intricately linked fabric of life on our planet is in obvious danger; a potential disaster is being sensed.

This emergent philosophy is now rapidly developing in stature, and there is a growing confidence that the Green view might prevail against its stubborn, deeply entrenched adversary. But the changes called for have not yet been completely perceived. For a whole cultural attitude to alter, we have to change more than our industrial processes – we have to change our minds. It will not be enough simply to try to alter our behaviour on a planet that is still conceptualized in the former way. If we are to survive as a species, we have to literally rearrange our worldview.

Many people in the Green and 'New Age' movements realize that the emergent philosophy is at heart a very ancient wisdom which states that the Earth is in some sense alive. Most cultures prior to our own held this view. It seems likely that we will somehow have to recover that belief, so that all our future actions can be governed by it.

The phrase 'the living Earth' means different things to different people. It is used somewhat glibly by various groups, virtually as a slogan, without the implications of the idea really being explored. Some New Age people use the idea as an emotional bath, relating to it simply on a *frisson* level. Others interpret the concept of the Earth being alive in the sense of the planet being the homebase of a complex skein of living things. Yet others use such phrases to denote the theory that the Earth regulates its processes – climate, interaction between living things and their habitat, and so on – as if it were a living organism. James Lovelock, the scientist whose Gaia hypothesis is discussed in this book, is the doyen of this group. He feels that biology and geology cannot really be separated, that life has interacted with its habitat in a single, 'tightly coupled process'. Although this falls short of any claim of the Earth being literally alive, Lovelock uses terms such as 'self-regulation' when referring to planetary processes – but how can a planet *self* regulate, if it does not possess some form of awareness? The question certainly requires serious consideration, because a process of regulation, of checks and balances, can only be achieved by use of a reference base, a memory of some kind. This cannot be effected without awareness – consciousness – being involved at some point in the process. It might be argued that non-living, non-sentient things such as computers contain memories, but the analogy does not hold. The mechanism is not the memory. However sophisticated the computer, its processes are initiated by human intelligence.

The idea of a living Earth is total anathema to conventional thinking within contemporary society, and even makes some Greens feel awkward. But despite the risks entailed, the purpose of this book is to pose the direct question: '*Is* the Earth alive?' Any consideration of such a profound and elusive aspect of the planet can only be an adventure of the mind at this stage, and the reader is asked to come along in that spirit. We must constantly bear in mind, however, that the idea of a living Earth would have been a perfectly normal, even self-evident, concept to most people living on our planet even a few hundred years ago. It is our present culture which is being eccentric in regarding the idea as a bizarre fantasy. The first part of this book, therefore, is a glance back at how the Earth was viewed in former ages and in traditional societies, and how we have virtually come to forget that view.

The second part of the book attempts to identify ways in which those old perspectives have started to come into our awareness again during the course of the twentieth century. These recollections have come in many unexpected forms: in the growing scientific knowledge of the interrelatedness of the different zones or 'spheres' of the planet, and of the way we are electromagnetically linked—body, brain and probably mind—with global processes and rhythms; in the study of sites left by ancient peoples; and in the ideas of modern, influential thinkers such as Lovelock, the scientist, Teilhard de Chardin, the priest—philospher who envisaged a 'noosphere' or zone of planetary consciousness, and the Irish nature mystic George William Russell, who wrote of his experiences of the magical nature of the landscape.

The final part of the book is a speculative inquiry into what the nature of the consciousness of Earth might be like, how it might be structured, and what the interfaces might possibly be between planetary and human sentience. Inevitably, these matters cannot be explored without considering the nature of our own consciousness.

Whether viewed simply as a mental exercise, or as a vital require-ment for future survival, the very nature of collating the living Earth concept means that many areas of human activity have to be brought together, even if it is too early yet for a full synthesis. There are endless narrow specialisms within science, and even the alternative and avant garde areas of research and awareness tend to be fragmented. From a purely pragmatic point of view, therefore, it is not possible in the following pages to go deeply into all the various aspects of the subject. Complex matters have been simplified as far as possible, keeping any technicalities to a bare minimum, so that the ideas and arguments can be shared by academics and non-specialists. Nevertheless, the text has all the necessary references in it for those who wish to follow up particular aspects in greater detail.

Various topics discussed in this book–for example, the new explorations of ancient sites–are in such early stages of research that little has been written about them before. As a result, some material is having its first public airing on these pages.

The provisional conclusions arrived at by the end of this adventure may differ from those of some readers, in which case let them by all means add their insights in their own ways. But let the process, once started, continue, for it is very urgent. The time is later than many of us like to think. Comments can be heard from even the ecologically aware that we are leaving a mess for our children to clear up. This is understating the situation. At this point on the cusp of the millennium, we can either make changes that will open up an entirely new era of human and planetary potential, or we will miss the last chance and not recover from the ecological slide which has so accelerated in our times. Just the single issue of the destruction of the rain forests could be the deciding factor. A whole chain of effects will be set in motion if they disappear. And when the global ecosystem starts to go down, it will go down like a stack of dominoes. The apparently isolated ecological problems we face now will develop into an avalanche effect. After that point, the matter will be too complex to put right.

Those who have to face the decisions are already present. We are not waiting for anyone else; no Space Brethren, no Star People, no 'male deities located off the planet' (to use Gary Snyder's phrase) are coming down to save us. We have drawn the short straw together. The new mental approaches that will be needed to underpin the necessary outer, material changes have to be sought now.

Paul Devereux

PART ONE

AMNESIA

Our modern culture is a little like a person suffering from amnesia. Something happened to cause a significant – but not total – loss of memory. Imagine that person, aware of having had a former life, but now cut off from it by a broken bridge of memory. Odd, isolated images can still be recalled, but connections cannot be made. Scraps of writings and occasional visits from acquaintances relating to that former life give fragmentary information about how it was. But, unable to make the connections, the amnesiac sets about making a new life, the former one gradually slipping away until it becomes like a hazy myth, no longer of any validity.

The record of archaeology, anthropology and history gives us a partial glimpse into the human mind as it was long before our own times. We can see the remains of objects and sites used by people in remote antiquity, and we can deduce from these how endless ages of nomadic human wandering (the Palaeolithic and Mesolithic periods, or Old and Middle Stone Ages) came to a relatively sudden end between about six and ten thousand years ago (the onset of the Neolithic period or New Stone Age), when settlement, agriculture and towns developed in Eurasia, the source of Western culture.

The overall picture which emerges shows quite clearly that most early peoples venerated the Earth, and their religious sensibilities gravitated around the worship of the land and nature. Earth was visualized as a goddess of birth and abundance: the nurturer and the destroyer. She was seen in the contours of the landscape, and represented in effigies – some of those found by archaeologists are over 20,000 years old.

We can trace the movement away from this awareness of the primordial Great Mother goddess towards the creation of dominant male deities and patriarchal societies as cultures became increasingly settled, defined and complex, and more warlike as territorial awareness hardened and the technological use of metal increased. These were all expressions of further changes in consciousness, from a diffused mental state merging like water with the environment, experiencing a slow, dreamy sense of time, to an increasingly isolated, 'harder' state of personal ego, separated from matter, running on the rails of linear logic and linear time.

In Europe these changes in mental perspective reached a climax around the seventeenth century, when the domination of nature replaced veneration for it. The soft-edged, intimate relationship with the Earth was finally replaced with the more distant, abstract outlook. This led on to the Age of Reason, the development of science as we know it today, and the foundation of our highly technological twentieth-century culture.

For a long time now we have been unable to remember our former closeness with the Earth. Due to this amnesia, the ecological problems now thrust upon us have come as a shock, unforeseen because of our condition. Perhaps that photographic image brought back to us from space stirred the long-forgotten feelings we used to have about our planet.

CHAPTER ONE

THE FORGOTTEN EARTH

While virtually all modern cultures consider the Earth to be deaf, dumb and inanimate, the people who lived on our planet for tens of thousands of years, from the dawn of the Upper Palaeolithic period some 40,000 years ago, experienced it as a great living being that was responsive, intelligent and nurturing. Following some of these early worldviews through the labyrinth of history, we shall notice the gradual emergence of an amnesia that is really a double forgetting, wherein a culture forgets, and then forgets that it has forgotten how to live in harmony with the planet. But even this double forgetting is not total. Awareness always leaves its tracks through the sands of time. The literal tracks may be obliterated, but there is always a seed of the perennial wisdom which endures through the millennia like some mythic spore awaiting the time for its revival.

In the archaic world, the mineral, plant and animal kingdoms were seen as inseparable elements of the web of life that arose, abided and dissolved in endless cycles. Ultimately, everything in this web was connected to the Earth, which was the stage on which the evolutionary drama was played out. As vast transitions took place, the Earth somehow managed to regulate all the changes, so that even as it changed it remained the same.

To our forebears, the Earth was awesome and surprising, warranting respect. Literally the Mother Land, she was primordial, there from the beginning, ancient beyond comprehension, yet she was reborn every moment in some new incarnation of the life force.

THE INTERACTIVE ENVIRONMENT

The Earth has witnessed everything that has happened over the five billion years of its history. The study of psychometry (the psychic ability some people claim to have to pick up information from objects or places) has shown that objects somehow record their interactions with other objects in proportion to the intensity and duration of the event.[1] Beyond our ordinary perception, there are always traces left in the aura associated with objects: the akasha, the ether, the morpho-genetic field (hypothesized by some modern biologists, see Chapter 3) – every age has a different name for a subtle environmental memory field, a frequency domain in which events are imprinted with vibrational patterns that we sense as the 'atmosphere' of a place. For our ancestors, landscapes were saturated with memories marking the places where significant interactions, confrontations, revelations and emotions took place between people, spirits, deities and the three kingdoms.

The mineral kingdom was considered to be inanimate matter to twentieth-century sensibilities until the recent re-awakening to the ability of crystals to transform energy and to store consciousness in various ways. To people of ancient traditions, however, who lived close to the Earth, not only crystals but ordinary rocks recorded memory and were responsive to consciousness. The American Indian, Chief Seattle, in his famous speech of 1854 remarked that 'even the rocks, which seem to be dumb as they swelter in the sun along the silent shore, thrill with memories of stirring events connected with the lives of my people'.[2] In the same vein, Claude Kuwanijuma, a Hopi spiritual leader, said that 'man does not have the only memory. The Earth remembers. The stones remember. If you know how to listen they will tell you many things'.[3]

There is a traditional Seneca Indian story, from New York State, which brings to life this theme of communication with the Earth through a rock called 'The Talking Stone':

'One day Orphan Boy was wandering through the forest . . . he lived with an old woman who sent him out to hunt for food each day. He already had a string of birds on his back, for he was very skilled with bow and arrows. When he came to the river, he sank to the ground wearily and pulled out a package of parched corn. As he ate, he gazed at the great rock face before him. To his surprise, he heard a voice say "Would you like to hear stories of the past?" Orphan Boy looked around but saw no one. Again the voice asked "Shall I tell you tales of long ago?" This time, Orphan Boy looked toward the cliff, for the voice seemed to come from the very rock face itself. A third time the voice asked "Shall I tell you legends of the days gone by?" Orphan Boy rose. He picked up his string of birds and climbed to the top of the cliff, toward the voice that had talked. He sat in quiet wonder as Gus-Tah-Ote, the Rock Spirit, began: "This happened in the time when men and animals lived as brothers and could understand each other's language. Listen!" The stories flowed one after another until the sun reddened the western sky. Then Gus-Tah-Ote said "Now leave the birds for me and return tomorrow." . . .

'The next day the same thing happened. Orphan Boy roamed farther and farther into the forest, and soon he did not return to the village even at night. But each day he came back to the rock for the story telling, which seemed to have no end, and each day he left some small offering of thanks. . . .

'One day Gus-Tah-Ote said "I have finished my stories. Do not forget them. Go back to your people, and tell them 'This is the way it happened.'" . . . Orphan Boy returned to the village of his childhood. That night, when all the people were assembled around the council fire, he took his place before them and began to speak. . . . On and on he spoke, one tale after another, just as he had heard them from the talking stone. And the people listened, with their ears and their hearts, and did not sleep.

'From that time, from the mouth of Gus-Tah-Ote, say the people of the longhouse, has come all the knowledge of the past.'[4]

Far from being inert matter, the Spirit of the Rock displays emotion, has a memory and can communicate with humans. Thus our earliest ancestors lived in what can be described as a conscious interactive environment. The biologist Lyall Watson observed that:

'. . . it is no longer possible to deny that our thoughts and desires might influence our environment. The most recent cosmologies all include consciousness as an active participating factor in reality. The new explanations of how the world works are strangely like the old beliefs of nonliterate people everywhere. . . . It seems that merely by admitting the possibility of unlikely events, you increase the probability of their occurrence.'[5]

Archaic people experienced the very act of perception as biological and reciprocally transformative, changing what you were looking at, as you were looking at it. Biological in this context does not refer to the physiological mechanics of seeing, but to seeing with a mind that is able to be influenced by other forms of mind. This interactive perception had an organic effect which could manifest, for example, as magical shape changing.

The concept of a conscious interactive environment extends equally to language, for embedded in language is the worldview which actually determines how people in a culture perceive reality. If words and concepts do not exist in a language, then for those people, these things simply do not exist. Before language was used to manipulate and control, words were creative vibratory patterns that were not merely heard, but were also magical agents of communication. For example, the Bella Coola Indians of Washington State knew that trees and people could speak to each other in the distant past, and even though humans had forgotten the language of the trees, the trees still comprehended human speech.[6]

In early cultures there was a pervasive sense of what Martin Buber called an I-Thou relationship with nature. This open reciprocity is well illustrated by the Eskimo poem, *Magic Words*:

In the earliest times
when both people and animals lived on earth
a person could become an animal if he wanted to
and an animal could become a human being
sometimes they were people
and sometimes animals
and there was no difference
all spoke the same language.
That was the time when words were like magic
the human mind had mysterious powers
a word spoken by chance
might have strange consequences
it would suddenly come alive
and what people wanted to happen could happen
all you had to do was say it.
Nobody could explain this:
that's the way it was.[7]

As ethnobotanical explorer Terence McKenna noted, 'this is our lost birthright, the gnosis of a partnership with an animate, linguistically active nature'.[8] Furthermore, our links to the Earth can be found in the very fabric of archaic languages. Biologist Lewis Thomas, drawing on nineteenth-century cross-cultural linguistic studies, wrote:

> 'It is nice to know that a common language perhaps 20,000 years ago, had a root word for the Earth which turned, much later, into the technical term for the complex polymers that make up the connective tissues of the soil, humus. There is a strangeness, though, in the emergence from the same root of words such as human and humane.'[9]

The French anthropologist Levy-Bruhl called this link with the environment 'participation mystique', which he saw as the essence of archaic consciousness.[10] It implied that there was a significant degree of non-differentiation between subject and object. But it was not a state of ego dissolution, for the ego was not yet formed as a distinct mental entity. Psychoanalyst Carl Jung commented on the psychological dynamics of this process:

> 'When there is no consciousness of the difference between subject and object, an unconscious identity prevails. The unconscious is then projected into the object, and the object is introjected into the subject, becoming part of his psychology. Then plants and animals behave like human beings, human beings are at the same time animals, and everything is alive with ghosts and gods.'[11]

This unitary experience is extended to the biosphere (the web of life on the planet) by many early cultures, for example by the mythic hero of the Jicarilla Apache of New Mexico who said: 'This earth is my body. The sky is my body. The seasons are my body. The water is my body too. The world is just as big as my body. The world is as large as my word. And the world is as large as my prayers.'[12] Similarly, the Australian Aborigine felt that to wound the Earth was to wound himself.

The communication of archaic humanity with the Earth was thus based on a completely different outlook, which in turn was determined by the value given to each sense in reading reality. Whereas today we weight our perception about 70 per cent by vision, followed by sound, with the other senses in the background, archaic participation mystique involved different sensory ratios, in which both sound and smell, for example, were more dominant, and cross-sensory experiences, such as listening to a scent, tasting a colour, or seeing the thunder, were more common. What an extraordinary sense of place could develop from this way of seeing. The more senses that an experience was registered in, the easier its recall became. When this cross-sensory perception was combined with an emotional bonding to the Earth, it became a reverential empathy, a deep ecological vision. As psychologist Ralph Metzner has pointed out, archaic cultures were 'symbiotically embedded in nature'.[13]

SHAMANISM

Shamanism was a worldwide Palaeolithic transformational technology which utilized controlled access to ecstatic states of consciousness for communication with plants, animals, ancestors, spirits and the four elements. The shaman was a healer, weather controller, diviner of food sources, enemies and lost objects – a spiritual ecologist who maintained the equilibrium between his tribe and their bio-region by being keenly sensitive to what D.H. Lawrence called the spirit of place:

> '. . . every people is polarized in some particular locality, which is home, the homeland. Different places on the face of the earth have different vital effluence, different vibration, different chemical exhalation, different polarity with different stars: call it what you like, but the spirit of place is a great reality.'[14]

This intuitive sense of place is an embryonic form of geomancy, the siting of dwellings, sacred places and burial grounds in harmony with local topography and subtle earth energies, which became more formalized as civilizations evolved.

'Shamans were those who had memory of the beginnings,' wrote religious historian Mircea Eliade.[15] The ability to recollect, to remember from an altered or trance state to an ordinary state of consciousness across what is normally a veil of forgetting – such as awakening from a mysterious dream – is called cross-state retention. Shamanic cross-state retention requires a deep knowledge of the biological cycles of birth, life, death and regeneration in all phenomena. In addition to chanting, praying, dancing, drumming and fasting, one of the most effective methods of entering into ecstatic states in the quest for cross-state knowledge is through the ritual use of power plants, such as psychoactive mushrooms, morning glory or peyote (the cactus also known as mescal). McKenna, who has done considerable ethnopharmacological research in the Amazon, suggests that such psychedelic plants may be cross-species pheromones,[16] which upon ingestion under proper guidance and in a suitable environmental setting, reveal that:

'. . . nature wants to be articulated, wants to be recognized as a source of information and as a cohesive being with intentionality. We are sharing this planet with something intelligent. Not abstractly intelligent, not incomprehensibly intelligent, but concretely intelligent and apprehendable to us.'[17]

The archaic communion with the living Earth through plants is a global shamanistic experience. Plants are not only sources of food, clothing, beverages, tobacco, medicines and perfumes, they are also very profound teachers. A psychedelic plant experience puts a shaman in touch with the heartbeat of the Earth. Anything out of balance or rhythm is immediately apparent, which is the signal for ritual correction by the shaman.

DREAMTIME

Throughout the archaic world, cross-state communication between humanity and nature took place in the Dreamtime, the name most commonly used to describe this unique temporal concept. It was experienced as a 'present time' which never ended, but stretched out to eternity, in which there was no past or future. This is very different from the evanescent present moment between past and future, which is over in the blink of an eye. In the Dreamtime time does not run out; it is always the first time that the gods, primordial ancestors and totemic animals have performed their mythic deeds and communicated directly with humans.

Hans Peter Duerr suggests that archaic cultures were 'outside' time, perceiving things in and of themselves, rather than seeing them from 'outside' time as an external observer.[18] It is this sensation of being 'outside' time that creates the dream aspect of the Dreamtime. Thus, whatever the cultural variation on its name, the Dreamtime is not just temporal eternity, but also the capacity to dream, to dissolve the boundaries of ordinary perception and communication between animate and inanimate, between humans and other species. Dreaming allowed cross-state perception to bloom 'outside' time. Dreaming, in this context, is the gateway to all altered states of consciousness and, as in dreaming, events in the Dreamtime were reversible to their origins. Through ritual reversing to their origins, a culture could regenerate both itself and the Earth.

The Australian Aboriginal tradition is the source of much of our information on the Dreamtime, which is known by many names throughout the continent. The Aborigines have inherited a 40,000-year-old history, the longest unsevered culture that the world has ever known. In a superb *National Geographic* article one of the last remaining Gagudju elders, Big Bill Neidjie, told the authors: 'Earth our mother, eagle our cousin. Tree, he is pumping our blood. Grass is growing. And water. And we are all one.'[19] Another Aboriginal leader explained that 'Aboriginals have a special connection with everything that is natural. . . . We see all things natural as apart of us. All things on earth we see as part human'.[20]

The Mimi spirits lived in the rocks, while the totemic ancestors, the crocodile, the kangaroo, the rainbow snake and many others, all left their imprint on a vibrant mythical landscape of hills, rocks, trees, waterholes and trackways. 'The whole countryside is his living, age-old family tree,' wrote the Aboriginal scholar T.H. Strelow.[21] But there is geomantic entropy, a running down, even in the Dreamtime landscape unless it is periodically looked after and awakened by the Aboriginal custodians of the land. In order to activate the Earth, they must hold ritual re-enactments of their mythical history which regenerates the life force that flows through everything. Eliade suggests that on their reanimating walkabouts the Aborigines experience a living memory of their entire ancestral totemic heritage.[22] It is a reciprocal experience, for as they remember the land, the land remembers and thus gives identity to them. This mythic recollection reanimates the sacred landscapes by recharging what biologist Rupert Sheldrake calls their morphogenetic, or form generating, memory fields. Sacred attention enhances these fields, for memory is a function of attention.

Finally, songlines or dreaming tracks were thought to be the primordial paths of the ancestors who sang the world into existence. They connected waterholes, caves of ancient totemic paintings, hills and prominent geological formations such as the Olgas or Uluru, Ayers Rock. In *Songlines*, Bruce Chatwin described this process of sonic geomancy:

> 'Regardless of the words, it seems the melodic contour of the song describes the nature of the land over which the song passes, so if the Lizard Man were dragging his heels across the saltpans of Lake Eyre, you would expect a succession of long flats, like Chopin's Funeral March. If he were skipping up and down the MacDonnell escarpments, you'd have a series of arpeggios and glissandos, like Liszt's Hungarian Rhapsodies. Certain phrases, certain combinations of musical notes, are thought to describe the action of the ancestor's feet. One phrase would say, "Salt-pan"; another "Creek-bed", "Spinifex", "Sandhill", "Mulga-scrub", "Rockface" and so forth. An expert songman, by listening to their order of succession, could count how many times his hero crossed a river, or scaled a ridge – and be able to calculate where, and how far along, a songline he was. Music is a memory bank for finding one's way about the world.'[23]

And the beat goes on. The Bushmen of the Kalahari Desert in Africa are more ancient than the most primitive of the black people of that continent. Laurens Van der Post, an explorer and writer who knew them intimately, observed that the Bushman 'lived in a state of extraordinary intimacy with nature, wherever he went he belonged, feeling kinship with everyone and everything he met on the way from birth to death'.[24] A Bushman hunter once told him that 'there is a dream dreaming us',[25] recalling the Aboriginal Dreamtime.

The American Indians, like the Aborigines, the Bushmen and other ancient peoples, lived in symbiotic harmony with the living Earth, and a language of empathic communication emerged from continued tribal interaction with the land, similar to the songlines. A traditional Hopi statement from Hotevilla declares: 'We have also said the earth is like a spotted fawn, the spots being areas with certain power and purpose. We are all provided with different vibration and frequency which is designed for communicating with the Great Spirit in order to accomplish certain life-supporting functions of Natural Laws in accordance with each one's customary ways.'[26] It is interesting to note that the linguist Benjamin Lee Whorf wrote that the Hopi 'actually have a language better equipped to deal with vibratile phenomena than our latest scientific technology'.[27]

In his perceptive book *American Indian Ecology*, religious historian Donald Hughes wrote that nature 'was to them a great, interrelated community, including animals, plants, human beings, and some things that Americans of the Western European tradition would call physical objects on the one hand, and purely spirits on the other. No person, tribe, or species within the living unity of nature was seen as self-sufficient, human beings possibly least of all. The Indian did not define himself or herself as primarily an autonomous individual, but as a part of a whole; and should hold a reciprocating mutually beneficial relationship with each type of being'.[28] These beings included earth spirits which could manifest as mysterious light phenomena. The Miday tribe, for instance, which inhabited the Lake Ontario region between New York and Canada, had a tradition known as 'shaking the tent' which was carried out to divine sites beneficial for villages. The shamans knew that some land had positive, life enhancing energy and that other land emitted disturbing, unhealthy energy. First reported in 1634 by a Catholic missionary, Father Lejeune, the spirit lights were described as cone-shaped with tapered tails, entering and violently shaking the tent where the entranced shaman lay after drumming and praying.[29]

The American Indians also believed that mountains were great living beings, and often described them in geo-biological imagery. The Black Hills of South Dakota, for example, are known by the Lakota as Paha Sapa – 'Heart of the Earth Mother'. For untold ages these hills have been used for sacred vision quests because they were considered to be gateways to spiritual dimensions. In the Four Corners area of the Colorado Plateau, Joan Price's atmospheric research has shown that mountains have cycles of breath just as humans do. At the base of the San Francisco Peaks in Arizona, amidst shrines of both the Hopi and the Navaho, the wind cave of Wupatki inhales and exhales air at 30 mph in six-hour cycles, and there are at least seven sacred breathing mountains with wind cave 'lung' systems which are thought to vitalize the Plateau.[30] The Indians' relationship to the Earth is felt through full body knowing, in which the senses and the spirit are unified. One of the most gifted contemporary Indian writers, N. Scott Momaday of the Kiowas, says:

> 'Once in his life a man ought to concentrate his mind upon the remembered earth, I believe. He ought to give himself up to a particular landscape in his experience, to look at it from as many angles as he can, to wonder about it, to dwell upon it. He ought to imagine that he touches it with his hands at every season and listens to the sounds that are made upon it.'[31]

Elsewhere he writes that '[to the Indian] a sense of place is paramount. Only in reference to the earth can he persist in his true identity'.[32] This seamless web of reciprocity echoes what Van der Post has said of the Kalahari Bushman: 'I believe [that his] way of knowing was through what knew him.'[33]

GODDESS

It was a common belief among many tribes that all life forms emerged from the womb of the Earth, and the Earth was deeply honoured and respected as a mother. In her coming of age ceremony, an Apache maiden became one with the fruitful Mother Earth or Earth Goddess. By her identification with the Goddess, she partook of her fertility.[34] Mother Earth was considered to be the continuing source of life for all living creatures, and all matter taken from her body was thought to share her aliveness. Thankful prayers were said to the Pueblo Clay Lady who gave her living flesh to potters. 'Similar ceremonies were used,' Hughes points out, 'to propitiate the spirits of turquoise, rock and salt.'[35]

Almost every Indian tribe had the tradition of a Mother Earth: Nuna of the Eskimo, Tacoma of the Salish, Maka Ina of the Oglala Sioux, Iyatiku of the Keres, Kokyang Wuhti of the Hopi, Changing Woman of the Navajo, Coatlicue of the Aztecs and many others. Nancy Zak of the Institute of the American Indian Arts summarizes the common elements of these sacred embodiments of the feminine:

> 'Overall we see a belief in the earth as a living being. In the Arctic as well as the Plains she is a deeply sensitive creature who is

grieved by death. She and her various embodied parts have feeling just as we do. These sacred figures may have a dark as well as a bright side – just as we do, just as life does. In many areas of the country, including the Arctic, the Northeast, and the Southeast, the life of the people – that is, the earth, its people and its foodstuffs – has as its source the voluntary or involuntary self-sacrifice of a mother figure.'[36]

As researcher Barbara Walker points out in her monumental study of women:

'Thousands of feminine names have been given to the earth. Continents – Asia, Africa, Europe – were named after manifestations of the Goddess. Countries bore the names of female ancestors or other manifestations of the Goddess: Libya, Russia, Anatolia, Latium, Holland, China, Ionia, Akkad, Chaldea, Scotland (Scotia), Ireland (Eriu, Hera) were but a few. Every nation gave its own territory the name of its own Mother Earth.'[37]

She was known as Mawu in Africa, as Ninhursag in Sumer, Hepat in Babylonia, Mami in Mesopotamia, Isis or Hathor in Egypt, Inanna, Astarte, Ishtar or Asherah in the Middle East, Rhea in Crete, Kubaba in Turkey, Cybele in Greece, Semele in Thrace and Phrygia, Zemyna in Lithuania, Pele in Hawaii – the list is endless. Art historian Merlin Stone comments on the significance of this widespread belief:

'We are not . . . confronting a confusing myriad of deities, but a variety of titles, resulting from diverse languages and dialectics, yet each referring to a most similar female divinity. . . . it becomes evident that the female deity in the Near and Middle East (and other parts of the world) was revered as Goddess – much as people today think of God.'[38]

The first depictions of an archetypal, living Earth Goddess are found in the Upper Palaeolithic roots of Old Europe in southern France. Pioneer archaeologist Marija Gimbutas has established that the earliest known vulva figurines supporting this belief are dated at about 33–35,000 BC.[39] Representations of the first pregnant Earth Goddess have been found between France and Czechoslovakia dating from around 25,000 BC.[40] It is important to emphasize, however, that

Palaeolithic and Neolithic goddesses of Old Europe (pre-Indo-European Europe from 6500–3500 BC) are not just fertility divinities. As Gimbutas stresses, they were life creatresses with three major functions: life-giver, death-wielder and regenerator. Birth, death and regeneration are the eternal processes which also correspond to the three phases of the moon: waxing, full and waning. These in turn are reflected in the three phases of women: the maid, the mother and the old woman.

The principal theme of the Goddess in her infinite forms is that there is no permanent death; death is always coupled with regeneration. Both the Dreamtime and the Goddess share the processes of boundary dissolution and continual cross-state transformation. The life force is always arising from, abiding in and dissolving back into the transpersonal source, the matrix of life and death. Gimbutas reports that the saying 'Mother, I come from you, you carry me, you nourish me, and you will take me after my death'[41] is still heard in European villages.

The anatomy of the Goddess is reflected in the body of the Earth. Each topographic form and contour was suffused with a different aspect of her power. The pregnant Goddess appears as Mother Earth in the form of a hill or mound potent with sprouting vegetation,[42] expressed by the poet Dylan Thomas as 'the force that through the green fuse drives the flower'. Art historian Michael Dames perceptively recognized that the largest prehistoric artificial mound in Europe, Silbury Hill, which lies on the Wiltshire downs in southwestern England, was an earthwork of the squatting pregnant Goddess in the position of childbirth.[43] The round summit of the hill was her omphalos or navel which held the essence of her creative power. The omphalos marked the centre of the Earth for archaic people. Gimbutas comments that these symbolic pregnant hills are also portrayed in Neolithic grave structures and incised on slabs of megalithic tombs in Brittany.[44] Mountains were also associated with the pregnant belly, buttocks, breasts, or mons veneris of the Great Mother. The sacred mountain and the omphalos are places where heaven, Earth and the underworld are connected. They are centres of the world from which life emanates. Sometimes they are associated with a World Tree or Tree of Life which also connects the three cosmological levels.

It is important to note that there are many centres in the archaic landscape. There are sacred hills, sacred mountains, sacred groves of trees, sacred springs and holy wells, which are all emanations of the Goddess. But they are not abstract, geometrical centres. They are all founts of a common underlying life force which reminds people that they themselves are a spark of the same Goddess life force. This is a fundamental premise of the perennial philosophy that is present in one form or another in every age. These sacred places are monuments in the truest sense of the word. They remind humanity of another reality in which there is a direct empathic experience of the One and the many at the same time.

Gimbutas commented that 'stone for archaic peoples was the concentrated power of the earth'.[45] For example, from prehistoric times the Goddess was venerated in the form of a black stone meteorite at Pessinus in Turkey. Crystal and other precious stones, such as the diamond, were considered to be frozen nectar of the divine matrix, the Mother. Crawling through the opening of a holed stone, such as Men-an-Tol in Cornwall, was believed to cleanse the body of both disease and sin.

Caves were the vaginal passageways to the womb of the Earth. It was within the dark recesses of the living body of the Earth Goddess that archaic people were in deepest communion with the cyclic mystery of birth and death. In Neolithic times people were buried in embryonic positions because they would be reborn again in the earth womb. Passage mounds in Ireland and Brittany, such as New Grange and Gavrinis, echoed the theme of a birth canal. Rachel Levy, in her study of the religious conceptions of the Stone Age, suggests that megalithic dolmens may have been gateways to the world of the dead. Dolmens are monuments made by laying a capstone across uprights, and this triadic form was perhaps abstracted from the entrance of the cave.[46] In southern Europe the cave tombs hewn from the rocks are either uterine, egg-shaped or anthropomorphic in form. From Palaeolithic and Neolithic evidence, we see how the biological template precedes the geometrical template in sacred architecture. This is not surprising, for as Eliade notes, the archaic sense of being born from the earth:

'. . . has created in man a sense of cosmic relatedness with his local environment. One might even say that in those times, man had not so much a consciousness of belonging to the human race as a sense of cosmobiological participation in the life around him. He knew, of course, that he had an "immediate" mother, whom he saw still near him, but he also knew that he came from farther away, that he had been brought to her by the storks or the frogs, that he had lived in the caves or in the rivers.'[47]

In Old Europe, Gimbutas points out, the Earth was also considered to be the collective social conscience – justice, in the form of goddesses such as the Greek Themis or the Russian Matushka zeml'ja. With regard to this theme, she wrote of Slavic peasants:

'If someone swore an oath after putting a clod of earth on his or her head or swallowing it, that oath was considered binding and incontestable. The Earth Mother listens to appeals, settles problems, and punishes all who dec -ive her or are disrespectful to her. She does not tolerate thieves, liars, or vain and proud people. In legends and tales, sinners are devoured by the earth. The earth closes over them.'[48]

Old European cultures persisted for almost 3,000 years, unbroken by internal social upheaval. After many years of field work, fitting the pieces of a vast archaeological puzzle together, Gimbutas concluded that the people lived in a peaceful egalitarian society based on a matrilineal system. They were settled agriculturalists, cultivating gardens and orchards. Their arts and crafts were inspired by their belief, respect and devotion to the Goddess. They had virtually no weapons of war until the final stages of their existence in the Copper Age.[49]

But all this was to come to an end in the latter half of the fifth millennium BC, and again in the fourth millennium, and once more from 3000–2800 BC.[50] These periods witnessed, according to Gimbutas, the dissolution of the Old European civilization by waves of nomadic horse-riding Kurgan people from South Russia. The Kurgan ideology was based on the strong male, the heroic warrior deities of sky and sun with shining faces like the burnished metal of their new weapons.

It was not metals themselves, but their use as agents of destruction that changed the course of history. The patriarchal Kurgans, like all Indo-Europeans, were hypnotized by the dominating power of the sharp metal blades of swords, spears, daggers and arrow points. The domesticated horse, which amplified the power of these lethal weapons, enabled them to spread quickly into the Danubian grasslands of central Europe. Gimbutas explains: 'Their arrival initiated a dramatic shift in the prehistory of Europe – a change in social structure, residence patterns, in art and in religion – and was a decisive factor in the formation of the Europe of the past five thousand years.'[51]

In spite of the shift to a powerful sky god tradition, the Goddess traditions, which were firmly rooted in the earth, lingered on for a long time before going underground in other cultures around the world. Nevertheless this turn in history represented the beginning of a trend towards geomantic amnesia. Contributing to this amnesia was the general Neolithic trend of object proliferation. When the Old Europeans stopped being hunter-gathèrers and began to settle in permanent villages, domesticating herds of animals and cultivating crops, more durable farming and household objects, such as pottery, rugs, metal tools and ornaments, furniture and clothing, began to multiply. Each generation of objects acted as a reflective matrix for the creation of new and improved objects. Design innovation began to feed upon itself, picking up speed as craftsmanship began to add individual variety to basic function. A more linear, logical 'left brain' accounting memory arose to keep records of the new objects. With this new aspect of memory came a gradual shift of attention towards the making and acquiring of more objects.

The Kurgan invasions effectively began to uncouple attention away from the primary Earth cycles of birth, death and regeneration. Hybrid cultures, later established by the Kurgans with the remnants of their captives, began to become more complex, stratified and territorial. As land became demarcated with boundaries, so too did consciousness become bounded in the crystallization of powerful warrior egos. The conscious interactive environment of the Goddess traditions became reduced to a dominating mastery of the land.

The Goddesses, at best, became the wives or consorts of the Kurgan war Gods. Male-female equality, inherent in the co-operative, egalitarian, Old European societies, was no longer the norm. This social imbalance was also reflected in the anima-animus division within individuals. As religious historian Riane Eisler emphasized, the Kurgans imposed a 'dominator model of social organization',[52] which instituted hierarchical boundaries in both landscape and mindscape.

These boundaries, the very opposite of the fluid Goddess and Dreamtime traditions, began to create state-specific perception and memory, by compartmentalizing reality in new ways. All of these boundary conditions, divine, social and individual, contributed towards the condition of geomantic amnesia.

The Hindu tradition of India, however, has an ancient connection with the Goddess tradition, dating from the Upper Palaeolithic. Hindus believe that the Earth is alive and permeated with different qualities of feminine energy. The Goddess not only rules the depths and surface of the Earth, but also its mountains. Several of the world's greatest peaks, known as the Primal Mothers, are in the Himalayas. Mount Everest is called Chomo-Lung-Ma, 'Goddess-Mother of the Universe'. Not far away is Annapurna, 'Great Breast full of Nourishment'. The melting white snow is the milk of the Goddess.[53]

SACRED SPACE AND TIME

In the Jain tradition, the great teachers of this ancient Hindu sect were known as tirthankras, which is derived from the word tirtha, a crossing over. Art historian Eleanor Gaddon explained that a tirtha literally meant a place where one crossed over a river. In a spiritual sense, it was a sacred site where a person crossed over to 'the other side', undergoing a religious experience.[54] This inner journey, from the profane to the sacred, is common to all holy sites. To enter sacred space is to enter sacred time, where the present time expands to eternity without past or future. It is a suspension from measured time. A tirtha is a place where the boundaries between dimensions dissolve, allowing cross-state communication with the memory or morpho-genetic field of the Goddess or God which has been established over centuries of worship. Sacred places often have an awesome atmosphere in which ordinary ratios of sensory perception are altered. The light, the colour, the sound, the fragrance may be unusual.

Transitional sites, such as tirthas, thus have an intrinsic awakening power, which shifts people out of their ordinary states of consciousness. At tirthas we remember to remember; we wake up to our life force connection not only with the Earth, but with the whole cosmos. We experience what anthropologist Gregory Bateson called 'the pattern that connects'.[55] This double remembering can be enhanced by rituals which include music, dance, food, song, prayer and meditation. Psychedelic plants (which could be termed morphogenetic field amplifiers) may also be used to open wide the doors of perception.

Mookerjee, in his book *Kali, The Feminine Force*, describes a number of tirthas such as 'a prehistoric megalith which is still worshipped as the shrine of the Earth Mother, Bolhai, in Madhya Pradesh, Central India. The Goddess is represented by a smooth, oval, red-coated stone. The capstone is about seven feet long, and rings like a bell when struck, or when rubbed with another stone in a ritual still practised'.[56] The Goddess Kali is often symbolized as a block of stone. It was considered auspicious to drink from or bathe in triangular-shaped pools, called yoni-kundas (vulva of the universe).[57] From Kashmir in the north, to the south of India, megalithic monuments emanating Shakti, the feminine life force, are found dating from 8000 to 2000 BC. As we have noted before, dolmens are constructed as wombs in the form of the Great Mother's vaginal or yonic passage. Caves and rock grottoes were used for ritual rebirthing. The Lakshmi Tantra tell us that Shakti operates through vibration, oscillating between phases of creation and dissolution throughout history.[58] The Goddess in India exists both within and beyond the universe; she is the universal life force and the very heartbeat and soil of the Earth.

LIFE FORCE AND GEOMANCY

Emanating from archaic divinities and spirits, the life force of the Earth was known by many different names. Each North American Indian tribe had its own term for this power. For example, there was *manitou* for the Algonkians, *wakonda* for the Sioux, *orenda* for the Iroquois, and *maxpe* for the Crows. In Melenesia it was called *mana*; in the Middle East *baraka* or *barak*; in Egypt, *sakhem*. To the Bantu of the Lower Congo in Africa it was known as *lunyensu* or *bu-nssi*; to the Kung Bushmen it was *n/um*; to the Australian Arunta Aborigines it was *arungquiltha*. The poet Federico Garcia Lorca defines the Spanish word *duende* as the earth force, this 'mysterious power that all may feel and no philosophy can explain'.[59] To the Japanese this force was known as *ki*. However, the Chinese word *chi* is the one most used today in connection with geomancy.

Around 2000 BC, Emperor Yu of China initiated an exploration into the quality of *chi* at building sites in order to prevent illness, such as arthritis, circulation problems or mental stress, which bad earth *chi* can cause.[60] A nineteenth-century Christian missionary, E.J. Eitel, wrote in his study of Chinese geomancy, *Feng Shui*:

> 'The Chinese look upon nature not as a dead inanimate fabric, but as a living, breathing organism. They see a golden chain of spirited life running through every form of existence and binding together, as in one living body, everything that subsists in heaven above or earth below.'[61]

Feng shui, which means wind-water, was the art of harmonizing the *chi* of the land and atmosphere with the *chi* of humanity, so that both benefited. Temples, homes, ancestral tombs and seats of government were all built in accordance with guidelines expanded upon in later chapters.

EGYPT

Ancient Egypt is an enigma because it never had a unified religious worldview. Each *nome* or region, such as Memphis, Thebes or Heliopolis, had its own creation myths. In predynastic Egypt there were many societies living along the Nile. Some of them were matriarchal Goddess oriented and others were patriarchal worshippers of Gods. Although the most familiar creator divinities in the Egyptian pantheon, such as Ptah, are male, there is also evidence of early female creatresses, such as Uatchat, a primordial snake Goddess who was prominent before the north and south kingdoms were united. Even Hapi, the male divinity of the life-giving Nile, was represented as an androgynous figure with female breasts. Isis, however, is the Earth Goddess supreme, whom the Roman writer Apuleius portrays as proclaiming:

> 'I am Nature, the universal Mother, mistress of all the elements, primordial child of time, sovereign of all things spiritual, queen of the dead, queen also of the immortals, the single manifestation of all gods and goddesses that are. My nod governs the shining heights of Heaven, the wholesome sea breezes, the lamentable

silences of the world below. Though I am known by countless names and propitiated with all manner of different rites, yet the whole round earth venerates me.'[62]

But it is on the walls of the temple at Edfu, in southern Egypt, that we begin to decipher in some detail one version of a predynastic Earth creation myth. In this Egyptian temple of the Ptolemaic period there are unique texts that have only recently been translated. Although the mythological history is written in an abbreviated form, based on more ancient texts, we can clearly see that the Egyptian theory of creation included an embryo of the Earth called *bnnt*. The new-born Earth, suggests Egyptologist E.A. Reymond, might be imagined as emerging from the embryonic *bnnt* floating in the primeval waters.[63] It took the form of a mound, which may have been a real prehistoric sacred cult site. This mound was understood to be a divine being.[64] While it can be argued that the emergence of the mound is an echo of the fertile sand islands emerging from the Nile after the river subsides, there is a distinct parallel here with the pregnant mound, hill and omphalos of the Palaeolithic and Neolithic Goddess traditions. (In fact, Devereux points out that there is an undoubtedly artificial predynastic mound – a tumulus – on the natural pyramidical peak that dominates the Valley of the Kings near Luxor.)

As a physical entity, the temple was believed to be an animate being commanded by its Ka,[65] the spirit double or astral body. From a magical spell, Reymond deduces that the Earth also was considered to have its own Ka. He further remarks that 'the historical temple was believed to have been built as the memorial for the Ka, the Ka of the Earth. This temple was believed to have been founded in a place where the Earth-Maker dwelt'.[66] From this statement it appears that the temple was magically animated to both commemorate and interact with the Ka of the living Earth.

Associated with the temple was the *dd*-pillar, which animated land that was particularly sacred. 'The Egyptians believed,' wrote Reymond, 'that where the *dd*-pillar was, there the sacred nature of the Earth was eternally vital but needed to be revivified by the creation of a new entity closely resembling in its physical appearance that which had once existed there.'[67] Apparently, the sakhem, the earth energy of a place, could run out of primordial juice! The texts on the temple walls reveal that the *dd*-pillar, which was present at the creation on the primeval mound and in each of the subsequent sacred domains, was ultimately situated at the temple of Edfu. Before a new world could be created, the previous vanished world of Gods had to be resurrected by erecting the *dd*-pillar, which Reymond said 'recalled from the underworld the immaterial forms of the deities who formerly lived in that place'.[68] Evidently the ancestral spirits of place, although never utterly extinct, went through cycles of existence, including a state of suspended animation, until they were magically reanimated by the presence of the *dd*-pillar.

To Reymond, the *dd*-pillar implied the idea of 'a continuance in time, the idea of an indefinite existence, thus ensuring the sanctity of the place which was about to be revivified'.[69] The *dd*-pillar functioned as a cross-state temporal integrator, connecting the Dreamtime of the previous divinities with the currently empowered deities. In other words, it was a sacred morphogenetic field regenerator, a more formalized version of a megalithic standing stone or menhir.

ALCHEMY

Egypt also formalized another arcane earth force. Alchemy, known in Egypt as 'black earth', later grew its mysterious flowers in ancient India, China, Greece and Rome. Yet, intimates polymath Richard Grossinger, the Egyptians in turn probably inherited 'the medicinal powders, the hieroglyphs, the potions from some older time'.[70] The archaic roots of alchemy are undoubtedly found in both shamanism and the Goddess traditions. Gimbutas remarks that the ancient Neolithic Bird Goddess, who is still recalled in Latvian mythological songs, was the protectress of metallurgy, like the later Greek Goddess Athena. Old European folklore, she said, had remnants of this alchemy.[71] She is not alone in this hypothesis. Mircea Eliade wrote:

> 'It was probably the old conception of the Earth Mother, bearer of embryo-ores, which crystallized faith in artificial transmutation (that is, operated in a laboratory). It was the encounter with the symbolisms, myths and techniques of the miners, smelters and smiths which probably gave rise to the first alchemical operations. But above all it was the discovery of the Living Substance which must have played the decisive role.'[72]

Metals were thought to have a life of their own, just like vegetables and animals. Grossinger explains the theory: 'Gradually, over the aeons, lead turns to copper, copper to iron, iron to tin, tin to mercury, mercury to silver, and finally silver to gold. The Earth is a loom in which the planets weave their vibrations. The vibrations may be thought of as musical notes that become concretized in the loom; transmutation is thus a changing of the planetary note.'[73] These living metallic vibrations are married in the Living Substance, the magically animated earth embryo-ores. The alchemists' goal was the production of the philosopher's stone, thought by some to be a conscious interactive state between spirit and matter.

The philosopher's stone, which was alleged to be an agent that changed base metals into gold, was also an agent of astounding physical healing and spiritual transformation. It can also develop in a more sinister direction: as a geochemical technology to make new metallic alloys used as weapons of war. This was the path the Kurgan warriors chose, to speed their destruction of the Goddess cultures of Old Europe.

JUDAISM

Elsewhere in the Middle East another important tradition arose which had a major impact upon the planet. In the Zohar (the Book of Radiance), one of the mystical books of the Judaic tradition, it is written:

> 'For there is not a member in the human body that does not have its counterpart in the world as a whole. For as man's body consists of members and parts of various ranks . . . reacting upon each other so as to form one organism, so does the world at large consist of a hierarchy of created things, which when they properly act and react upon each other form literally one organic body.'[74]

This biological theme is also found in the growth of the Earth from its centre, Mount Zion in Jerusalem: 'The Holy One created the world like an embryo. As the embryo proceeds from the navel onwards, so God began to create the world from its navel outwards and from there it was spread out in different directions.'[75] In the same vein, Walker points out that the Hebrew word 'hara' could be translated as both 'mountain' and 'pregnant belly',[76] as we observed in the probable Neolithic Goddess associations with places such as Silbury Hill.

Furthermore, the belief that the Earth is alive is connected with the Shekinah, the feminine power of God. In Hebrew, Shekinah means the divine presence dwelling in the world. The jealous, strong, patriarchal God of the Torah is balanced by the benevolent gracious Shekinah of the Kabalah, of which the Zohar is a part. Judaic scholar Daniel Matt, who translated the Zohar, described the Shekinah as 'the Goddess ruling over the Earth. She is given numerous names in the Kabalah: the Earth, the Ocean in which all the rivers stream, the Holy Apple Orchard. She is the animating life force of the universe and is called simply Chaya, the Living Creature. She is the Mother of the World. By uniting with the masculine half of God she engenders all earthly existence, the world is blessed and vitalized'.[77] The Shekinah restores and balances the Earth. She has also been interpreted as being the breath and radiance of the world. At other times, she is symbolized by the plain unleavened bread of Passover. Bread, made from grains, is considered to be the fruit of the Earth.

The Kabalistic tradition was the gnostic wisdom aspect of Judaism, but the official rabbinic and talmudic body of teachings and laws presents us with the victory of transcendent monotheism over the Goddess cults of Asherah, Astarte, Anath and Elat in Canaan. 'Here we see the first glimmerings,' wrote historian Morris Berman, 'of what I have called non-participating consciousness: knowledge is acquired by recognizing the distance between ourselves and nature. Ecstatic merger with nature is judged not merely as ignorance, but as idolatry.'[78]

The Old Testament legacy was that God was the creator of the Earth, but separate from his creation. Although the land was seen as bountiful, flowing with milk and honey, the archaic engagement with an animate world was severed. The world was seen as a secondary effect of God. And yet on several momentous occasions, such as his manifestation to Moses in the burning bush, God did manifest in the physical world. He said to Moses, 'Put off thy shoes from thy feet, for the place whereon thou standest is holy ground.'[79] Another time, Jacob spent the night at Har Hamoria, the future site of the first temple in Jerusalem.[80] He went to sleep using a stone as a pillow.[81] God appeared in Jacob's dream of angels ascending and descending a ladder that reached to heaven. When he awoke, Jacob said 'This is the gate of heaven',[82] and erected the stone as a pillar. He anointed it with oil, calling the place Beth-el, house of God. This hierophany, or divine manifestation in an ordinary object, was not thought to be pagan animism; it was understood that the stone was only a vehicle for the vision. Nevertheless, it was still considered to be sacred as a monument, as a reminder of a numinous event.

We see in Judaism, therefore, two apparently divergent perspectives of divinity relating to the Earth: one which is natural, mystical, nourishing, lunar and feminine, and another which is supernatural, creative, commanding, solar and masculine. In truth they are both aspects of a greater unity that is without gender, but the supernatural masculine aspect proved to be one of the dominant historical forces which have shaped Western history.

GAIA

There is evidence in Minoan Crete, from about 1400 BC, of a powerful female Earth deity, known as the bare-breasted Serpent Goddess. However, it is not until the period of the Homeric Hymns (850 BC) and the later poet Hesiod that we begin to have a formal mythological genealogy tracing the origins of Ge or Gaia, the Greek Earth Goddess. Hesiod's *Theogony* relates that 'first of all did Chaos come into being, and then broad-bosomed Gaia, a firm seat of all things forever'.[83] Gaia gave birth to the starry heavens, the mountains and the seas. In the Homeric Hymn XXX, we read that Earth is the 'mother of all, eldest of all beings'.[84] It is through her agricultural fertility, which was the heart of early Aegean religions, that we are most familiar with her. Yet in earlier times she was the Goddess of wild vegetation, untamed animals and the dark, primeval mystery of the underworld, which was the dwelling place of ancestral ghosts. This last aspect of Gaia has roots that go back to the Palaeolithic belief that the Earth was both womb and tomb to humanity.

Gaia was also considered to be the source of dreams which rose like vapours from her depths. Dream incubation, in a sacred cave, grove or temple, was believed to be a method of bypassing the images of the conscious mind and thus receiving guidance from the spirit of place. In Greece and Asia Minor there were pits in many temples called abatons in which people would incubate, sleeping as if they were unconscious in a womb. This cross-state process was later brought to a very sophisticated level at the therapeutic dream temples of Asclepius in which remedies for mental and physical diseases were sought. Gaia also ruled over several oracular sites, including Delphi on Mount Parnassus, the omphalos or navel of the world, where through the mouth of her entranced prophetess she foretold the future.

Even though Gaia was supplanted at her shrines and oracles in 2700 BC by the male deities of the Indo-European raiders, and again in 1200 BC by the patriarchal Olympian sky gods, such as the Zeus of the Doric invaders, as Themis she still remained the Goddess of justice, a function of Earth since at least Neolithic times. As the embodiment of justice, the Earth responded in the form of earthquakes, plagues and poor crops if she was abused. The patina of the Olympian pantheon, which Riane Eisler aptly describes as 'a group of quarrelsome, competitive, and generally unpredictable deities',[85] never totally concealed the vital connection to the Earth Goddess.

THE GREEK PHILOSOPHERS

At the beginning of the sixth century BC, Thales emerged as the first of the pre-Socratic philosophers. He was also considered to be the first Greek physicist, the vanguard of a scientific investigation into the underlying principles and dynamics of nature. But even though the emphasis was on empirical observation of nature, the worldview of these early philosophers was in some aspects more like the earlier pre-Olympian animism. In this respect Thales believed that apparently inanimate chunks of matter, such as magnetic stone or amber, could be alive. This doctrine, called hylozoism, implied that all matter has life. We are left with the impression, however, that Thales was more concerned with the theory that particular chunks of matter were animated, rather than an outright extension of this idea to an entire animated planet.

At best, Thales presents us with a paradoxical animism in which there is the beginning of an objective distance between humanity and nature. Classical scholars Kirk and Raven conclude that the most reasonable interpretation of Thales' hylozoism was 'the belief that the world is interpenetrated by life, that many of its parts which appear to be inanimate are in fact animate'.[86]

Anaximenes, a generation later than Thales and from the same Milesian school, was also hylozoistic in outlook. He believed that air was the primary substance, functioning as the breath of the world. Anaxagoras, who may have been his student, was a metaphysical philosopher who believed that an omnipotent Mind controlled all matter, animate and inanimate, even though it was not in all matter. This separation of mind and matter establishes him as the first dualist of Greek thought.

The physician Hippocrates (460–357 BC), a contemporary of Anaxagoras, presented a contrasting holistic vision of life. He wrote that 'there is one common flow, one common breathing, all things are in sympathy. The whole organism and each one of its parts are working in conjunction for the same purpose'.[87] As a healer, Hippocrates was aware that some places were beneficial for healing specific diseases, while others had a detrimental effect.

But the idea that the Earth was an integral, living, intelligent being was developed by Pythagoras and his school at Crotona in southern Italy around 500 BC. His concept of recycling of the life force, of the transmigration of souls, is a curious echo of the Palaeolithic theme of perpetual regeneration of life. As a consequence of this theory, he also believed in the kinship of all living things.

'Whereas the Milesians were impelled by innate intellectual curiosity and dissatisfaction with the old mythological accounts to attempt a rational explanation of physical phenomena,' comment Kirk and Raven, 'the impulse underlying Pythagoreanism seems to have been a religious or emotional one.'[88]

It is apparent that there is a spectrum of different pre-Socratic philosophies, ranging from physics, to metaphysics, to biology, health and mysticism. Plato, who lived almost a century after Pythagoras, was influenced by the earlier philosopher's vision of a living Earth. In the *Timaeus*, Plato proclaims that the Earth itself, via a cosmic intelligence, not the Olympian Gods, animates all life on the planet. The world is 'that Living Creature of which all other living creatures severally and generically are portions'.[89] Just as human life emanates from the life of the Earth, so do our souls emanate from the world soul. 'Whence can a human body have received its soul,' writes Plato, 'if the body of the world does not possess soul?'[90] He believed that all life on the Earth was interdependent with the life of the Earth, forming a symbiotic planetary unity. This unity is more concretely formulated in his geomantic musings in *The Laws*: 'Some localities have a more marked tendency than others to produce better or worse men. Most markedly conspicuous of all will be localities which are the homes of some supernatural influences, or the haunts of spirits who give a gracious or ungracious reception to successive bodies of settlers.'[91] Once again we see the interaction of the mind with the landscape. This interaction, however, is not one way, it is reciprocal: 'Earth as being your mother, delivered you,' Plato remarks in *The Republic*. 'Now as if your land were your mother and nurse, you ought to take thought for her.'[92]

According to Theophrastus (371–288 BC), a philosopher who studied with both Plato and Aristotle in Athens, there is an optimum environment for every living organism, an *oikos topos* which provides the most beneficial combination of nourishment, security and well-being for survival.[93] '*Oikos*' is the root of the Greek word for ecology, the study of harmonic interactions between organisms and environment. Ecology became recognized as the biological dimension of geomancy.

The Romans inherited from the Greeks a deep respect for the Earth. The great orator Cicero proclaimed that 'the world is an intelligent being, and indeed also a wise being'.[94] The Neo-Platonic philosopher Plotinus revivified Plato's doctrine of a world soul or *anima mundi*, and the historian Tacitus remarked that Mother Earth was the 'all-ruling deity, to whom all else is subject and obedient'.[95]

The Roman omphalos or navel of the world was situated in the temple of Vesta in the Roman Forum. Her shrine was the most sacred in the Roman religion. Vesta is the Latin for Hestia, one of the most ancient Greek Goddesses. Hestia symbolized the hearth, the fireplace, the centre of every family's home, in effect its personal navel of the Earth. The fireplace was the axis around which the household revolved for warmth, light, cooking, eating, relaxing and story-telling. Hearth is another form of earth – (h)earth.

NUMINOSITY

Like other early people, the Romans believed in a supernatural life force which they identified as *numen*. Akin to the Melanesian *mana* or the Iroquois *orenda*, it is not a deity but is possessed by deities.

Although it may emanate from gods or goddesses, it is not exclusive to them. It confers exceptional qualities on men and women.

Numen is also the essence of the intangible spirit of place, the charged aura of places of power. The astrologer-poet Manilius, a contemporary of Tacitus, wrote that Hesiod sang of 'the gods of the woodland and the *numina* sacred to the nymphs'.[96] Classicist H.J. Rose suggests that he can only be referring to the fact that the wild places which the nymphs and their Italian counterparts were thought to inhabit were themselves suffused with *numen*.

The biographer Plutarch (AD 41–54) pointed out that these numinous places, the wild regions far from human habitation, where nature was undisturbed, were essential to the vitality of the rest of the Earth. *Numen* exudes the atmosphere of 'the other world'. Ovid, the Roman poet, described an ancient grove of holm-oaks on the Aventine Hill of the capital, 'at sight whereof you might say, "there is *numen* here"'.[97]

In the springtime offerings were made to the Earth Goddess, Tellus Mater. She was thought to give an unimaginable amount of *numen* for the fertility of agricultural fields, so it was wise to tend her in a caring and reverent manner. Rose makes it clear that Tellus was not an abstract 'personification of the planet on which we live, but much more nearly the owner of the *numen* of those portions of the surface which the Latin-speaking farmers cultivated'.[98] Treaties were made with foreign nations in which the Italian officials were first purified and energized by touching the *numen*-charged soil of the Roman citadel with their heads. Thus the idea of a living Earth was recognized and honoured by the Romans in many aspects of their life, from the mysterious sense of nature to farming and politics.

CHRISTIANITY

The genesis of Christianity in the Middle East, and its subsequent spread to Old Europe and the rest of the world, completely altered the way in which the Earth spirit was regarded and produced a tide of moral judgement against anything that the Goddess traditions held sacred. Following Judaism, from which it emerged, orthodox Christianity sought to maintain the separation between the creation and the creator. When there is a religious division of this magnitude, participation mystique and cross-state communication with nature are forgotten.

Paul the Apostle taught that the natural world had fallen into sin along with humanity and needed to be redeemed by the saving grace of Christ. The realm of matter in nature was considered to be an impediment to the spirit. Life on Earth was just a stopping place on the path to absolution from original sin. This was because Christianity, as educator Dolores LaChapelle observed, 'focused on the endings of things, preferring to concentrate on the "ideal" of life after death in a perfect state called heaven. Life on this "plane of being" was transitory, unimportant, even illusory; therefore the earth itself became expendable, of no real value, thus permitting total exploitation of nature'.[99]

This emphasis on the afterlife isolated the static end phase of a linear progression towards salvation which was not integral to the archaic cycle of birth, life, death and regeneration. The fragmentation of the continuous cycle of existence contributed to the emerging geomantic amnesia in which humanity began to disengage from primordial planetary rhythms. Psychiatrist George Talland defined amnesia as 'the premature closure of a searching cycle'.[100] Although he was giving a modern clinical description of this condition, it gives us an insight into the collective psyche of this transitional time. It must have been very disturbing to many early Christians, especially those who lived in the country and were still closely allied with the old Earth traditions.

For the more orthodox believers, pre-Christian sacred places, such as stone circles, standing stones and earthworks, were seen as reminders of an opposing worldview and were later reclassified as works of the Devil. Groves of venerated sacred trees were chopped down. However, total obliteration of the ancient monuments proved to be an impossible task. A more prudent strategy was to take over the sacred sites, temples and holidays of the ancient world and bring them into the Christian fold. This was a subtle form of spiritual conquest, in which the original place or time was still held sacred, while the old spirits and deities were absorbed into the Christian tradition. The archaic Earth rites were considered pagan ('of the countryside', implying pre-Christian nature religions) and were not encouraged. Thus as the new urban religion spread, the ancient bond with the Earth gradually dissolved.

One of Plutarch's later works was a lament entitled *On the Decline of*

Oracles, in which a story is told of a ship passing some islands near Greece. When it was suddenly becalmed, a mysterious voice was heard saying: 'Great Pan is dead.' Plutarch also relates that at the same time in Britain the Druids saw portents, including violent winds and lightning flashes, indicating that 'one of the Mightier Souls had fallen. Their passing and dissolution fosters tempests and storms and often infests the air with pestilential properties'.[101] Without human reciprocity, the spirits of place effectively exist in a state of suspended animation until they are recognized again.

So the sun began to set on the conscious interactive environment of the Goddess. This gradual uncoupling made civilized humanity aware that they were no longer 'outside' Earth time. There was a sense of being caught between two times: the nostalgia of the past and the promise of future redemption.

A CHANGE OF MIND

THE CHRISTIAN WEST c 400–1180

The religious and political victory of Christianity in Europe inflicted a grave, though not fatal, wound on the body of belief in a living planet, the mother of all life.

Christianity emerged as a distinctly urban religion, borrowing freely nonetheless from the myths and symbols of many of the pagan religions with which, in those heady times of temporal and spiritual breakdown, Christianity shared the Mediterranean stage.[1] As it became increasingly institutionalized, the new religion rested on two major pillars: Christ's redemption of an inherently sinful humanity, and the world itself as a place of unhappiness to be endured until we reached God, far removed from the debased material world.

This new God was worshipped in darkened chapels, rather than outside, and decidedly not by dancing in the woods or fields in the moonlight. The pleasures of this life, this body and this Earth were at best diversions that took our minds and souls from their real aim. Sexuality ceased to be one of the mysteries at the very heart of life and became degraded, as was the body itself, to a regrettable, though necessary, means to procreation. Indeed, indifference if not out and out hostility to the joyful and celebratory aspects of sexuality followed from a theology that no longer centred on an Earth that itself was alive, for an Earth seen as fecund mother necessarily put the procreative and the pleasurable near the centre of both myth and worship. A constant complaint made against the pagans by early Christians, as well as Christian missionaries who would later engage in proselytizing and subjugating the nature people and their religions in Ireland, Africa, North and South America, Asia and elsewhere down through the centuries, was that the non-Christians acted in a 'sinful' manner by celebrating the blessings of life.

At a very basic level, Christian theology undermined belief in a living nature by reconceptualizing the underlying structure of time. The cycles of nature – the seasons, the tides and the stages in people's lives – still existed as a physical reality for most people, but the time of theology was now a one-way process, from Creation to apocalypse, punctuated, to be sure, by the divine incarnation in Bethlehem. For Christians, real time, the time of their faith, was now seriously out of joint with nature's time.

We see all this very clearly in one of the central texts that emerged as the Church became an official religion of the declining Roman Empire, Augustine's *Concerning the City of God* . . . , begun in 410 after the fall of Rome to the Goths and finished in 426, just as Augustine's own city of Hippo was about to be taken over by the invading Vandals. Significantly, the work was subtitled *contra pagani* – against the pagans. After condemning the blasphemous and irreligious idea that 'God is the Soul of the World' and that the world is therefore to God 'as the body is to the soul' as a terrible heresy that leaves nothing at all 'which is not a part of God', Augustine takes pains to explain that 'the earth is the work of God, not his mother'.[2]

Similarly, although the body was not created as a prison for the soul, since the Fall that is what, in effect, it has become. To Augustine, 'the soul makes war with the body'; our flesh has 'come under deserved punishment. . . .' Augustine's divorce from nature was so extreme, in fact, that he noted with approval that Genesis says 'And God saw that the light was good', following the creation of light, while the advent of darkness or night gets no such approval – the dark night was associated not only with the fallen angels, but with evil in general.[3]

A second teaching of the early Roman Church undermining the idea of a living Earth took hold in the years after 553, when the Council of Constantinople supposedly condemned as anathema the teachings of Origen (AD 185–253 or 254), especially his theory concerning the pre-existence of souls. Recent scholarship has shown that the attack on Origen was not really an official Church position, but for the next 14 centuries it was thought to be, and the historical association between Origen's theories and the heresy of denying Christ's divinity made it unlikely that the mistake would be easily realized.[4] And if souls cannot be pre-existent, then ideas concerning prior lives or future lives – that is, ideas about reincarnation – are similarly false. Accepted by many early Christians, and central to numerous pre-industrial cultures, belief in reincarnation established a vital connection between people and the Earth. Interring their relatives' bones in soil that literally contained their family roots, early peoples continuously resanctified their land. If, on the other hand, this life on Earth is but a stage we must endure before reaching our real, afterlife goal, then it is of little matter if the land is honoured, or if it is seen as of our flesh and blood.

Yet religious belief dies hard, especially if rooted in the day-to-day experiences of those who live within the cycles of nature. Despite an apparent incompatibility between believing in a living Earth and Christian theology, such tenets remained fairly widespread throughout the Middle Ages. These ideas of a living nature were, to be sure, watered down until they were but pale reflections of the original pagan traditions, living on sometimes only in the symbolism of a harvest rite carried on at a notable local rock or spring for centuries; in such a case it is difficult to know how many of the participants would have been able to articulate their belief in the living Earth. In other instances the substratum of a living, animated nature – assumed, rather than spelled out – would have been quite clearly evident to virtually all its practitioners (as, for example, in alchemy). Disapproved of, branded as heretical, and often practised under the threat of horrible tortures and executions, the pagan tradition had to go underground.

It is certainly clear that the Church fathers saw their fight against pagan traditions as continuous. Correspondingly, they grew to recognize its signs, and, unless compromise were necessary for strategic reasons, to spare no resources to wipe it out. A touch of compromise, for example, seems hinted at when Pope Gregory I wrote to Abbot Mellitus in 601 that instead of destroying pagan temples in England he should Christianize them. Although Gregory focused on not having to duplicate 'well-built temples', he could not have been unaware of the widespread understanding that worship, celebrations and healings traditionally took place at particular power spots where the life-giving energies of the Earth Mother were especially accessible and powerful. Such power spots could not be ignored; their power had to be redirected to Christianity as part of its effort to 'assume spiritual control of the country'.[5]

A couple of centuries later, at the Council of Nantes, the practice of venerating stones at ruins was condemned; those who neglected to destroy such 'idols' were considered guilty of sacrilege.[6] Nevertheless, worship has continued at many until modern times. Reports from the British Isles, Italy, southern France, Hungary, Germany and elsewhere indicate on-going and widespread worship at stones; together with the large numbers of rituals incorporating images of fertility at holy wells, springs, sacred groves, or around maypoles, often in association with a 'Diana' figure, these incidents clearly argue a persistence of ancient traditions.[7]

Among Christian women mystics of the later Middle Ages the older tradition of the Earth as the mother also remained strong. For example, Hildegard of Bringen (1098–1179), from the Rhineland, in her poem 'Cosmos: the Manifestation of God', writes that the Earth is '. . . mother of all, for contained in her are the seeds of all'.[8] The Earth, she says, is 'the fleshly material of people, nourishing them with its sap, as a mother nurses her sons or daughters'.[9] Using imagery that reveals the association between this living Earth and concern for fertility and sensual pleasure that was at the heart of its worship, Mechthild of Magedburg (1210–80), also from the Rhineland, claimed that her soul was loved by God 'with great passion in the bed of love'.[10]

Those who read the works of the major philosophers of Classical Greece (known rather imprecisely in the West until the twelfth century) found substantial support for an Earth that was organic in nature. As we have seen, to the Stoics, Plato and the Neo-Platonics, the Earth was an animal and could be understood physiologically. Plato's student, Aristotle, based his cosmology and physics on categories that were vital, as in, for example, his explanations of the fall of heavy bodies, ideas used later by Augustine. Aristotle's analysis of the world emphasized, unlike Plato, its changes, mutability and growth.

One of the first signs of the expansionism that was to engulf the histories and fortunes of the West occurred when the Roman Church called for a crusade to recapture the Holy Land from the Muslims. That crusade and several others that followed unleashed powerful forces that would transform the world for many centuries. Significantly, when in 1095 Pope Urban II issued the call for the First Crusade, he repeated another claim from antiquity, that Jerusalem was, as the Vulgate, the Latin Bible, had described it, the *umbilicus terrae*. The Crusade was necessary, the Pope claimed, because 'Jerusalem is the navel of the world, a land which . . . the Redeemer of mankind illuminated by his coming'.[11]

THE CHRISTIAN WEST, c 1180–1600

Three fairly widespread areas of medieval belief or practice in the late Middle Ages had at their core belief in a living nature: the lore of gems, crystals and other stones; alchemy; and certain geomantic practices followed in choosing sites and designs for sacred buildings.

According to an eleventh-century work, agate possesses eight principal virtues, including giving protection from snakes, witches, hidden fiends, thunder and disease; sapphires, another work from the thirteenth century maintained, prevented poverty.[12] The particular powers that specific gems or stones had came from a complex web of interrelationships that ultimately derived from the living cosmos of which they were a part.

Alchemical practices similarly presupposed a living matrix from which all substances had arisen.[13] For example, veins through the Earth in which water and the 'seeds' of metals or other chemicals ran were commonly likened, as in ancient texts, to the veins of blood in human and animal bodies. The alchemist helped to deliver only what had come to term within the 'womb' of his or her retort, according to a popular metaphor, although the alchemical midwife certainly tried to speed up the process of the material (and spiritual) transmutations. Not only is the context the ways in which living creatures function, but several of the alchemical laboratory practices are also commonly explained using the terms and imagery of lovemaking.

Finally, it was not uncommon for medieval church architects and builders to function within a hidden tradition of geomancy. For example, the cathedral at Chartres, a centre of Neo-Platonic theology,[14] was designed in this way. Locations for sacred buildings were chosen by means of dowsing techniques, portents from dreams, or other divination techniques. As we have seen in Chapter 1, these traditions too arose from a sense of a living, animate Earth, of which the medieval geomancers, even when working within a specifically Christian mystic vision, would still be well aware.

It is certainly not true that alchemy existed as a discipline totally separate from those of geomancy or the lore of gem magic, and that their individual practitioners did not share some of the same legends, vocabulary, texts and practices. Neither is it true, however, that these remnants of the old pagan tradition practised by geomancers, alchemists and magicians – and by witches or peasants celebrating the old calendrical rituals around a maypole – really represent a cult still hanging on, albeit in an underground, less visible, form. Something tangible has been broken; the tradition of the Goddess has gone or has survived by the thinnest of threads, and many who continued to carry on her rituals did so entirely or mainly ignorant of their significance or original context.

But undoubtedly there were places where a continuous family tradition survived through the centuries, and others where enough of the original fabric of the magical teachings held on so as to give a not unrealistic picture of ancient beliefs. In some instances, so consciously were the old symbols used as to make us realize that a clearly recognizable aspect of the Goddess of ancient times is being invoked, together with her association with a living Earth. For example, the classic English text of the late Middle Ages, *Sir Gawain and the Green Knight,* is an adventure tale concerning Sir Gawain, who represents the Christian court of King Arthur, and the Green Knight who comes from a pagan court.[15] The Green Knight is consort to a Lady, later identified as Morgan Le Fay, who is explicitly linked to sorcery and at one point is called 'goddess'. Consciously using a variety of symbols of the ancient Goddess, this unknown Christian author explicitly invoked the themes, associations and values of ancient paganism to comment on the Arthurian, Christian court.

Other examples of the conscious use of explicit symbols dating back to such ancient traditions are found in the numerous English church carvings that depict women displaying their exaggerated vulvas, sometimes alongside male figures with erect penises. These mostly date from the eleventh to the fifteenth centuries.[16] Called 'sheela-na-gigs', according to Brian Branston, their number, distribution and variety leaves little doubt that they are not just a Celtic phenomenon, but are rooted more in medieval English culture.[17] In this context it is interesting to note that in 1263 the English Church tried to halt the common practice of making the communion Host in the shape of testicles.[18]

Also found in churches built before 1500 are carvings of heads whose hair is depicted as green foliage. These tend to lend credence to Branston's conclusion:

'[There] was from the earliest times among English country-folk a reverence for a female figure with an exaggerated sexual organ. . . . the figure is pagan but firmly set in the centre of Christian worship, the church, and is therefore numinous or divine. . . . [The] sheela [is] the actual representation of the Great Goddess Earth Mother on English soil. [It is] surprising . . . that the 'idol' should so clearly retain characteristics which go back to . . . the Stone Age.'

Indeed, attempts to remove such figures from local churches have led to protests from church members and, in one instance, to the sheelas being replaced.[19]

The Protestant Reformation and Catholic Counter-Reformation of the sixteenth century created a new social and ideological context for debating the issue of magic – and by extension, the question of the lifefulness of nature. One important charge against the Catholics by the Protestants was the extent to which Catholic dogma was based on magic; the sacrament of the mass was an obvious example. For while the Catholic Church generally condemned magic, the function of the priest was precisely to be a vessel for magical power. According to the Church, however, the priest – unlike the sorcerer – was an authorized agent of God. Many Protesant reformers objected strongly to resemblances to pagan idolatry. Catholics, in turn, became defensive, initially denying the charges and attempting to put a damper on some church practices; but they went on to level countercharges of magical practices against some reform leaders. It was not exactly an auspicious time for either Catholic or Protestant natural philosophers to advance speculations based on animist notions.[20]

The decades of warfare between Protestant and Catholic countries that dominated the early modern European historical stage, and the devastating civil unrest and warfare that broke out in many European countries as Catholics and Protestants vied for control, had a profound effect on ideas about the world. The widespread killing and devastation led some, particularly among the intelligentsia, to suspect and even reject religious dogma, fuelling a wave of scepticism in the late 1500s and 1600s against belief in general. Seventeenth-century philosophers anxiously demanded new criteria, so that mere belief could be replaced by unequivocal true knowledge. This was a central thread running through the works of Francis Bacon, Galileo, René Descartes and Isaac Newton, among many others. Their quest was ultimately to lead to an emphasis on independent, objective knowledge. Such knowledge, it was finally decided, could be based only on the shape, size and mobility (quantitative and spatial characteristics) of the assumed tiny atoms and molecules underlying all phenomena.[21] These changes in thought were nearly fatal to the idea of a living Earth.

EUROPE, c *1600–1750*

By around 1600 it was still widely thought that the Earth was a living creature. Yet by the end of the seventeenth century educated people in England and large areas of Europe were certain that the planet was a mere lump of dead matter, a view they persistently sought to impose on everyone else throughout Europe and the rest of the world. The essence of all such matter was its inertness; according to the seventeenth-century mechanical philosophy, the quantitative measure of its 'matter and motion' wholly accounted for the properties of any substance.

It was the scientific revolution and especially Sir Isaac Newton's theories (discussed later in this chapter) that provided the intellectual framework for what became known as the 'machine universe'. Yet, paradoxically, for most of his life Newton himself continued to believe that nature, and the Earth, were alive. It was a view he dared not publish, as we shall see, because of its associations with ideas that, during England's Civil War, had formed a significant part of the ideological arsenal of leaders of land seizures and peasant movements against fen draining, deforestation, and so on.

From ancient times, in fact, but with greater frequency since the Reformation, 'enthusiastic' movements have arisen periodically, imbued with a millennarian vision and an insurrectionary politics that respected no authority but their own divinely-inspired 'inner voice'. Some of these movements, such as the Quakers, have managed to survive into modern times and attain an institutional base; but the Quakers had originally been a moderate compromise that arose after the wilder, less accommodating times of the English Civil War, when such groups began to be labelled 'enthusiasts'. Historically these enthusiastic groups have struck fear into the hearts of authorities. And many of them have had their roots in forms of magic.

In the period prior to the scientific revolution, England was becoming one of the first nation-states, as well as separating from the Roman Catholic Church. Following Henry VIII's break from Rome in 1534, the dissolution of the monasteries led to land speculation which had been unknown in feudal times. For the lower classes, this was a catastrophic development.

Much of the common land that had traditionally been used by peasants for gathering wood, cultivating small gardens, or grazing cattle now began to be 'enclosed', most often for the exclusive purpose of raising sheep for the expanding woollen industry. Vast numbers of peasants were torn from their customary sources of food and warmth and were thus forced from their land. They joined masses of other expropriated peasants, along with large numbers of what have been called 'masterless people' – beggars, vagabonds, immigrants, outlaws, wandering labourers – who, by the early 1600s, spent much of their time squatting on the margins of society, often in the forests.[22] Those forests themselves had been under attack, however, for timber was needed to construct the buttresses and beams used to shore up the coal mines, or to build England's rapidly growing fleet of navy, merchant and pirate ships (by no means separate categories at that time). England's already sparse woods were being rapidly depleted, and there was pressure to move the squatters off.[23] Other areas of the countryside were similarly affected by the emergence in the sixteenth and seventeenth centuries of England's first significant enterprises organized along capitalist lines – centralized production, large-scale investment and an advanced division of labour.[24]

The effect of all these developments on the rural population might be clearer if we examine the explosive rise of the British coal industry.[25] By the sixteenth century England's limited timber supply was near exhaustion; expeditions were sent to fell extensive forests in Ireland and Canada during the following century, but for growing cottage industry and domestic heating needs, it became increasingly necessary to dig for coal, which Britain was blessed to have in good measure. Dig they did. From the 1560s to the 1680s, for example, shipments of coal out of Newcastle rose from 33,000 tons a year to 620,000 tons, an increase of nearly 20 times in only 12 decades. The mines went deeper and more shafts were opened; the owners built larger and more complicated machinery, and worked their miners, many of whom came from the surrounding countryside, harder and longer. The new mining methods were costly: by 1700 it was not unusual to spend £2000 to reach just one seam. One mine owner paid £20,000 to install drainage tubes against flooding.[26] Such investments required 'efficient' use of resources, especially the people working the mines. As a result, there was a rise in the number of people suffering from long-term debilitating diseases and an increase in the number of fatal accidents.[27]

In England it was coal, in Germany and elsewhere on the Continent precious metals and metals for warfare. But everywhere mining was on the increase – even in the New World, where the conquistadores drove the Indians into the Earth for as much gold and silver as could be had, shipping it back to Europe to pay for their greater trade with Asia.

To those who believe that the Earth is alive, mining traditionally bears tremendous symbolic significance, and if done at all is carried out with a certain reverence, or even reluctance.[28] One American Indian explained why mining was so repugnant to him:

> 'You ask me to dig for stone? Shall I dig under [my mother's] skin for her bones? Then when I die I cannot enter her body to be born again.'[29]

In his *Re-enchantment of the World,* Morris Berman remarks that up until the fifteenth century 'the sinking of a new mine was accompanied by religious ceremonies, in which miners fasted, prayed, and observed a particular series of rites'.[30] Miners' rituals sometimes symbolically requested permission from the Earth to remove her minerals and treasures – just as an American Indian hunter would ask the spirit of an animal to give up its life so that humans might eat. In other ceremonies, a commitment to take only measured amounts was made, or a symbolic offering, such as food or a valuable object, was given in exchange. But such commitments, and the attitudes of respect for the Earth that they reflect, were clearly anachronistic in an age that was shipping more than six hundred thousand tons of coal a year out of Newcastle. If the maximum number of seams were to be mined, dictated only by market conditions and the availability of transport, such attitudes had to be banished.

In seventeenth-century England, according to Christopher Hill, 'virtually all industry was a matter of collecting and processing natural products'.[31] The growth of mining, forestry and the wool trade meant that for the first time in England's history new forms of economic activity were based on viewing the Earth primarily as a source of profit.

This new attitude had a brutalizing impact on the natural world. We should not be surprised, therefore, to find contemporary protests against the view that the Earth should be plundered for her riches. As early as the end of the fifteenth century, an allegory was written revealing strong local opinions about the effects of mining on the farmlands of Lichtenstat in Saxony. In this work, Mother Earth is testifying as a plaintiff, having filed charges of matricide against a miner. To support her claim she calls upon the pagan deities as expert witnesses:

> 'Bacchus complained that his vines were uprooted and fed to the flames and his most sacred places desecrated. Ceres . . . that her fields were devastated; Pluto that the blows of the miners resound like thunder through the depths . . . the Naiad, that the subterranean waters were diverted and her fountains dried up; Charon that the underground waters had been so diminished that [his boat] was unable to carry the souls across to Pluto's realm, and the Fauns protested that the charcoal burners had destroyed whole forests to smelt the miners' ores.'[32]

In response to this and other protests, pro-mining apologetics were published, the most famous by Georg Agricola. His encyclopedic treatment of the various aspects of mining practice and technology, *de re Metallica* (1556), opens with a discussion of fears that mining was extremely dangerous. People were saying, Agricola acknowledged, that mining was an occupation fraught with various perils, but most of these he blames (in a managerial style still with us) on the carelessness of the mine-workers. Agricola also admitted to contemporary complaints that mining devastated the air, soil and water – '. . . when the ores are washed, the water which has been used poisons the brooks and streams, and either destroys the fish or drives them away' – but his reply was simply that without the wealth and materials dug out of the ground, civilization would be impossible. Besides, mines tend to be located in mountains or valleys otherwise unproductive or 'invested in gloom' so any damage caused will be of little consequence.[33]

Such radical social and natural transformations extending across the face of early modern Europe and England were not, of course, painless. Peasant uprisings and plebeian urban movements imbued with class resentments and sometimes egalitarian beliefs spread, frequently among those classes most victimized by the new land policies. In Provence in 1578, for example, Catholic and Protestant peasants joined together to burn chateaux and massacre local nobles. Earlier, in the German Peasant Wars of 1525, the expansion of landlord privileges at the expense of traditional peasant rights surfaced as a central issue.[34]

In the first half of the seventeenth century England had a series of bad harvests, which particularly affected the poor.[35] There were widespread riots against enclosures and rebellions also against the draining of the Fens – it was as leader of such resistance that Oliver Cromwell, 'Lord of the Fens', first rose to prominence.[36] In the cheese district of Wiltshire, the county of Avebury and Stonehenge, violence erupted over deforestation. In Buckinghamshire, 'tumultuous pro-ceedings' lasting from 1647 to 1649 threatened to tear down enclosures. Gerrard Winstanley, the Digger, led a number of labourers to the common on St. George's Hill on 1 April 1649, to manure and work it, with the vision that 'the Earth should be made a common treasure of livelihood to whole mankind [sic]'.[37]

Writing about traditional agricultural societies, especially in Britain, Janet and Colin Bord have commented that the 'importance of [harvest time] is shown by the widespread nature of harvest customs and rituals, and by their vitality. Most of them only died out when machinery took over the harvest, and even now traces still remain'. They cite the example noted by the folklorist Alexandre Carmichael in the Highlands and islands of Scotland:

'The day the people began to reap the corn was a day of commotion and ceremonial. . . . The whole family repaired to the field dressed in their best attire to hail the God of the harvest. Laying his bonnet on the ground, the father of the family took up his sickle, and facing the sun, he cut a handful of corn. Putting the handful of corn three times sunwise round his head, the man raised the "Iolach Buana" reaping salutation.'[38]

With the outbreak of the English Civil War in 1642 and the breakdown of censorship and central power, magical practices and beliefs, already rather common in the countryside, became even more prevalent. More books on astrology, alchemy and the medicine of the holistic thinker Paracelsus were published in the ten years from 1650 to 1660 than in the previous century, and many foreign works on magic were translated into English. German mystical theology, too, acquired a large English following at the time.[39]

Among many of the Independent sects most active in Civil War political and religious agitation interest in magic ran especially high. John Everard, a Familist, translated works of Hermes Trismegistus, the apocryphal Egyptian sage whose writings became central to the body of ideas known as Hermetic thought. Leaders and many of the most prominent members of the Ranters, the Familists (including the apothecary Nicolaus Culpeper and probably the astrologer William Lilly), the Fifth Monarch Men, the Seekers, the Quakers, the Muggletonians, and Gerrard Winstanley, the Digger, were partisans of astrology, magic, or the alchemy of the German shoemaker, Jacob Boehme. Magic was proposed as a course of study at the universities by reformers, and debates about magic took place at Oxford.[40] The Czech philosopher Comenius, whose ideas were so influential in the 1640s, merged Hermetic ideas with Baconian philosophy – and in the hands of Samuel Hartlib and his plan for social, economic, religious and educational reforms, gained an even wider support, including leaders of Parliament and many craftsmen. No wonder that one historian has concluded that 'the natural magic tradition attained unprecedented influence and attention in England during the Puritan Revolution.'[41]

It is certainly not true, however, that every magus was on the left or identified with the dispossessed during England's upheaval. Specifically aristocratic and royalist alchemists, magicians and probably even witches existed. What is true, however, is that in the minds of the mid-seventeenth-century critics of magic a strong link connected magic and left-wing politics.

At first glance it is not obvious why in the middle of debates ranging from the question of suffrage to the issue of collective farming, men and women trying to rebuild their social world should turn to magic. There are, however, several concrete areas where opponents of a centralized Church of England or the other glaring social and religious inequalities of the time would have overlapping interests or points of view with visionaries of the occult. Most significantly, the exponents of magic and the left sectarians shared a philosophical premise that, quite differently from traditional Aristotelian logic, emphasized contradiction and polar oppositions. For example, in 1652 the alchemist Thomas Vaughan wrote that the first matter of Creation was:

> '. . . a miraculous *substance* . . . of which you may affirme *contraries* without *Inconvenience*. It is very *weake*, and yet most *strong*, it is excessively *soft*, and yet there is nothing so *hard*. It is *one* and *all*: *spirit* and *body*: *fixt* and *volatile*, *Male* and *Female*: *visible* and *invisible*. It is *fire* and *burns not*: it is *water* and *wets not*: it is *earth* that runs, and *Aire* that stands still.'[42]

According to Vaughan and the other exponents of magic, change arises less from outside causes than from internal reasons, arising out of the contradictions inherent in any thing or situation. The social and political movements of the Civil War, relying as they did on inner authority rather than outside leaders for spiritual or political direction, might well have noticed how such a logic provided justification for their actions. That is, the logic based on opposites easily fed the 'enthusiastic' temper of the times – that style of feeling, believing, thinking, and especially acting that, according to contemporary critics, characterized radicals during the Civil War and allowed them to commit such outrages against order and decency as their insubordination within the (Parliamentary) armed forces, the regicide of Charles I, the abolition of the Church of England and House of Lords, and, not least, the seizure of property and the sexual excesses that were said to have taken place, even inside the churches, by some of the left-wing sectarian groups.[43] Precisely because magic emphasized the individual man or woman's ability to act upon the world and was capable of giving eager people a path to an inner source of power, it emboldened the would-be 'gnostic saviours' that the Civil War literally brought out of the woods.[44]

Additionally, opposition to desecrations of the Earth was common both among the dispossessed who migrated to the ranks of the Independent sects and among those whose practice of magic took them to the remaining wild places in England for their rituals. Assaults on the Earth by the forces of modernization struck hard at peasants and ex-peasants, but we may presume that the remaining forests and moors where these marginal people squatted would have frequently been the very same place where the astrologers, fortune tellers and witches performed their sacred rituals in celebration of the lifefulness and fertility of the planet, the mother to us all. For the lifefulness of nature – and hence the need to work with her in a different manner from that of 'objective' science – is at the core of all magical traditions. As Janet and Colin Bord wrote:

> 'Observation of the natural cycle, together with experience, taught the first farmers how they could promote the fertility of their land and crops and livestock. They knew, however, that good crops and healthy cattle were not achieved solely by keeping the land fertile, important as that was; there were other invisible forces at work. Innumerable rituals were followed as men attempted to reinforce these subtle forces and to influence them to work in their favour: rituals to encourage the return of the life-giving sun, rituals to energize the sprouting seed, rituals to cause the rain to fall. . . .'[45]

These themes may be traced back through the centuries; in classical Greek times and even beyond, there was a Goddess, often called Diana, connected with a religion of visions, whose following was especially strong among women, slaves and the lower classes, ruling 'over all those who lived *outside* the social order'. By the time of classical Greece, her following, along with that of a God often associated with her, Dionysus, was apparently causing consternation among the upper classes. By the Middle Roman Republic a campaign of annihilation, with countless executions, an army to hunt down leaders of the religion, and a ban on all night-time assemblies was being waged. One reason for upper-class disgust at these cults was their horror in thinking that 'men who have wallowed in their own and in others' debauchery' could ever be called upon 'to fight with sword for decency of your wives and children'.[46]

Some writers have recently found evidence of an archaic cultural and religious continuity reaching from Portugal, through Europe, Asia Minor, Arabia, and into India and parts of North Africa, concerning a common myth of a male horned god who had powers derived from an archetypal connection with both animals and plants, and was associated with orgiastic celebrations. A goddess with similar powers and associations, prior to him in origin, was similarly worshipped in revels in the wilds. She reflects earlier times when women had greater religious, political, sexual and economic power. Both deities 'persist as the most popular gods among people from the lower classes, even when the political establishment puts great money and effort into propping up the official war gods and the gods that personify the authority of clan and state. In some cases, the Great Goddess and the horned god also become the focus for an assault against the basic world-view of the established religion'.[47]

Whatever the reasons for the coming together of the Independent left and enthusiasts of the occult in seventeenth-century England, when in mid-century critics began to mount their attacks on the ideas and practices of the left-wing groups, the overlap between magic and the disaffected in the rebellion formed one of their prime themes. John Wilkins, a founder of the Royal Society, was an outspoken critic of the magical enthusiasts, linking some to the left-wing Levellers. John Webster, the educational reformer, was attacked as having the 'Familistical-Levelling-Magical temper,' and Samuel Parker denounced the 'Enthusiastical Fanatacisme' of the Rosicrucians as encouraging disorder. These criticisms were echoed by many in the community of natural philosophers, both in England and on the Continent, beginning around the middle of the seventeenth century, as they sought a new natural philosophy, based on sobriety, capable of countering widespread disorder and threats of subversion. For the influential continental critic of magic, Pierre Gassendi, 'there was no place for spontaneity in nature itself, nor could it be sanctioned in the human soul.'[48]

As the ideological campaign against 'enthusiasm' grew in strength, large numbers of influential intellectuals made a striking turn against the magic at its core; this was followed by their wholesale embracing of the new alternative, what was called, fittingly, the mechanical philosophy. That the campaign was so widespread in different areas of Europe reflects the fact that by mid-century what has been called 'the crisis of the seventeenth century' was felt nearly everywhere in Western Europe, even though it was only in England that the monarchy was deposed as a result of a full-scale civil war.[49]

During the whole of this period European civilization was extending itself, both inwardly and outwardly, in the most remarkable manner. Inwardly, it was a time when natural philosophers and craftspeople began to devise instruments that could enhance the human sensory organs. Stunning inventions such as the telescope (1609), microscope (c 1665), pendulum clock (1656), thermometer (from c 1600 on), and vacuum pump (1654) transformed our power to know the natural world in far-reaching ways. In a subtle manner, naked-eye observations were rendered less central, less real, our bodily sensory organs in effect now subservient to mechanical devices that would enhance their powers. And somewhat earlier there had been the printing press, the magnetic compass – as well as, in a perverse sense, the invention of cannon, which was less an extension of man's senses than of his brute strength.

The cannon, in turn, was the key to Europe's external extension, the tool that opened up its expansion out of the Mediterranean basin and northern Europe to explore and eventually colonize the rest of the world. And what did the Europeans discover in these distant lands? Varieties of paganism, cultures which took for granted that the world they lived in was a fellow creature.

Against the pantheistic world of the enthusiasts, where every tree, rock or stream reflected the wonders of the Creation, the many new voices of philosophical moderation put forth the doctrine that reality at the deepest level consisted only of the 'matter and motion' of the underlying atoms or particles that formed the cosmos. For any particular thing it was the amount of matter and motion, quantitative measures of the world, that defined it; all else, the sounds, colours, textures and smells, were only 'secondary' qualities. The world was said to consist only of 'inert', entirely passive bodies. John Keill, a disciple of Isaac Newton, explained at the beginning of the eighteenth century that 'every Mutation induced in a natural Body, proceeds from an external Agent; for every Body is a listless Heap of Matter, and cannot induce any Mutation in itself'.[50] In other words, according to the mechanical philosophy, matter, in essence incapable of self-activity, is dead. All change – in contrast to the logic of opposites – came from without.

During the scientific revolution, the growing commitment to the mechanical philosophy in effect provided an ideological justification for the new way of seeing the planet primarily as a source of minerals and other marketable resources. Nature dead is nature allowing – if not inviting – the power of measurement and calculation. Henry More's influential *Enthusiasmus Triumphatus* (1653) inveighed against the imagination, ecstasy and lust as the causes of enthusiasm, and found the philosophical roots of that delusion in Paracelsian alchemy, which taught that nature 'is the Body of God'. The newly founded (1660) Royal Society, in response to heavy criticism, issued a defence of its work in 1667, seven years after the restoration of the monarchy, that promised that the new science, because of its methods and assumptions, would ensure the defeat of enthusiasm, by allowing room for intellectual disputes 'without any danger of a *Civil War*'.[51]

To be sure, even as late as the last part of the seventeenth century there were still those, such as Spinoza in the Netherlands and Leibniz in Germany, with different visions, more closely tuned to the vitality in nature. Their visions, however, had trouble bearing fruit in succeeding centuries in the arid intellectual soil of Europe, where, owing to the mechanical philosophy, barrenness was seen as a virtue.

It would be a serious error to conceive of the battle against the enthusiasts as an intellectual campaign alone. Historians have long been puzzled over the fact that the bulk of European witchcraft persecutions and executions occurred not in the 'dark' medieval period, but rather in the sixteenth and seventeenth centuries, when the development of 'reason' and science would have supposedly made belief in witchcraft a vanishing phenomenon. It was during this period – and in England especially during the Civil War and interregnum – that persecution of witches reached its height.[52] In witchcraft circles today, this period is known as 'Burning Times', a nightmarish era of torture, forced confessions and widespread executions.

The campaign against witches goes back to much earlier times, of course, as in a sense does the more general fight against enthusiasm. But despite the condemnation of witches in the Bible, there were times when the practice of witchcraft was tolerated and even taken for granted – sometimes because of protection from powerful believers amongst the nobility, at court, or among the Church hierarchy; and perhaps often because the activities and beliefs of witches overlapped and shaded into any number of practices and ideas of other, more established, occult traditions having deep roots in the countryside.[53] Yet in the last half of the fifteenth century this all changed, and for the next two centuries what became essentially an extermination campaign against witches broke out in Europe. According to varying estimates (none of which, given the scattered and fragmentary documentation, will ever be proven) from one quarter of a million to nine million people were executed for being witches, the bulk of whom were poor and female.[54]

Around the middle of the seventeenth century and in connection with fears of additional uprisings in England, France and elsewhere, this war of extermination against witches broadened into a more general and sustained attack on magic itself, identified now as the root system growing under the wild tree of enthusiasm.

The rise of a specifically mechanical science at this time had a dual function in the campaign against enthusiasm in general and witches in particular. It served to certify, through the teachings about motion, space, time, causality, matter, life and death, precisely what reality was, and by implication what it could not be – what had, therefore, to be mere hallucinations.[55]

A third function of mechanical science, although this took longer to reveal itself, was that of helping to 'tame' nature. This showed up first in the advent of 'scientific farming', a long-term process that has amounted to nothing less than a new form of warfare against the Earth, as manure and compost were remorselessly replaced by synthetic substitutes. This has been compounded in the twentieth century by the use of heavy machinery. The compacted and deadened soil that is the result has been an enormous loss. Farmer and poet Wendell Berry writes:

> '[A healthy soil] is the great connector of lives, the source and destination of all. It is the healer and restorer and resurrector, by which disease passes into health, age into youth, death into life. Without proper care for it we can have no community, because without proper care for it we can have no life.
>
> 'It is alive itself. It is a grave, too, of course. Or a healthy soil is. It is full of dead animals and plants, bodies that have passed through other bodies. . . . If a healthy soil is full of death it is also full of life: worms, fungi, micro-organisms of all kinds. . . . Given only the health of the soil, nothing that dies is dead for very long'.[56]

The violations against the life of the soil described by Berry arose, he argues, from the desire 'to impose scientific (that is, laboratory) exactitude upon living complexities that are ultimately mysterious'.[57] By the seventeenth century, this process was already well under way, and the rise of the mechanical philosophy at the very least reflected, if it did not in some sense cause, this process.

Until around the 1500s, the general distrust of 'enthusiastic' behaviour on the part of the property-owning and conservative classes usually co-existed with other, contradictory, views. Even in the most proscriptive of Christian moralities, for example, it was customary throughout much of late medieval and early modern Europe to recognize the 'lord of misrule' at carnival times, to throw off the restraints ostensibly guiding one throughout most of the year. At such times, boisterous, drunken and licentious behaviour was tolerated and even encouraged.

In his *Popular Culture in Early Modern Europe*, Peter Burke traces the long-term campaign against such excesses, showing that from the sixteenth century onwards the clergy (and, later, certain members of the laity) led campaigns throughout Europe – Catholic and Protestant areas alike – specifically to 'reform or suppress many popular festivities' and, indeed, popular culture itself, partly because they considered many areas to be infected with people who seemed closer to 'savages' than to Christians. In 1509, for example, Erasmus complained that the Siena carnival had 'traces of ancient paganism'.[58] In place of the older ethic which stressed 'the values of generosity and spontaneity and a greater tolerance of disorder', reformers tried to shift popular sensibilities in the direction of self-control, frugality, hard work, order and (a significant change from earlier times) keeping firm distinctions between matters sacred and profane.[59] What is particularly interesting here is how, when the reformers singled out specific practices to condemn, emphasis fell heavily on magic; along with dancing and playing cards were listed divining, fortune telling, masks, magic, puppets, witchcraft and the use of folk healers. Even Christian plays were unhealthy and dangerous, no doubt because theatre itself excited the imagination.[60]

Popular culture, Burke argues persuasively, became particularly worrisome when, after the Reformation, widespread civil wars, peasant uprisings and urban unrest spread through parts of Europe. Making matters worse was the increasing literacy and a new phenomenon –

popular newspapers that spread news and opinion rapidly and widely. When in 1594 a group of rebellious peasants in Bergerac ended their assembly with cries of 'Liberté!', it was a clear sign of present and future dangers.[61] Popular rituals quite often had particularly egalitarian structures and festivals were frequently occasions of riot or rebellion – all this would have played a large part in the desire to suppress them, given the growing political involvement of peasants, craftspeople and other plebeian elements. Huge demonstrations occurred during the English Civil War. Burke concludes that the 'English in the mid-seventeenth century were the most politically conscious society in Europe'. This was upsetting to some. In 1690, after the Glorious Revolution, societies formed in England for the 'reformation of manners' were determined to stamp out gambling, taverns, whoring, licentious songs, as well as theatre, masquerades and fairs.[62]

These strictures were effective; between 1550 and 1650 many traditional customs were stamped out. A second phase of the reform campaign, lasting from about 1650 to the end of the eighteenth century, set out to build on the remarkable results so far, and placed even greater emphasis on the repression of any belief in a (non-Christian) supernatural.[63]

Throughout the British Isles literally hundreds of megalithic circles or standing stones are still intact, despite the campaigns to pull them down. That so many have survived after several thousands of years is testimony to their remarkable construction (far beyond the techno-logical ability of our civilization); but beyond their durability in the face of the elements, their continued presence speaks eloquently of the awe, or fear, with which they are viewed by their human neighbours, few of whom dared tamper with them.

With the outbreak of Civil War in England, the most far-reaching discussions and debates about church organization, hierarchy and doctrine erupted; in their first meetings, the Parliament of 1640 argued in particular about the extent to which under Charles I the Church of England had adopted liturgies, prayers and accoutrements closer to Roman Catholicism than to the spirit of English Protestantism. Committees were sent to all English counties by the House of Commons to deface, demolish and remove 'all images, altars or tables turned altar-wise, crucifixes, superstitious pictures, ornaments and relics of idolatry' from the churches and chapels. The Commons also appointed a committee of nine men with the power to demolish any monuments of superstition or idolatry that they found offensive.[64]

Whether it was an extension of such sentiments is probably impossible for us to be sure, but at least once during the Civil War a Cromwellian governor of Cornwall demolished the Men-Amber stone, fearing the veneration it commanded from those nearby.[65] By the eighteenth century, however, it seems to have been more for economic reasons that stones were knocked down, either to create more arable land or to provide building materials.[66] Given the extensive encroachment made over the previous century to the woods, moors, fens and commons, this should not be the least surprising.

ISAAC NEWTON

Isaac Newton was born in 1642, just as the Civil War between King and Parliament broke out. Shortly after the Restoration he went to study at Cambridge, one of the intellectual centres in the campaign against enthusiasm in general and witchcraft in particular, where he learned Cartesian philosophy as well as the limitations of any science based wholly on inert bodies.[67]

In effect, Newton's scientific career was spent trying to comprehend the all-too-elusive sources of activity in the supposedly inert world – as well as reconciling them with both the observed phenomena of the motion of bodies and the structure of geometry. In his earliest student notebook on natural philosophy, he had already begun to ruminate on what he was to call a 'secret principle of unsocialness' in nature to explain some of the behaviour of matter.[68] By the time of his *de Gravitatione et Aequipondio Fluidorum* (probably written in the late 1660s), Newton had developed a theory of matter as an emanation of the omnipresent God's will, who had imposed on certain spaces the attributes of impenetrability and mobility. Thus nearly two decades before his *Principia* (1687), Newton had come to see that the existence and mobility of matter can be best understood by an analogy with the will: sometimes God's, at other times that of Newton or his readers:

'. . . so God may appear (to our innermost consciousness) to have created the world solely by the act of will, just as we move our bodies by an act of will alone.'[69]

Thus at the core of his philosophy was one of the central concerns of the occult tradition: how mind can control matter. This emphasis on will would be a recurrent theme in Newton's work. It was will, perception, vegetation, the processes of putrefaction and ferment-ation, growth – all processes of living bodies – that from an early age Newton turned to in his quest to understand the world and its manifold appearances. At around the time that he wrote *de Gravitatione*, Newton composed two important alchemical papers. One, called by historians the *Vegetation of Metals*, was based on a set of four propositions:

All things are corruptible;
All things are generable;
Nature only works in moyst substances
And [with] a gentle heat.[70]

Both essays focused on the 'vital agent diffused through everything in the earth'. When introduced into a mixture of matter, this vital agent would first act 'to putrefy and confound [them] into chaos; then it proceeds to generation'. He carefully distinguished the 'vegetative' actions of nature based on this vital spirit from those actions which were 'purely mechanical'.[71] Newton believed that this spirit arose out of the bowels of the Earth to become fixed in minerals and salts, although some of it rises up into the air, becoming ether. And as this ether crowds into the atmosphere, it causes other ether to descend back down to the Earth, making bodies it passes through become heavy. Given this rise and fall of ether, Newton noted:

'Thus this Earth resembles a great animall or rather inanimate vegetable, draws in aethereal breath for its dayly refreshment and vitall ferment & transpires again [with] grosses exhalations. And, according to the condition of all other things living, ought to have its time of beginning, youth, old age, and perishing.'[72]

These concerns for the spirit pervading nature, for the source of activity in matter, remained Newton's central preoccupations; it was in alchemy that he was convinced the answers to his questions lay. His assistant and amanuensis, Humphrey Newton, recounted that Newton's 'fires were almost perpetual', and the extent to which he neglected food and sleep 'made me think he aim'd at something beyond ye Reach of humane Art & Industry'.[73] Given the extensive alchemical experiments and reading Newton undertook throughout the 1680s and into the early 1690s, his recent biographer has concluded that the *Principia* was 'an intrusion' into his primary concern, alchemy.[74] In alchemy Newton found the inherent sexuality of nature and parallels to other life processes were emphasized. In one alchemical paper, written in the late 1670s, for example, Newton remarked that he had produced 'a mercury as living and mobile as any found in the world. For it makes gold begin to swell, to be swollen, and to putrefy, and to spring forth into sprouts and branches, changing colours daily, the appearances of which fascinate me every day. I reckon this a great secret in Alchemy'.[75]

From such laboratory notes and essays there is reason to believe that Newton was able to find some of the elusive and wondrous substances hinted at in the alchemical corpus, though not the legendary philosopher's stone itself. Yet his labouring over his alchemical furnaces slackened and then, according to Westfall, stopped altogether sometime in the mid-1690s, after his move to London, even though he continued to buy alchemical books – 75 per cent of his recorded book purchases, in fact, between 1701 and 1705.[76] Following the death in 1702 of his arch rival and *bête noire*, Robert Hooke, Newton prepared his long-awaited *Opticks* for the press, and at its end set down his thoughts in a number of projected *Queries*, which, in their unpublished form, vividly portray his continued animist view of the world: '. . . since all matter duly formed is attended with signes of life . . . those laws of motion arising from life or will may be of universal extent' reads one draft, while another, in a cautious double negative, claimed that 'We cannot say all Nature is not alive'.[77] He emphasized that the laws of motion in his *Principia* were passive laws, in themselves insufficient to explain the manifold complexity of the observed world. There were other, active principles, underlying them – and these were his real goal, Newton hinted more than once.[78]

But both of the above quotations are from manuscripts Newton chose not to print, a reticence reflecting a profound philosophical re-orientation from the mid-1690s onwards. Working on an aborted second edition of the *Principia* in the middle of the decade, a couple of years after he had undergone a mental breakdown, Newton tried to improve his flawed theories of the moon and comets, as well as drafting replies to criticisms that had been raised about the first edition. No problem was more glaring than the question of universal gravitational attraction, the basis on which the whole of the *Principia* rests and also its most vulnerable theory. Newton saw all matter as mutually attracting – 'action at a distance' – even across the reaches of empty space, according to a precise mathematical formula. This contradicted the touchstone of the mechanical philosophy, the notion that matter was inert and able to interact only through impact. Trying to reconcile these inconsistencies for this stillborn second edition, Newton for the first time adopted the theory that certain qualities of bodies were the 'essential' ones.[79]

Two other important shifts in Newton's thinking around this time similarly represented a partial retreat from his notion of the lifefulness of nature. Both in treatises published by disciples and in hints and changes inserted in later editions of his *Principia* and *Opticks* (1704), Newton constructed a theory of cosmogony – a doctrine of the birth and development of the Earth – in opposition to the theory announced by Robert Hooke. Whereas for Hooke the sources of change to the Earth were internal to the Earth, the Newtonians proposed a complex celestial machinery which utilized the impact or near approach of comets as the major agent of terrestrial transformation. In other words, Hooke's Earth was vital, while Newton's was – like the inert bodies of the mechanical philosophy – primarily a passive body.[80]

Soon after Hooke's death, Newton announced in the *Queries* to his *Opticks* that even to debate such topics as the development of the Earth was 'unphilosophical'; but if the Earth were a living body, avoiding questions of its origin and major stages of subsequent development would be to turn away from the most interesting and central questions, so in the meantime, secretly, Newton debated precisely those topics.[81] In addition, that enthusiasm still posed a serious threat to society was vividly shown to him by the example of the notorious freethinker and Deist, John Toland, who borrowed freely from Newton's theories for his own unorthodox political and religious writings. In response, Newton used the Queries to the *Opticks* to back off from some of his earlier notions.[82]

In all three of these shifts in his worldview, made at the time that he was leaving his scholar's study at Cambridge to come to London to immerse himself in the world of politics and finance, Newton backed away from his earlier magical and animist belief in a world filled with life. He did not entirely leave off his former speculations, he merely became more discreet in the expression of them. Nonetheless, there is a marked change. No longer were Newton's eyes focused on a world 'delighted with Transmutations' and governed by 'secret principles of unsocialness' or by nature's 'secret fire'. No more did he write, as far as we know, about gold which swells and putrefies, 'to spring forth into sprouts and branches, changing colours daily, the appearances of which fasccinate me every day'. We do not find in his later writings speculations that 'the vast aethereall Spaces between us & the stars are for a sufficient repository for . . . food of the Sunn & Planets'. And, symbolically, in 1717 Newton bought a maypole, first erected in London in the Strand to celebrate the return of Charles II, putting it to a new use of supporting a telescope.[83]

Given Newton's role in sanctifying a new scientific worldview, and the influence that worldview has had on the world as successive national and tribal cultures have undergone modernization, it would be no exaggeration to claim that Newton's crisis of belief and the subsequent changes to his philosophy were also a crisis of the first order for the whole of Western and, hence, world culture. Despite any logical absurdities in the universal attraction of 'passive' matter, educated people came to see the world as an elaborate machine, a far cry from the widespread earlier view of the Earth as an organism, a mother who provided for her many children.

Not long after 1700 the battle was essentially won, for few were privy to the carefully hidden views of the great discoverer of the laws of nature, and when Newton died, most of the manuscripts reflecting his inner thoughts were labelled 'Not fit to be printed'.[84]

CONCLUSIONS

The Restoration attack on enthusiasm was, as we have seen, a product of the Civil War and revolution in England. Radical left-wing religious sectarians, subscribing to animate, magical views of the world, had urged the adoption of new ways of looking at nature, property, authority, relations between the sexes, and religion; new ways which, among other things, threatened to stop the forces of economic and political development in England in their tracks. Especially important were questions about the nature of nature. For, if alchemists and others were right about matter being alive, then mining's brutal assault on the Earth's skin would continue to be seen by many as an unthinkable violation.

Even though three of the foremost English intellectuals of the second half of the seventeenth century, Robert Boyle, Isaac Newton and John Locke, had a long-lasting interest in alchemy, corresponding about it and exchanging secret recipes, by the beginning of the eighteenth century no 'serious' English thinker would dare pursue the alchemical art. This reveals that a fundamental transformation in English consciousness had taken place – although not, we should be clear, because of a dramatic or systematic rebuttal of alchemy in the scientific literature of the time. Boyle and Newton, at least, went to their deaths still believing in the possibility of alchemical transmutation,[85] despite their popular reputations since the eighteenth century for having irrefutably disproved it. It is clear that here science was being used to construct an ideological barricade behind which the forces of order could defend themselves against the wilderness that lay beyond. Scientists proved all too willing to play the intellectual 'police force' in erecting the barricades and deciding which were the allowable categories for views wanting to be 'taken seriously'.[86]

Just when we are desperately in need of such knowledge, it is finally possible to pierce that veil of obfuscation and chicanery that consigned alternative images of reality to oblivion back in the seventeenth century. Whether nature and the Earth are to be seen and honoured as both alive and the source of all other life, or whether they shall be considered a mere collection of resources to be tapped, was implicitly at the heart of Newton's crisis. It is hard to think of a more pressing question for our times.

PART TWO

RECOLLECTION

Just as the traditional worldview disappears over time's horizon, there are signs that we may be reaching out to halt the process.

Let us return for a moment to our hypothetical amnesiac, our metaphor for the present cultural state of mind. He has forged ahead in a new life, relegating his former existence before his loss of memory to insignificance. Let us suppose, however, that after a period of time he encounters information in his new life that jogs old memories from his past. He begins to feel that he can glimpse something of what he knew then, and starts to recollect themes he used to consider important before the amnesia. Recollection – collecting together again the fragments. Then the recovering amnesiac has a catalytic experience: he sees a photograph that stirs deep feelings, dredging up further memories. This comes at a time of crisis in his new life, when his very existence is in jeopardy. He knows that if he can piece together the information he is uncovering to form a new jigsaw of his old understanding, he may be able to save himself. He starts talking to himself to clarify his thoughts.

As our generation moves towards ecological crisis, some of the old wisdom is beginning to filter back into our awareness in some curiously varied ways.

This part of our adventure deals with the doors being opened by some aspects of science, by broad-ranging study of ancient sites and traditions, and by the minds of individual scientists, visionaries and mystics.

CHAPTER THREE

WHOLE EARTH

To approach the idea of a living planet with its own sentience – of such a scale and structure that we have failed to recognize it in modern times – we first have to identify what it is we actually mean when we refer to 'the Earth'.

It is a natural tendency to think of the world simply as a hard body winging its way through space, but scientists have now come to view the planet as being composed of up to five zones or 'spheres'. These embrace and interact with one another in such a way that we can think meaningfully of the Earth only in terms of the whole they create.

THE SPHERES OF EARTH

The first Earth is the lithosphere, the solid body we most readily identify. At its heart is the core, about 4,350 miles (7,000 kilometres) in diameter and largely molten, probably composed of nickel and iron at very high temperatures. The central region or inner core could be solid. The core as a whole is surrounded by the mantle, about 7,880 miles (12,686 kilometres) across its outer diameter, which is composed of silicate minerals and has various zones within it. The uppermost division is thought to be a 'crystal slush'. The outer layer enclosing the mantle is topped by the crust, only about 22 miles (35 kilometres) thick or less, like the skin of an apple compared to the volume of the whole fruit. It is made up of three types of rock: igneous (heat-originated rocks formed from volcanic action or processes deep within the crust) such as granite; sedimentary (particles of weathered rock deposited – usually by water – in strata within the Earth's crust) such as sandstone and limestone, or of organic origin like coal; and metamorphic (rocks changed by heat, pressure or chemical action) such as gneiss, marble or slate.

Only in recent decades have we come to learn that the crust is composed of sections called 'tectonic plates' that move relative to one another, floating on the top layer of the mantle. At plate boundaries, where various forms of pressure are created, there is a high level of earthquake and volcanic activity.

Sedimentary rocks contain fossils which give us a geological time scale. The Earth was formed about four and a half billion years ago, and the fossil record suggests that life first appeared about 600 million years ago, with human beings beginning to appear perhaps four million years ago. We have thus been present on the planet for about 0.09 per cent of the Earth's history, while civilization has existed for a tiny 0.0001 per cent.

The second Earth is formed by the waters of the world, and is known as the hydrosphere. Water covers about 70 per cent of the world's surface in liquid or frozen form. On the surface there are oceans, lakes and rivers. Within the crust there are teeming volumes of subterranean groundwater. There is gaseous water in the atmosphere, too. The waters of Earth, the waters of life, form a global circulation system between land, sea and air. Water evaporates from large bodies of open water, rising into the air where it forms clouds. It falls back as rain. On land, part of this is returned to the atmosphere by the action of plant life and evaporation, while some of it joins rivers and streams and is returned to the sea, or leaks into the crust to join the subterranean groundwater systems.

The vast majority of Earth's waters are in ocean or glacier form, but rivers and streams, while holding a relatively small amount of global water at any given time, nevertheless allow the passage of a high volume of water over the course of a year.

A controversial view is that some of the groundwater is formed directly by processes deep within the Earth – 'primary waters' welling up from the depths through rock strata.

The third Earth comprises all the living organisms, known collectively as the biosphere – Gaia's brood, as it were. It encompasses all that grows, swims, slithers, crawls, walks or flies: the great mammals and fish of the oceans; trees – some of them the oldest living things on Earth; plant life; animal life; insects; microscopic lifeforms; birds and . . . human beings. The biosphere exists on or within the topmost layer of the Earth's crust, in the lower atmosphere (the 'sky') and within most of the bodies of water on the planet.

With the advent of space exploration, the biosphere has begun to move out into regions beyond the gaseous zone of Earth, the atmosphere. This fourth Earth, composed of gases, vapour and aerosol (airborne) particles, interacts with living things. It surrounds the Earth's crust and rises hundreds of miles before merging into outer space. It is produced by exhalation of the lithosphere in volcanic action and by all the processes of the biosphere. Without it there would be no sound, smell, golden sunsets, blue sky, or life itself – the atmosphere filters out dangerous radiations from the Sun and outer space.

Hanging in haloes around the solid body of the planet, the atmosphere is closer in at the poles than at the equator. About three-quarters of the atmospheric mass is concentrated in the lowest level, the troposphere, which we know as 'air'. This is composed of several gases, but mainly nitrogen and oxygen, and weather is created within this level. Air is constantly on the move, swirling and shifting in great currents and small eddies, due to temperature variations around the globe, producing wind action from the gentlest breeze to fierce, destructive hurricanes and tornadoes.

The troposphere becomes colder with altitude, but at a height of about seven miles (11 kilometres) at mid-latitudes, at a region known as the tropopause, temperatures begin to rise again with the start of the next atmospheric layer, the stratosphere. The upper levels of this region contain ozone molecules which filter out dangerous solar ultraviolet rays – it is damage to this atmospheric layer that is one of today's most pressing ecological concerns.

Above the stratosphere, the atmosphere merges into the iono-sphere. This is composed of layers of charged particles (ions), which humanity uses as a kind of ceiling off which it can bounce radio signals between distant stations on the ground. The electrical activity within the ionosphere causes it to glow; its dull green or red light has been recorded by satellites and in the right conditions can even be seen by the naked eye from the ground. Significant currents of electricity (DC) are continually flowing within the charged ionospheric gases, and it is thought these may be linked with little-understood electrical currents (telluric or earth currents) flowing through the crust about 47 miles (75 kilometres) below.

The fifth Earth is the energy body of the planet, called the magnetosphere. Strictly speaking, this could be considered an extension of the atmosphere, but it makes more sense to treat it as another manifestation of the Earth as a whole. Electromagnetic activity interpenetrates all the other spheres and extends many thousands of miles beyond the ionosphere, forming an 'energy envelope' around the Earth where its influence overrides the Sun's electromagnetic fields. This bubble of energy around the planet contains the Van Allen belts: rings of radiation containing trapped particles from outer space, created and moulded by the Earth's magnetic field (called the geomagnetic field) into a doughnut shape surrounding the planet and protecting it from the onslaught of much cosmic and solar radiation. The pressure of charged particles from the Sun – the 'solar wind' gusting at about a million miles an hour – affects the overall shape of the magnetosphere, so it is compressed where it faces into the solar wind but trails into space behind the planet in the opposite direction.

The magnetosphere is thus the interface between Earth and extraterrestrial energies and is in constant activity.

A particularly visible and beautiful expression of the magnetosphere occurs in the upper atmosphere above polar regions when air molecules come in contact with charged solar particles, accelerated and channelled by the Earth's magnetic field, producing shimmering, shifting displays of polar lights – the aurora borealis or australis.

Exactly how the Earth generates its own magnetic field is not fully understood, but it probably arises as a result of a kind of dynamo action caused by the varying rotational speeds of the core and the mantle. This geomagnetism varies in intensity over the Earth's crust due to mineral deposits, and is also subject to influences superimposed on it by solar, lunar, planetary and galactic sources.

Cyclic sunspot and associated solar flare activity, in addition to the 27-day rotational period of the Sun and its segmented magnetic field, have a definite effect on both magnetic and electrical conditions on Earth, which can indirectly affect weather, growth cycles, and even earthquake activity. In other words, through the terrestrial magnetosphere the Sun can influence the atmosphere, biosphere and lithosphere. Much the same is also true of the Moon. We will be encountering specific examples of these solar and lunar effects later in the book.

We have only gradually become aware of the carefully balanced interrelationships the biosphere has with its environment. The study of these relationships, ecology, has moved from being popularly perceived as a bizarre, unnecessary or 'trendy' activity to occupying an increasing amount of serious, general attention. The lesson of the delicate balances of nature has taken a long while for our modern culture to begin to absorb. We are now becoming increasingly aware of how, for example, human activity can interfere with the interactions between biosphere and atmosphere. If we cut down and burn rain forests to a great extent, as we are doing, then the balance of gases in the atmosphere will be affected. We will also remove the habitat of many species, with the consequent breakdown of food chains producing unforeseen effects. This sort of destruction will feed back to the biosphere in terms of temperature changes, weather alterations and so on.

Again, if we pollute the atmosphere directly with chemicals and gases, features such as the ozone layer become damaged, with a whole chain of possible effects being initiated – reduced protection of the biosphere from cosmic radiations may be only one of them. Similarly, if we continue to pollute the hydrosphere, all kinds of effects can be triggered. Creatures that live in the water die, or abnormal algae growth develops and the water becomes deoxygenated leading to a sequence of biological catastrophies.

But this sort of material is now becoming readily available and it is not the purpose of this book to produce some kind of ecological catalogue – we are looking for even deeper connections. Towards that end, we must look at an even more subtle form of ecology that is only just coming to light at this time, but which may yield insights into undreamt of connections between the biosphere and the planetary body, and between the human mind and the physical Earth.

THE ELECTROMAGNETIC WEB

The geomagnetic field exists because of what goes on within the lithosphere, and is further influenced by extraterrestrial factors. The biosphere and atmosphere react in turn to the global magnetic and electric fields. Further chains of effects result from this.

Western science has, in general, tended to consider that the low energy levels involved (the strength of the geomagnetic field averages at around half a gauss, for example) could not possibly affect living organisms. There has been resistance to Western research and published claims of Soviet work indicating that life *does* respond at these levels. Yet such sensitivity to natural energy fields is only to be expected. As A.P. Dubrov, the great Russian pioneer in the study of living organisms and geomagnetism, has written: '. . . life came into being and has evolved in the presence of the geomagnetic field.' The situation is well put by Guy Lyon Playfair and Scott Hill: '. . . the history of life on Earth may have been governed throughout its whole span by a geomagnetic influence so subtle that it is only recently that we have been able even to measure it accurately.'[1]

Living things have their biological sensitivities tuned to the levels of the natural environment, usually for their own specialist needs, but sometimes for purposes that remain obscure. The Indian liquorice plant (*arbrus precatorius*) is keenly sensitive to both magnetic and electrical stimuli, and is often used as a weather plant. Experiments with it have apparently shown that it can predict cyclones, hurricanes, tornadoes and even earthquakes.[2] The leaves of plants such as mugwort or chicory will turn themselves towards the north. In 1960, British botanist L.J. Audus fortuitously discovered that the roots of plants were sensitive to magnetic fields – magnetropism. In Canada, Dr V.J. Pittman noted that the roots of certain North American cereal plants, and some weeds, consistently aligned themselves in a north-south plane, parallel to the horizontal force of the geomagnetic field. He also discovered that the germination of some cereals could be accelerated if their seeds were pointed towards the north magnetic pole. When Dr H.L. Cox of Denver, Colorado, grew vegetables in soil sifted with magnetised ferrous ore (magnetite), growth rates increased dramatically. Illinois researcher J.D. Palmer was able to demonstrate that thousands of *volvox aureus* – a tiny spherical plant composed of a number of cells and one of the simplest of all living organisms – could not only respond to a bar magnet but could also sense the direction of lines of force in a magnetic field. Frank Brown, a great American pioneer of the study of biomagnetism in the 1950s and 1960s, discovered in an experiment with potatoes lasting nine years that their metabolic data revealed that the vegetables possessed an 'awareness' of when the moon was rising, overhead, or setting. He felt this must be due to some 'common physical fluctuation having a lunar period'. The prime candidate for that is, of course, the geomagnetic field, because measurements show that it is responsive to the lunar day and month, as it is to the solar cycles.

In carrying out directional experiments with 34,000 New England mud snails, Brown provided convincing evidence that they could respond to both solar and lunar effects on the geomagnetic field. The snails' morning tendency was to turn east, and in the afternoon to the west. When Brown introduced a magnet a little stronger than the Earth's field, and aligned with it, the snails continued to react to the Sun's passage; but when he put the magnet at right angles to the geomagnetic field, the molluscs began to follow a lunar pattern. In a later experiment with the more nocturnal flatworm, the creature followed the lunar influence directly.

In 1975 Richard P. Blakemore at the University of Massachusetts at Amherst found out to everyone's surprise that some bacteria had a magnetic sense. The discovery came about because he noticed that a type of bacterium he was studying from the salt marshes of Cape Cod always oriented itself north-south on his microscope slides. Experiments with a bar magnet soon showed that it was responsive to magnetism. He then found other examples of bacteria with this ability. Investigation by means of electron microscope revealed that each bacterium had a chain of tiny magnetite crystals within it. Each piece of the mineral was surrounded by a thin membrane, so it could act like a magnet, and the pull exerted on the chain as a whole by the geomagnetic field was sufficient to direct the bacterium.

These findings led other researchers to hunt for magnetic material in a wider range of living organisms. Magnetic crystals were found in bees and pigeons. In both cases these built-in compasses seem to act as back-up directional aids to other methods such as navigation by the Sun, the use of polarized light, and so on. Bees have been trained to come to sugar solutions by means of artificial magnetic fields, and the orientation of honeycomb-building can be affected by applying such a field to the hive.

Magnetic sense is undoubtedly involved in the great migrations of some species. North America's monarch butterfly, for example, travels thousands of miles south in winter, always to the same regions. While they probably use solar navigation as well, monarchs contain the most magnetite yet found in any butterfly, so they almost certainly 'read' the geomagnetic field. Even more impressively, the Arctic tern flies to Antarctica for the southern summer, a distance of 11,000 miles (17,700 kilometres). Such prodigious feats of navigation are certainly accomplished by the sensing of geomagnetism. Indeed, this was demonstrated as long ago as the 1950s, even before magnetite deposits began to be found in living things. Hans Fromme of the Frankfurt Zoological Institute observed that at the appropriate season caged robins began facing towards the southwest, their migratory direction, even when the stars and the Sun were kept from their sight. Fromme's co-worker, Freidrich Merkel, put the birds inside a steel cage, insulating them from the Earth's field. They no longer faced in any particular direction.

Whales and dolphins are now believed to be able to use 'magnetic stripes' on the ocean floor as navigational aids on their long submarine journeys. These stripes are produced by geological, tectonic action causing spreading of the seabed. The cetaceans seem able to use areas of high magnetism – which tend to occur in localized areas – as geomagnetic 'landmarks', and the long troughs of low geomagnetism, the stripes, as routeways. These mammals have both fine and coarse magnetic materials embedded in their bodies, but researchers feel that their refined magnetic sensitivity may be due to large magnetic particles in the inner ear, recently discovered by Michael Fuller of the University of California at Santa Barbara.

Some creatures sense magnetic fields in other ways, however; magnetite (which is sometimes produced in living organisms for its hardness rather than for its magnetic properties) need not always be involved. In sharks, rays and skates, for example, the field is comprehended as electrical impulses created as the animals move through the water, and thus through the geomagnetic field. They achieve this electrical sensitivity by means of long conductive channels (known as 'the ampullae of Lorenzini') connecting electrically sensitive cells in the snout with pores on the skin.[3]

Research has continued to increase the roll call of creatures with magnetic sensitivity. The German researcher G. Becker has shown that even flies align themselves to the direction of the geomagnetic field when landing. Some creatures can detect magnetic changes as small as a thousandth of a gauss, or even less. The yellowfin tuna, for instance, is believed to be able to distinguish variations as minute as one twenty-thousandth of the Earth's field!

We are only just beginning to realize how exquisitely attuned the biosphere is to the energy fields of Earth. Forces do not have to be powerful, just appropriate. As French researcher Michel Gauquelin has correctly observed: 'Organisms sometimes respond more readily to weaker energy levels to be found in nature.'[4]

The biosphere can interact in terms of magnetism, electricity, infrared, ultrasound and other ways with the other spheres of Earth and within itself. How does the human being fit into this web?

Although we can be sure nature did not leave humans out of the scheme of things, there is still great resistance to the idea that we are sensitive to invisible and subtle environmental stimuli. This is partially because of a legacy of a stubborn mechanistic attitude still pervading many areas of science – a quite inappropriate mental perspective with which to enter the next millennium, incidentally – and partly because an admission that human beings can be affected by electromagnetism in many different ways would leave power companies and whole industries open to questions and doubts regarding health hazards. The economic problems such a situation might entail could be enormous, and we must always remember who pays the bill for establishment science.

Nevertheless, the human being is an electromagnetic creature in many respects. Let us take sensitivity to magnetism first of all.

Dr Robin Baker, reader in zoology at Manchester University, says: 'If humans have such a [magnetic] sense, we should expect them also to have to learn how to use it effectively. Most people, because of the modern way of life and the many aids to navigation with which they are surrounded, have little cause to make use of a geomagnetic sense.'[5] Since 1979, Baker has been conducting experiments to see if people do possess a sense of direction. In one test a group of students were taken by bus from a 'home' base. They were earmuffed and blindfolded, and wore helmets containing either magnets or non-magnetic brass bars. The subjects were asked to estimate the direction home at two points on the journey. On analysis, those without magnets in their helmets scored more accurately than those affected by the magnetic field in their helmets. In another series of tests, Baker and co-worker Janice Mather rotated blindfolded subjects on a frictionless swivel chair in an environment free of magnetic interference. Afterwards, the subjects were asked to indicate a compass bearing. The researchers obtained statistically consistent success rates. Baker has since appealed on British television for volunteers to take part in further human navigation experiments.

Some of Baker's tests have been repeated by other researchers with unclear results, but there may be a number of variables accounting for this. In 1983, Baker and his colleagues felt confident that they had located a human magnetite source in the sinuses of the ethmoid bone, close to the pituitary and pineal glands in the brain.[6]

Researchers working with dowsers (water diviners or water witchers) have revealed what appears to be a great magnetic sensitivity in humans. In the 1940s Dutch scientist Solco W. Tromp found in reliable experiments that blindfolded dowsers could detect changes in artificial magnetic fields. Later work by French physicist Yves Rocard similarly showed sensitivity in dowsers to magnetic fields, down to tiny fractions of a gauss. Moreover, he found that dowsers could not function if magnets were placed at certain points on their bodies. Russian researcher Aleksandr Dubrov has confirmed such orders of human magnetic sensitivity and postulates the existence of superconducting factors within the human body. Extensive tests carried out by physicist Zaboj Harvalik in the United States during the 1970s likewise demonstrated human sensitivity to small, changing magnetic fields. Incredibly, he found that many subjects can detect variations as weak as a hundred-thousandth of the geomagnetic field. With his most sensitive subject, the late Wilhelm de Boer, a master dowser from Bremen, West Germany, a change of one billionth of a gauss was accurately recorded.

Harvalik used special alloy shielding to try to see if there were any specific centres of magnetic sensitivity within the human body. He came up with two candidates: the adrenal glands (near the kidneys), and a location 'in the vicinity of either the pituitary or the pineal gland'[7] – the very same area singled out by Robin Baker's research. The pineal gland has long been claimed by occultists as being important in paranormal functioning.

There is evidence that people under hypnosis or the influence of hallucinogenic substances can sometimes actually perceive a static magnetic field as a flickering effect. It is also known that magnets of certain strengths applied to the temples can create the sensation of light in subjects in a normal state of consciousness, even when in total darkness. There have also been many reports of people being able to 'hear' aurora effects in the sky, meteoric displays and radar beams ('like buzzing bees'). Indeed, there are prototype versions of electrical aids to hearing, for nerve-deaf individuals, with which the person can 'hear' through any part of the body. This ability of human beings to perceive electromagnetic effects in sensory ways has lead former NASA engineer James Beal to wonder 'How many people are now in mental institutions or psychologically affected because they are afflicted with hypersensitivity to electric fields and hear voices, buzzing sounds, and strange signals?'[8]

Dr Michael Shallis of the Department of External Studies at Oxford University has been studying possible connections between electrical hypersensitivity, allergy symptoms and psychic ability in selected people.[9] One of his subjects is also supersensitive to magnetism. When this person is suffering from a bout of his allergy, he finds it helpful to pick up a telephone – the magnet in the earpiece seems to stabilize his condition. At certain times this same man becomes so sensitive to the geomagnetic field that when facing south his symptoms become worse and can actually provoke unconsciousness. On the other hand, when he turns to the north he feels better, and even euphoric. The north 'calls him'. This subject has been objectively tested in special laboratories and can quite definitely respond to magnetic field directions.

Shallis's work has particularly pointed up the remarkable electrical sensitivity the human being can possess in extreme cases. One subject would almost pass out if people crossed their arms or legs in her vicinity. Shallis tested this effect carefully, having the crossing actions done out of the woman's sight, but she still responded instantaneously. 'The effect was genuine,' Shallis concluded, 'not a trick of the mind. Somehow our actions were affecting the electromagnetic environment to which she was so sensitive.' Other subjects would begin to feel ill a few hundred yards from high-tension cables, while underneath them they would go into convulsions or even faint. Another woman became incredibly sensitive to electricity when she had temporary tooth fillings containing aluminium; these turned her into a human aerial, causing her to collapse near street lights, hear electrical sounds, and develop uncomfortable static charges on her skin. Other subjects were at times unable to use electric appliances because of allergic reactions.

These people are excessively sensitive, it is true, but if the mechanisms exist in them, they must be able to exist to some degree in us all. Certainly particular animals can have specialized electrical sensitivity equivalent to the above examples. For instance, Frank Brown commented that his snails and flatworms had 'more than one hundred times the sensitivity which would be required . . . to "perceive" the electrical field created by a thundercloud rising miles away on the horizon'.

We know people can react to electrical effects in the environment in a general way, because of mass reactions to air ions. Ions are atoms or molecules that have lost or gained an electron so they are no longer balanced, and thus become charged. Decades of research have shown that negative ions have a bracing, healthy effect on human metabolism, while positive ions tend to lead to psychologially depressed states, tiredness and even illness. Negative ions are produced around water that is being disturbed, such as waves on the seashore, waterfalls or cascading streams. They are also plentiful in clear mountain air. Conversely, closed, occupied rooms and other interior spaces tend to have high positive ion counts. Major producers of positive ions in nature are certain winds that seasonally affect specific regions: the khamsin of the Middle East; the sirocco of Italy; the Swiss foehn; the French mistral; and the santa ana and chinook winds of North America. Records show that when these dry winds blow, crime rates, traffic accidents and admission of mental patients tend to increase. People become irritable, fatigued or depressed. Asthmatic conditions deteriorate, and other ailments can be made worse.

Another electrical condition hugging the Earth's surface is the electrostatic field which exists between the ground and the ionosphere. Its strength can be in the order of several hundred volts per metre. Volunteers who have been experimentally excluded from this field for prolonged periods in laboratory Faraday cages – which have metal walls to screen out electromagnetism – have shown marked changes in their normal daily rhythms of metabolic factors such as body temperature, sleep-waking cycles, urinary excretion of certain chemicals, and other bodily processes. We all suffer such disruption to some extent when we are in screened spaces such as aircraft, metal-framed buildings and cars. Exposure to the electrical field of our planet seems to be necessary for our health.

Electromagnetic fields can affect all kinds of processes within the human body. The pineal gland (once again) has been shown to vary its production of the hormones melatonin and serotonin when subjected to various orientations of magnetic fields no stronger than that of the Earth (half a gauss). These hormones act on the nervous system in a variety of ways, including the control of all biocycles within the body.

Another example is the cell. Cells are now known to be complex structures involving the use of electromagnetism; cell walls may even act as semiconductors. (Indeed, there are a number of structures in the human body that researchers following the lead of Nobel prize winner Albert Szent-Gyorgyi have suggested may act as biological semiconductors, and some may even become superconductors in certain circumstances.) Applied electromagnetic fields can thus influence cells – for example, by changing their rate of division. This could have all sorts of implications for the production (and healing) of tumours and cancers.

'In the last two decades nearly all tissues have been proven to produce or carry various kinds of electrical charge,' the American orthopaedic surgeon Robert O. Becker has written.[10] Becker has been a great researcher into bioelectricity and the relationship of organisms with their electromagnetic environment. He has pioneered the application of weak electromagnetic fields in the healing of bone fractures and processes leading to possible regeneration of limbs. In the course of this research he also discovered a direct current (DC) pattern within the human body.

In 1938 unusual effects in human blood began to be noted. Japanese physician Maki Takata had developed a chemical test for albumin in blood serum which became known as the 'Takata reaction'. He was able to provide a way of measuring albumin's propensity for curdling into small lumps, a process called flocculation. In men this index was supposedly constant, but in women it varied with their menstrual cycles. In January 1938, however, researchers started to notice that the flocculation index had suddenly begun to rise for both women *and* men. Detailed analysis of the behaviour of the index in geographically widely separated subjects began. It became clear that people's flocculation indices were varying as if responding to some worldwide influence. After years of work, the primary agent was identified as the Sun. This showed up in two ways: the flocculation index, very low at the end of the night, gives a sudden rise at daybreak, and general rises in the index for men and women precisely coincided with the appearance of sunspots – and it transpired that 1937 had been a peak sunspot year. Changes in blood serum were noted as sunspots crossed the centre of the Sun's disc, when charged particles were at their strongest flow towards the Earth. Takata even discovered that the indices declined during solar eclipses, when the Moon stands between the Earth and the Sun.

But how was the Sun's influence able to affect our blood? Subsequent research has shown that electrical and magnetic fields can affect the blood's ability to coagulate quickly, and it is thought that one aspect of the solar-blood connection could be extremely low frequency (ELF) waves set up in the atmosphere shortly before the Sun rises.[11] These ELF waves could have an important part to play in the dynamics of the Earth taken as a whole. As Robert Becker points out: '. . . there are primary effects on all life-forms at ELF frequencies.' Most significantly, ELF waves may directly connect the workings of the human brain with the terrestrial environment.

EARTH RESONANCE

Natural ELF and VLF (very low frequency) waves are produced by cosmic influences and a variety of weather conditions, particularly lightning, although details of their origins are by no means clear. They occur in the space between the Earth's surface and the ionosphere and are very small but continuous pulsations superimposed on both the magnetic and electrical fields of Earth. H.L. König has shown that natural ELF signals vary on a daily and seasonal basis. In 1952 W.O. Schumann of Munich University published a paper showing that the Earth–ionosphere cavity is an electrodynamic resonator and that when ELF wavelengths approximate the circumference of the Earth a resonant system is set up. This has become known as the 'Schumann resonance'. Frequencies peak at 7.8, 14.1, 20.3, 26.4 and 32.5 Hz (hertz – one hertz is one cycle per second), and most of the energy is concentrated at around 10 Hz. A 10 Hz wave is about 18,600 miles (29,930 kilometres) long. ELF waves can travel all around the world with very little loss of energy and can penetrate just about anywhere.

The known emission frequencies of parts of the human body fall within the ELF range, from just above zero to around 100 Hz. In particular, the brain produces a curious set of electrical rhythms ranging between 0.5 and 30 Hz. These brainwaves were first measured by Hans Berger in Germany in 1925, although their existence had been noted a few decades earlier by British physiologist Richard Caton. No one is completely certain how these cerebral sweeps of electrical waves are formed.

The lowest frequency (0.5–4 Hz) waves, termed the delta rhythm, are principally associated with deep sleep, and some researchers feel they may also be connected with the onset of paranormal experiences and higher levels of consciousness. Next are theta waves (4–7 Hz), which occur during dreaming and half-waking states, and also in deep meditation. The alpha rhythm (8–13 Hz) occurs during states of passive alertness, an empty rather than relaxed mind, a 'scanning or waiting' mode of consciousness.[12] Alpha seems to be a prerequisite condition for altered states, but has to combine with other rhythms to achieve them. The fourth brainwave rhythm is the beta (13–30 Hz) range of frequencies, which occurs in normal waking states, being associated with active thinking, problem-solving and attention to the outside world.

Clearly the human brain contains electrical frequencies that relate to those found naturally in the energy fields of the planet itself. Some researchers are convinced that this came about because life evolved within the influence of these fields, and the brain rhythms became entrained by them – in other words, planetary pulsations began to 'drive' the electrical activity of the brain.

We can see, therefore, that the 10 Hz focus of the Schumann resonance more or less centres on the brain's alpha frequency range, and researchers have found that the 10 Hz band can be used to restore normal metabolic rhythms in human volunteers experimentally cut off from the natural fields of Earth, Sun and Moon.[13] Life, it seems, needs to hear the 'heartbeat' of its mother planet.

The temporal lobe region of the brain is particularly sensitive to electromagnetic fields. A feature of the temporal cortex is the hippocampus, which is associated with memory and dreaming. Clinical stimulation of the hippocampus with very small electrical currents can produce apparitions, time and space alterations, auditory effects and so on. These can even interject into waking consciousness. San Franciscan researcher Francis Ivanhoe has suggested that Ammon's horn, a part of the hippocampus, is able to read out the field strength of the Earth. Moreover, neural activity in the hippocampus is increased with electrical stimulation, maximizing at the 'Earth frequency' of 10–15 Hz. One way or another, it really does seem that we have an electromagnetic umbilical cord connecting us with Mother Earth.

Flashing lights and certain kinds of sounds can also set up specific brainwave patterns. Alpha/theta states, for example, can be induced by gazing at the flickering flames of a fire, the glint and sparkle of sunshine on rippling water, the dapple of sunlight through breeze-blown foliage, or by listening to the 'pink noise' roar of a waterfall, a babbling brook, rain on leaves or wind in the trees. In the laboratory, precise brain rhythm frequencies can be induced by the controlled flashes of a stroboscope. Yoga and other meditation systems can also promote certain brainwave frequencies, and by using electronic biofeedback techniques, in which instrumentation indicates brainwave conditions, a person can quickly learn what mental and physiological behaviour to adopt in order to enter, for example, an alpha state.

What all this means is that in certain mental states our brainwaves are resonating with the rhythms of Earth. We can attune ourselves to the planet. Some of those states (such as the drowsy hypnogogic state that we enter just before we fall asleep) seem to enhance the entry of visionary and paranormal information into our awareness. And in hypnotic and hallucinogenic states, as we have noted above, it is even possible to perceive external low-level electromagnetic fields. Perhaps in certain states we can directly open up to the vast ocean of biological-frequency natural forces of the planet. And perhaps there is two-way traffic between mind and planet. . . .

We will be returning to some of these considerations in later chapters.

FIELDS

The apparent links between the brain's electrical rhythms and built-in electromagnetic sensitivity with terrestrial energy fields may be facilitated by energy effects surrounding the body. Robert Becker has floated the idea that the body's DC system could be the means by which we can 'log in' to the ELF rhythms of the planet. Another candidate could be the magnetic field that surrounds the head. This results from the electrical activity in the brain and is very subtle. Indeed, it was only discovered in the 1970s with the advent of the extremely sensitive SQUID magnetometer. Also, as we have already noted, the body produces a number of other electromagnetic emissions – the heart generates its own magnetic field, for instance.

The idea of there being an energy field surrounding the body was given some of its earliest experimental support by the work of two professors at Yale University in the 1930s and 1940s. F.S.C. Northrop and Harold Saxton Burr proposed the idea of such a field and Burr developed a voltmeter to measure biological electric fields. He found them on a wide range of organisms, from trees to reptiles to humans and other mammals. In a famous experiment he 'hooked up' a tree for many years, and found that its electrical field responded to lunar phases, sunspots and storms, as well as showing the more expected changes due to light and moisture variations. Burr and Northrop referred to these fields – which they found both surrounded and penetrated organisms – as 'L-fields', or life fields. They saw them as 'organizing' fields that accompanied an organism from its beginning and provided a kind of electromagnetic mould or template for its growth pattern. Burr's findings and ideas were ignored or dismissed for many years, but they are now more readily seen as being of greater validity than they seemed at the time, even if they were of a relatively primitive, pioneering nature.

The whole question of living things being associated with electromagnetic fields and currents is still viewed by much of orthodox Western science with varying degrees of scepticism. For many scientists, it all smacks too much of old 'vitalist' ideas, which are discredited concepts consigned to the scientific dustbin. Nevertheless, modern work cannot be dismissed and the sceptical stance is doomed to change as research continues. As Lyall Watson has pointed out: 'In 1960 there were just three papers on the subject in the scientific literature. By 1984, there were over 10,000. . . .'[14]

But the idea of organizing fields as proposed by Burr goes somewhat beyond merely recording the presence of electromagnetic fields around and within living organisms, and did not just spring out of nowhere. Some of the nineteenth-century vitalists postulated that something had to be acting on organisms to account for their growth and shapes – a process summarized in the term morphogenesis. In the 1900s Hans Dreisch called such an influence, force or vital principle, entelechy. In the 1920s a few biologists proposed that morphogenesis was organized by fields, and one of them, Paul Weiss, therefore called his concept the 'morphogenetic field'. In recent years biochemist Rupert Sheldrake has caused a storm of controversy by proposing a more sophisticated version of such L-fields, morphogenetic fields and the rest. He calls his hypothesis 'formative causation'. In this he suggests that we are not dealing merely with fields around individual organisms, but that we have to consider whole species fields:

> 'What is new in the hypothesis of formative causation is that the structure of these fields . . . results from the actual forms of previous similar organisms. In other words, the structure of the fields depends on what has happened before. . . . They represent a kind of pooled or collective memory of the species. Each member of the species is moulded by these species fields, and in turn contributes to them, influencing future members of the species.
>
> 'How could such a memory possibly work? The hypothesis of formative causation postulates that it depends on a kind of resonance, called morphic resonance.'[15]

Sheldrake distinguishes such a resonance from other examples known to science, including electromagnetic resonance. Morphic resonance does not involve a transfer of energy from one system to another, he suggests, but 'a non-energetic transfer of information'. Nevertheless, it does resemble known kinds of resonance in that it requires rhythmic patterns of activity.

So Sheldrake's fields are, essentially, memory fields – as he says, 'Our memories may not be stored inside our brains, as we usually assume they must be.' But what are these memory fields? Indeed, what is a field? We have used the term repeatedly during this chapter, and we will encounter it in later pages, too. It is not a term that can be easily defined. Robert Becker handles the question with a measure of caustic humour:

'A field is "something" that exists in space around an object that produces it. We know there's a field around a permanent magnet because it can make an iron particle jump through space to the magnet. Obviously there's an invisible entity that exerts a force on the iron, but as to just what it consists of – don't ask!'[16]

Lyall Watson also recognizes the enigmatic nature of the field concept:

'The idea of having an electrical field we cannot see or hear or taste is in itself rather mysterious, so it is worth explaining that a field does not exist in its own right. It is simply an area in which certain things happen.'[17]

Sheldrake similarly notes that:

'The nature of fields is inevitably mysterious. According to modern physics, these entities are more fundamental than matter. Fields cannot be explained in terms of matter; rather, matter is explained in terms of energy within fields.'[18]

He considers that his morphic fields 'like the known fields of physics, are non-material regions of influence extending in space and continuing in time'.

The field concept is an essential mental tool for modern science, because it needs to explain how things can act on one another at a distance. Since at least the days of the physicist Faraday (1791–1867), the problem has been tackled either by the invention of some kind of ether (which Maxwell, Faraday's contemporary, referred to as a useful 'collection of imaginary properties') physically existing at some level in space, or by supposing fields to be 'a state of space', which is at once both a simple and infinitely complex idea. Modern science basically sees fields in terms of the latter concept. Einstein, for example, proposed a space-time continuum, of which gravity is an expression, conceptualized as curved space. This may all sound incredibly abstract, rarified stuff to the layperson, but fields are certainly real – who could deny the existence of gravity? (Some materialists probably would if they could get away with it.)

We cannot directly experience the nature of fields, except, possibly, in certain altered states of consciousness. While they are continuous and holistic (one cannot cut up a piece of field and put it in a pocket), fields are nevertheless distinct entities. They can relate to and interact with one another yet occupy the same space. Electromagnetic fields, for instance, differ in kind from the quantum matter fields of modern physicists. These strange quantum fields underpin manifest existence: particles do not exist surrounded by these fields but are in themselves 'manifestations of the underlying reality of the fields', as Sheldrake puts it. Matter consists 'of rhythmic processes of activity, of energy bound and patterned within fields'.[19]

We simply do not know how many or what range of fields may exist, but it is the conservative nature of science (although by no means all scientists) to assume at any given moment that only the currently known fields exist. If a field helps describe something, as is the case with Sheldrake's morphic fields, it has a use, if not a reality. It may have both, of course. (In Part Three we shall propose a field to describe something for which we currently do not have a usable mental handle.)

Thus fields may be the means by which humanity, and the biosphere in general, is merged with the Earth as a whole.

PSYCHOSPHERE

This deepening understanding of fields may lead the way to the recognition of a further sphere of Earth – that of mind. It has been proposed that ELF fields, at least, may be associated with some forms of extrasensory perception (ESP or *psi*). Varying forms of this theory have been put forward from the early 1970s onwards. No one seems to have looked at it in greater depth than neuroscientist Michael Persinger, a professor in the psychology department at Laurentian University in Ontario, Canada. In a series of studies[20] Persinger and his colleagues have carefully and statistically compared data bases of various kinds of ESP – telepathy, clairvoyance, precognition (pro-phetic awareness), seeing 'ghosts' – with a worldwide index of geomagnetic activity. The work has to be seen to be properly appreciated – astounding correlations have been found between the faculties of telepathy and clairvoyance specifically and days of quiet geomagnetic activity. The correlation is not so good for other forms of ESP. In a 1987 study[21] of 109 cases of telepathy, most of the experiences were reported to have occurred during intense dreams (suggesting theta level activity). The cases in this particular study were taken from a reliable, late-nineteenth-century source, a period when, as Persinger points out, there would have been much less artificially produced ELF waves in the atmosphere and the people involved would not be in modern, steel-framed buildings which, as we have noted, can affect the geomagnetic field locally. In his discussion on the results of this study, Persinger wrote:

'These results clearly indicate that spontaneous ESP experiences were more likely on days when geomagnetic activity was much lower than on days before or after the experiences. This . . . suggests an ELF mechanism. Quiet geomagnetic days would be less disruptive to the natural resonances that are generated between the earth and the ionosphere or that propagate within the quiet geomagnetic field.

'Most ELF hypotheses . . . have directly or implicitly embraced the Schumann resonances. These ELF fields are generated within the earth-ionospheric cavity. Their specific wavelengths are due to the absolute circumference of the earth and the spatial and electrical properties of the ionosphere. There are a multitude of different sources that can contribute to ELF in this mode. . . .

'. . .Whatever mechanism is involved with the association, the correlation between ESP and geomagnetic activity appears to be persistent and strong . . . .

'. . . If ESP phenomena are coupled with geomagnetic activity, then perhaps their elusive nature is tied to the day-to-day or even hour-to-hour variations of the geomagnetic environment within which we are all immersed.'

Disturbance of the geomagnetic field would be caused by phenomena such as sunspot activity, the phases of the Moon and so on. As Persinger states, quiet periods would provide 'less disturbance of the Schumann wave guide'. Another possibility, Persinger points out, could be that a quiet geomagnetic environment has an effect upon the person undergoing the ESP experience, increasing his susceptibility to it.

Persinger proposes that telepathy-clairvoyant stimuli utilize the ELF 'channel' and interact with the temporal lobe in the human brain. He remarks that 'essentially all of the major experiences and characteristics of telepathic-clairvoyant phenomena have been evoked by experimental or spontaneous (epileptic) stimulation of the human temporal lobe'.[22] We have already noted the electromagnetic links between the hippocampus (in the temporal lobe area) and the key frequencies of the Schumann resonance. As well as the hippocampus, Persinger suggests the involvement of the amygdala, as the two are connected. While the hippocampus is associated with memory, dreaming and altered states, the amygdala is associated with emotional experiences. Electrical stimulation of these structures produces a whole range of paranormal sensations, even out-of-the-body feelings, as has been indicated earlier in this chapter. Experimental stimulation within theta and other ELF frequency ranges seems to have produced particularly noteworthy effects on these features within the brain.

Basing his ideas on important work carried out on the hippocampus by T.J. Teyler and P. DiScenna,[23] Persinger pictures[24] the hippocampus as a sort of mental card-index system within a cerebral 'library'. It can gain access to specific memory-based imagery coded in nerve cells within microscopic columns of the brain's cortex if the appropriate 'card' – pattern of electrical discharging sequences within the hippocampus – is read. In this way, the telepathic or clairvoyant message does not have to be in the form of actual imagery or feeling somehow carried by the ELF waves, but merely an energy pattern that uses the person's own store of mental imagery, analogous to the way that the electronic transmission of sound or images is being increasingly digitized by computers nowadays.

Most cases of telepathic and clairvoyant experience seem to involve peak moments or crises. Perhaps these circumstances give the broadcasting pattern an extra boost of some kind, rendering it more likely to be picked up by the human brain with the most appropriate decoding patterns, when electromagnetic conditions allow.

Many years ago the American independent scientist Dr Andrija Puharich noted distinct correlations between telepathic performances and the phases of the Moon which may relate to the mechanism Persinger and others have been suggesting, although at the time Puharich felt that gravity was the most likely connection.[25] Puharich also noted the effects of electrical storms and other energetic environmental factors on *psi* functioning. Robert Becker and his colleagues have shown that magnetic storms caused by cosmic factors definitely appear to influence mental states. Over a four year period they checked the admissions of over 28,000 patients to eight mental hospitals in the United States against 67 magnetic storms which occurred during the same period, and found that significantly more people were admitted just after magnetic disturbances than when the field was stable. They went further and followed the detailed behaviour of a dozen schizophrenics. There was a tight correlation between various behavioural changes and cosmic ray incidence.

Finally, Russian work has shown that alterations in alpha rhythms can occur during telepathy experiments; similar alterations occur in theta waves when the subjects are successfully producing psychokinetic effects (moving physical objects by the action of mind alone).[26]

ENERGY POLLUTION

Earlier we noted the problems of human pollution of the environment and how this can upset the interactions between the terrestrial spheres. The same is true at the invisible levels of energy. In the twentieth century we have pumped out a virtually incomprehensible amount of electromagnetic pollution. In terms of environmental energy, we inhabit a completely different world to that of a century ago. Robert Becker and Gary Selden put it well:

'For billions of years . . . the energies that life grew up among were relatively simple. There was a weak electromagnetic field modulated by micropulsations within it and further sculpted by the solar and lunar cycles. There was a burst of static centred at 10,000 hertz and reverberating over the whole earth whenever lightning flashed in the scores of thunderstorms in progress at any one time. There were a few weak radio waves from the sun and other stars. Light, including some infrared and ultraviolet, was the most abundant form of electromagnetic energy. At higher frequencies, living things absorbed only small amounts of ionizing X-rays and gamma rays from space and from radioactive minerals in rocks. Large parts of the energy spectrum were silent.
'We'll never experience that quiet world again.'[27]

Now we churn out artificial ELF waves from power cables, electrical appliances and communications systems. Our domestic wiring, high-tension cables, office and home equipment radiate electro-magnetic fields. We occupy environments that shut us off from the natural energy fields, and in which pallid artificial light shines onto us. We dispense a bluster of radio waves and microwaves. We leak and explode radioactivity into the atmosphere, hydrosphere and lithosphere.

Our architects design huge steel-framed buildings with reflective glass; throbbing with internal energy systems, they stand in an environment humming with a seething mass of artifically produced energies. People argue about the aesthetics of buildings, but who considers their energy characteristics – their materials, shape, energy resonances, usuage of electrical power? Cities are electromagnetic energy vortices.

Many of these energy radiations may be at high frequency levels that do not harm us unless we come into direct, unprotected contact with them. But some of the fields are at what we can now identify as biological frequencies, those frequencies to which life is tuned. What are these doing to our physical and mental health?

There is growing concern at the way power cables, microwave communications, domestic cycles of AC (alternating current) electricity and other features of our modern, artificial energy environment may be affecting us. This is, of course, a factor in the reluctance of establishment science to accept the enormous body of data relating to bioelectricity and biomagnetism. The implications could be extensive – and that is just with regard to physical and recognized psychological effects. How these new influences could also be affecting our psychic lives has hardly been broached, yet even from the brief summary provided in this chapter, it is clear that we might be justified in adding a sixth 'sphere' to the other five – a mental or psychosphere, the very means whereby our consciousness is linked to planetary processes, and perhaps to other individuals of the species.

ALL THINGS ARE CONNECTED

The review of energy ecology in this chapter has of necessity been simplified, but it is sufficient to show that the terrestrial spheres are interconnected on even the most subtle levels. The Earth is one pulsing, resonating organism. Viewed in this way, we can see that we do not live on the Earth, but in it. Even when we gaze out at the stars at night we are looking through less dense spheres of the Earth. In fact, we are an aspect or expression of the planet ourselves.

In 1854 Chief Seattle expressed traditional knowledge when he stated:

> 'This we know, the Earth does not belong to Man; Man belongs to the Earth. This we know, all things are connected like the blood that unites one family. All things are connected.'

Such a traditional sense of relatedness has been fading from our planet. But perhaps, at the eleventh hour, we are recollecting that ancient wisdom in the language of our times and culture. That recollection can be rapidly augmented within the modern psyche because, ironically, the acceleration of the development of the technological processes that enable us to leave Earth has provided us with a means of communicating with each other at a speed and on a scale never known before. We call it information technology. It is not an end in itself, however, only a means. How we use it is the vital factor. As T.S. Eliot warned: 'Where is the wisdom we have lost in knowledge? Where is the knowledge we have lost in information?'

To recollect fully the ancient wisdom, to translate it into modern understanding, we have to embrace more than physical ecology, crucial as that is. We must not exclude the deeper aspects of wholeness, the mental, psychic and spiritual levels. We have to understand their place, too, for they are part of our heritage, part of our experience of being conscious. Gaining acceptance for this aspect of the problem is even more difficult than for physical ecological concerns, because it is inherent in the outlook of our times that such matters are dismissed as occult, unimportant or fraudulent. The mentality that has fashioned our culture has not only rendered us blind to the subtle planetary web that we are part of, it has also closed off vast areas of the inner world of consciousness.

CHAPTER FOUR

MONUMENT TRANSMISSIONS

If mainstream awareness in our culture is just beginning to appreciate openly the ecological responsibilities involved with being a part of the world, and is only reluctantly realizing to what extent we are also electromagnetically enmeshed with the planet, then there is still some way to go before it perceives the significance of a curious development that has been taking place since World War II: the burgeoning interest in ancient, sacred sites.

As we noted in Chapter 1, early peoples either identified or created special places that they saw as being sacred, of a different order to the rest of the landscape. It was a phenomenon that occurred throughout the world, and the sacred sites took many forms. Some were natural locations – outcrops of rock, caves, springs, trees, mountain peaks. We find examples of these sanctified spots in Australian Aboriginal traditions, in Amerindian shamanic caves, in the sacred oaks and holy wells of Iron Age Europe and the worldwide population of holy hills and mountains. People as separated as the ancient Greeks and the South American Ayamara Indians viewed spots where lightning or a meteorite had struck as holy. Other sites were minimally marked locations, what the Pueblo Indian scholar Rina Swentzell refers to as 'an understated sacredness'. She notes a shrine site on Tsikumu, one of the Pueblo's sacred mountains in the Santa Clara range in New Mexico, where 'a few well-placed stones . . . define an area scattered with cornmeal and a deeply-worn path in the bedrock. No special structure celebrates the sacredness of this place. Architecturally, it is under-stated, almost inconspicuous'.[1]

Then there are the more substantial examples of spiritual engineering which we tend to refer to today as 'monuments': the great stone and earth structures such as Egypt's Great Pyramid, France's rows of standing stones in Brittany, England's Stonehenge and Avebury, Ireland's Newgrange, the serpentine earthwork in the United States called Serpent Mound, and Peru's Machu Picchu. In addition to these and other celebrated sites throughout the world, there are many thousands of lesser-known ones. Stone circles, for instance, abound in various forms in the Middle East, in Africa, in Europe and elsewhere. In the British Isles alone there are around 900 surviving stone circles, and there are nearly that many in the Senegambian area of West Africa. Legions of sacred places dot the Earth's body.

Traditional peoples resorted to these places to contact the spirit world, to dream, to worship, to be initiated or healed; they also cursed or invoked at them. But after the seventeenth century watershed, as the Age of Reason arose, a different approach to these sites developed. People called 'antiquarians' emerged and an intellectual interest was generated about the sites. Who built them? How old were they? What was their purpose? They became objects of curiosity and study, instead of use. It was a consequence of the final veils of amnesia that had fallen across the face of the former world.

The country folk remembered a little better; they still had their legends and stories about the old stones and mounds, and they still revered the wise women and men who secretly, quietly, went to the old places. But it was a fading memory. As we noted in Chapter 2, it is estimated that possibly nine million people were executed in Europe as witches.[2] Although this massacre, mainly of women, included victims of personal vendettas, local gossip and intrigue, it undoubtedly also removed large numbers of practitioners of the Old Religion, interpreted by the Church as Devil worship. After the butchery resulting from the witch-hunting hysteria, only a ragged remnant of those possessing the old knowledge was left. This was further dissipated by the effects of the Industrial Revolution and the hardship of life experienced by the peasantry.

So the rural folk-memory and knowledge declined as antiquarianism developed into archaeology. By the twentieth century, the sacred sites were seen as monuments to former superstitions. But although scientific archaeology became more sophisticated, and more removed mentally from the nature of the sites it studied, a background sense of the special nature of the places remained within the contemporary psyche.

POWER PLACES

This residual sense of the specialness of sacred places was partially explained by the legacy provided by the garbled remnants of folklore. These stated that the old sites had strange properties: the old stones could heal, they could move, they could not be counted. The ancient mounds contained secret treasures, and were the abodes of fairies and elemental spirits. The stone circles were places of enchantment. The sites issued sounds at certain times of the day; fairy lights appeared at them. Spirits of the dead appeared as globes of light (called *haug eldir* in Scandinavia) above the prehistoric burial cairns. All the legendary beliefs made the same point: the ancient sacred sites possessed magical, supernatural qualities. They were places of power.

People also recognized the awesome skill that went into the construction of many of the monuments, and wondered where such knowledge and ability came from, and why the ancients would have expended so much time and trouble. It was fashionable in the early years of the twentieth century for psychometrists to visit ancient sites. The overall consensus of these sensitives was that the old sites had been used for the magical concentration of cosmic forces.

This type of work at prehistoric sites was branded by British archaeology as 'lunatic fringe', as was 'ley hunting' also. Since at least the closing decades of the nineteenth century it had been suggested by various researchers in Britain and continental Europe that ancient sites fell into straight lines. In 1921 the most comprehensive version of the theory was put forward by Alfred Watkins of Hereford, a well-known businessman, photographer and inventor. He thought the alignments were the remains of old traders' tracks laid down in the Neolithic period (roughly the third and fourth millennia BC in Britain). Watkins called his lines 'leys' for a time, as he thought the Saxon word, which meant meadow, could be logically traced back to the creation of waymarked straight tracks through prehistoric forest, causing strip clearance of land. He published books on the subject, his main work being *The Old Straight Track* (1925), which produced hostile reactions within archaeology but elicited a positive response from many other people. A club was formed and ley hunting enthusiasts carried out much fieldwork until the onset of World War II. Unknown to the British, similar work was going on at the same time in Germany, where the alignments were called 'holy lines' (*Heilige Linien*), but unfortunately this became contaminated with the rise of Nazism.

The twentieth century also saw the revival of the Old Religion as 'witchcraft', although in specialized forms with modern accretions. The magician Aleister Crowley was anxious to see the formation of a 'new and greater pagan cult', for he felt the time was ripe for 'a natural religion'. That was in 1915. The process was probably given a boost with the publication in 1921 of Margaret Murray's scholarly work, *The Witch-Cult in Western Europe*. But it was in the decades after World War II that the greatest explosion of esoteric occult interest broke forth. In the 1940s and 1950s Gerald Gardner acted as a catalyst in the development of modern witchcraft, a process further facilitated in Britain by the repeal of the Witchcraft Act in 1951. Today there are many thousands of people involved in 'Wicca' and nature religions of various kinds around the Western world. People resort to the old sites again, with various motives and versions of paganism. Their rites and ceremonies are mainly invented and only loosely based on what might have been the actual procedures and practices carried out at the sites. But the essential thing is that people are trying to use the old stones, the holy wells and springs and other places of sanctity once more.

This interest in the Old Religions has found an intellectual corollary in a revived interest and study of former Goddess-oriented cultures, a theme particularly close to the hearts of feminist scholars. Those involved with the Old Religions, in whatever form, also tend to be ecologically aware, and see themselves as guardians of the natural world. The ethos of this widespread movement is aptly summed up in the term 'ecopagan' which is sometimes used to describe it.

The decades since World War II have also seen a tremendous development of popular interest in paranormal phenomena, UFOs, and mind-altering substances (LSD being the most important and controversial new psychoactive agent to appear in recent times). In addition, interest has been shown in how hallucinogenics were used in traditional cultures.

THE GEOMANTIC REVIVAL

By the beginning of the 1960s a new, holistic way of studying prehistoric sites began to form. Watkins' ley theory had almost disappeared from view, but came back with a vengeance, curiously, through the agency of certain people associated with the new interest in UFOs. How this happened is explained fully elsewhere;[3] it is enough for our purposes here simply to know it happened.

Throughout the 1960s, interest grew in the ancient sites, how they formed 'ley lines', how strange energies could be dowsed at them, how the megalith builders might have been 'ancient astronauts', and so on. Bizarre and erroneous though some of the psychedelic generation's notions may have been, they nevertheless expressed a new awareness regarding the ancient places in the landscape that was dawning at that time.

There were even revolutions occurring in archaeology itself: the Carbon-14 system used to date organic material discovered at sites was found to be inexact, and was recalibrated by means of the tree-rings within the trunks of the ancient Bristlecone pines of California. The new dating charts appeared in 1967,[4] and when the ages of prehistoric sites were ascertained against this information, it was found that places such as Stonehenge, Newgrange and other sites throughout the world were in fact many centuries older than had been realized. Whole archaeological theories concerning the spread of cultural influences had to be abandoned or modified.

Also in 1967, a book was published by a former engineering don at Oxford University, Alexander Thom, which provided detailed evidence drawn from decades of meticulous research showing that stone circle sites in Britain had been laid out to deliberate geometrical schemes, probably using a basic unit of prehistoric measure, and could have been used for quite sophisticated astronomical observations, beyond the needs of a basic agricultural society.[5] (It was Thom's work which provided the final stimulus to the formation of archaeo-astronomy, an area of research which has now become academically respectable.) The ancient monument builders began to be seen as being older and wiser than had been previously accepted by archaeologists.

After the excesses of naive enthusiasm in the 1960s, a new generation of 'ley hunters' emerged in Britain, and started to explore the countryside and the ancient sites from more inclusive perspectives than conventional archaeology allowed. Specialist groups and magazines such as *The Ley Hunter* emerged. Books on ancient sites and 'mysteries' began to appear. A whole category of publishing if not initiated, was certainly expanded. Nor was it just the domain of writers and researchers: artists too began to draw inspiration from the forms, geometry and atmosphere of ancient sacred places. This whole area of holistic research into ancient sites and their landscapes is often referred to as 'Earth Mysteries', an appellation conjured up in 1974 by an unknown sub-editor clearly exasperated with trying to sum up succinctly the new multidisciplinary area of interest surrounding the evaluation of ancient sites.

Some Earth Mysteries researchers, such as Nigel Pennick and his Cambridge-based Institute of Geomantic Research, were busy discovering and republishing old texts, including the writings of Victorian missionaries to China who described the strange feng shui practices they found there, which they dubbed 'geomancy'. This word originally meant divination (mancy) by means of casting soil on the ground and reading the patterns thus produced – a little like the more humble divinatory form of tea-leaf reading – but these Victorian commentators used the word to describe the huge, landscape-scale arrangements of sites and detailed rules regarding building layouts and orientations that they encountered in China, and Earth Mysteries researchers readily adopted this Victorian application of the word to sacred geography in general. Not only in China, the modern geomants learned, but also in numerous other countries, practices involving the layout of sites with regard to local topography and conceptions of terrestrial forces once existed, sometimes surviving in vestigial form or documented in widely scattered archival material. In Europe, people such as Pennick have been busy uncovering what can be gleaned of Northern European geomantic traditions in the early historical epoch, but as regards the prehistoric megalith builders, only the gaunt sites themselves remain, and it is from them that the nature of the geomancy of those periods has to be reconstructed.

In recent years some orthodox archaeologists have taken to calling the more serious, responsible Earth Mysteries researchers the 'alternative academy', which at least is an improvement on 'lunatic fringe'.

But whatever name it goes by – Earth Mysteries, geomancy, alternative academy – this wide-ranging research area is a new dynamic approach to the study of the old sacred places, and has a growing number of adherents in Europe and North America. It is not passive antiquarianism; it is a search for the principles governing ancient knowledge that might be found encoded in ancient sites and landscapes. The hope is that we may be able to integrate some of these principles into our modern mentality. If this can be achieved, they may help create a new geomantic philosophy for the twenty-first century.

Another development spawned in the 1960s was the 'New Age' movement, a potpourri of Oriental and Western spiritual traditions, avant-garde science, psychology, anthropology, consciousness studies and paranormal research. Geomantic concerns have naturally found a niche within this amalgam. Although some aspects of the New Age movement have taken on a bland flavour (rather strongly influenced, it has to be said, by primarily white American ideas and fantasies about spirituality and ancient cultures), and some of the material bandied around within its circles is based on inaccurate or partial information seasoned with generous doses of pseudospirituality, it is nevertheless an authentic expression of a major recollection beginning to occur within the modern psyche. Magazines, books, conference centres and communities extolling New Age views have steadily been appearing and establishing themselves.

Unfortunately, there has also been an 'anti-science' element developing within both New Age and ecopagan areas. Some people have confused the narrow, pedantic strain in many aspects of orthodox science with the more open-minded approach that is really the true spirit of science – the human delight in discovery and comprehension. Science has also been confused with technology, in particular with the more reprehensible aspects such as fearsome weaponry and inhumane and ecologically damaging mechanical and industrial processes. This is careless thinking. Science is not technology, and technology has always been used by human beings. Even in the time of Goddess-oriented cultures, people knapped flint, engineered megalithic constructions, made use of the flora and fauna (both classical names for deities) in the environment, and made garments. And, as we shall shortly see, there was also a form of 'shamanic physics', in which geophysical factors were incorporated into the repertoire of shamanic techniques.

In 1987, as a result of highly individualistic interpretations of the Mayan calendar by José Arguelles,[6] there was a 'Harmonic Convergence' event, during which people were encouraged to go to a

hell is the burning
away of memories
and attachments to
free the soul

Jacobs ladder

If you have really made
your peace, the devils
are really angels freeing
your soul from the earth.

death mask — denial of your own death
memories (immediate) past, imagined future

sacred site in their vicinity. Thousands of New Agers around the world complied. Although one may question the rationale behind the supposed purposes of the overall event, the fact that many people did visit a number of the old places was in itself of value, and in many ways symbolic of what has been going on for many years now.

THE RETURN

There is a return to the old, sacred places of power. This is going on in numerous ways. At a mundane level, modern transportation and increased incomes in the First World have made it possible for people to visit ancient sites on a scale never seen before. Stonehenge, for example, is visited by around three-quarters of a million people every year. As the veteran geomantic writer John Michell has observed, 'Tourism is a modern form of pilgrimage'. The return has also happened in the more deliberate, conscious ways indicated in the preceding paragraphs. It is as if these points on the Earth's body are calling us back again. They have a special quality, recognized by former inhabitants of the planet. Their essential characteristics if natural and unadorned, or their placing, structural materials, measurements and orientations if engineered, make them veritable schools of stone and earth, places of perennial learning. Locked into them is information about the planet, about ourselves, and about ancient wisdom. Parts of this timeless information can be accessed by use and study of the sites.

It often seems as if just by being at an ancient site, especially if it is well-preserved, remote and rarely visited, something is communicated by the Earth to the person by some kind of mental osmosis. This effect – intellectual, aesthetic or intuitive – can be instant or can occur more subtly long after the visit, but once 'the call of the stones' is heard (what Michell calls 'megalithomania'[7]), an individual is bound by an irresistible, magnetic pull to ancient sacred places everywhere. It is one particular way the planet has of connecting with us. If this seems an over-poetic way of putting it, it is nevertheless a real phenomenon.

The Earth Mysteries approach to ancient monuments is, as has already been noted, holistic. The modern geomant's brief is broader than that of the archaeologist, but no less valid. Indeed, archaeology is encompassed in the methodology of the alternative academy, which is both multidisciplinary and multimode. More exactly, it is a 'systems' approach to ancient sites; things are looked at in an interconnected manner rather than in isolation. What physicist Fritjof Capra says of living systems in *The Turning Point* (1982) can be more or less generally applied to the systems approach:

> 'At each level of complexity we encounter systems that are integrated, self-organizing wholes consisting of smaller parts and, at the same time, acting as parts of larger wholes. For example, the human organism contains organ systems composed of several organs, each organ being made up of tissues and each tissue made up of cells. The relations between these systems levels can be represented by a "systems tree".
>
> 'As in a real tree, there are interconnections and inter-dependencies between all systems levels; each level interacts and communicates with its total environment.'

What has come to be called the 'General Systems Theory' has emerged from new attitudes developed by scientists and other researchers in the middle of this century. In *The Awakening Earth* (1982), Peter Russell says:

> 'The term "theory" is in fact rather misleading. General Systems Theory is not so much a specific theory as a way of looking at the world. It sees the world as an interconnected hierarchy of matter and energy. According to this view, nothing can be understood on its own; everything is part of a system (a system being defined in its most general sense as a set of units which are related to each other and interact). Systems may be abstract, as in mathematical systems and metaphysical systems, or concrete, as in a telephone or transport system.'

The systems approach allows different areas of knowledge to yield information about one another. For instance, certain engineering principles might be found to apply to areas such as biology or sociology. The systems method is really a quest for what Gregory Bateson, as we noted in Chapter 1, called 'the pattern that connects'. The new geomancy is systems archaeology.

THE PATTERN THAT CONNECTS

In Earth Mysteries, the pattern that connects is the site itself. A stone circle, for example, as the root or trunk of a 'systems tree', yields many branches of information when studied. Standard archaeology would usually be the first branch to be climbed. The basic facts could be determined in this way: what does archaeology reveal about the date of this place? Has it been excavated, and, if so, what finds were made? Where do the stones come from, and what are their dimensions, weight, geology? Are all the stones original? Are any missing or misplaced? Is this site part of a regional group of monuments? The answers to specific questions such as these would be added to the background knowledge obtained by archaeological research on the type of monument and the period of prehistory concerned.

Although such information is essential for any study of a site, archaeology can tell us little more. But the site itself can. So the next 'branch' of the site the modern geomant might consider in an attempt to build up a mosaic of understanding about the place, would be the folklore surrounding the feature: what the country people who for generations had shared the landscape with it had to say about the place. How was the site founded? Was it built where an arrow fell? Who shot the arrow – the Devil, a giant, a holy man? Or was the site erected where oxen decided to sit? Perhaps the stones are really people who were petrified while dancing on the Sabbath? Do the stones heal? If so, which ones? Which are supposed to move at midnight? Have fairies been seen here, and what did they look like – little people or mysterious lights? Does a secret tunnel link this site with another one several miles away? And so on; the alternative researcher does not take the legendary imagery literally, but knows that authentic fragments of information, of memory, may be encoded in it.

Next, the ground-plan geometry might be inspected, especially if the site is a stone circle. The work of people like Thom or the researchers into sacred geometry such as Keith Critchlow[8] would be consulted. Is the ring a true circle, or does it create a special geometrical figure? If the latter, what is it? By studying such geometry, we can gain access to esoteric thinking through the ages. Sacred or canonical geometry is the geometry of nature, the patterns of growth, structure and movement that underpin all manifestations of the physical universe. The geometry of snowflakes; the spiral curves of microscopic sea creatures and the swirl of galaxies; the unfolding of a fern or the growth of a shell; the branching pattern of a tree or the proportional structure of the human skeleton. Because it is the pattern of nature, the old temple builders used sacred geometry in the structure of their sacred places, for a temple is a microcosm of the universe, whether it be a stone ring on a windswept moorland in northwest Europe, a pyramid in the aridity of Egypt's sands, or a site anywhere else. This geometry is not a human invention, but simply the formalization of the inherent patterns governing nature. It depicts the invisible 'doorways' whereby energy shimmers into material reality, and as such has always been associated with spiritual and magical activity since human beings have been on the planet.

After examining the pattern on the ground, the modern geomant will check the skies above a site, since holy places were often designed to link heaven and Earth. Do the stones point to distant features (outlying standing stones or skyline peaks or notches) indicating the rising or setting of the Sun at key times in the year – the solstices and equinoxes, or the intervening cross-quarter days, all important in the pre-industrial calendar? Or does the site relate to the Moon during important points in its 18.6-year cycle (often called the 'Metonic cycle' after Meton, an ancient Greek astronomer who knew of it)?

As well as marking the cosmic cycles of time in this way, the light of the Sun or Moon – and perhaps planets and stars too – might have been 'brought down' to Earth in particular ways. Many examples of this are now emerging. At the picturesque stone circle of Castlerigg, near Keswick in the English Lake District, researcher John Glover discovered that what he termed a 'shadow-path' was cast by the tallest stone in the ring at midsummer sunset.[9] When surveyed, this line of shadow was found to have originally extended for about two miles and indicated a line of ancient sites along its axis. Moreover, evidence was revealed which suggested that the land around the site had been sloped to maximize the length of the shadow.

In Ireland the American researcher Martin Brennan discovered that on important dates not only did the Sun's rays reach inside at least some of the ancient Neolithic chambered mounds, casting laser-like sunbeams on interior rock carvings, but also that outlying stones at sites such as Newgrange cast fingers of shadow over the enigmatic rock carvings on edging stones surrounding the mounds.[10] In other words, the earth and stone monuments are the hardware that allow the software of light and shadow to run the programs encoded in the strange symbols carved six thousand years ago. The megalith builders can still speak to us directly across gulfs of time. In a similar way, high on Fajada Butte in Chaco Canyon, New Mexico, slits in a construction of stone slabs allow a 'dagger' of sunlight to interact with a carved stone spiral design, marking accurately the solstices and equinoxes.[11] This feature is believed to have been left by the vanished Anasazi people more than a millennium ago. In Mexico one of the serrated corners of the Toltec-Maya stepped pyramid known as the Castillo at Chichen Itza, throws a moving shadow onto the northern balustrade in the last hour before equinox sunset, creating the illusion of an undulating body connecting with the stone head of a serpent at the bottom of the balustrade.[12] Around the turn of the century, Sir Norman Lockyer noted that the central axis of the Karnak temple at Luxor in Egypt was oriented on the setting midsummer sun.

A great many similar examples exist. We have come to learn that around the world and through vast periods of time the temple builders knew the movements of the heavens and incorporated them into their sites.

Another important branch of knowledge relating to a site is its geomancy: how does it relate to the local topography and geology and to other sites? At some British megalithic sites it has been noted that the tops of stones echo the shape of the distant skyline when viewed from certain positions, or their dominant axes mark specific directions.[13,14,15,16] These could be subtle, but enduring, waymarking systems.

A related characteristic is the way some groups of ancient sites align across the landscape. Awareness of this emerged in modern times with Alfred Watkins' ley concept and is a major plank of the alternative academy. The alignment theory has been considered heretical and contentious by orthodox archaeologists for several decades, but sufficient evidence has now accumulated[17] for such resistance to be obsolete. Sites align, or old straight tracks exist, all over the world. In continental Europe there are alignments of prehistoric sites or places that have evolved on such locations. In Britain, aerial photography is revealing dozens of extraordinary straight-line features surveyed and dug into the ground during the third and fourth millennia BC. Called cursuses, these can run for miles, often linking prehistoric mounds even older than themselves. Partially or completely invisible at ground level, most cursuses are now 'ghost sites', perceptible only as markings in vegetation when viewed from the air. (The course of a major cursus, the first to be discovered, is signposted close to the car park at Stonehenge.)

In Indonesia, the great temple of Borobudur on Java aligns with other temples to the East – Pawon, Mendut and the site of another now destroyed – an alignment celebrated by an annual procession. These Buddhist shrines almost certainly stand on the locations of earlier sacred sites.

In the Americas, old straight tracks occur in several areas. In the United States, Indians left mysterious straight tracks running for dozens of miles in the Californian sierras and in other southwestern states. Some of these lines run from mountain peak to mountain peak without deviation. No one knows why they were built. The best-researched set of these centuries-old lines is around Chaco Canyon. Here Anasazi sites of largely unknown function stand on the old trackways, which the folklore of the present Navajo says were 'not really roads' and refers to as tunnels along which the Anasazi could travel with 'invisibility'.[18] In Mexico, there are the remains of pre-Hispanic straight roads, and in the Yucatan and areas further south in Central America are the straight *sacbeob* or ritual roads of the Maya. In South America, in the Andes of Peru and Bolivia especially, there are perfectly straight lines or tracks on the ground, running for miles (the most famous, but not the most extensive, being the so-called 'Nasca lines'). Shrine sites are dotted along the lines in exactly the pattern foreseen by Watkins half the world away in Britain. These old straight tracks or leys were built by ancestors of the present Ayamara and other Indian groups. Later lines were built by the Inca, the most enigmatic being the *ceques* radiating out of Cuzco. These lines were for the ritual use of the emperor, and had sacred sites aligned along them. Although referred to in early Spanish texts, no one knew quite what form the now invisible *ceques* took until they were revealed as old straight tracks by means of infrared photography undertaken by researcher Tony Morrison.

No one today really understands why traditional societies, widely separated chronologically and geographically, made these mysterious straight lines. Some came to be used for travel, but without doubt that was not their original purpose. They were magical lines in some way, and current research suggests they were spirit lines used by shamans in traditional societies and by the king or emperor in more hierarchical ones. It has been found that a proto-Indo-European linguistic root, *reg*, meant 'movement along a straight line' and this eventually found its way, in one form or another, into the structure of words associated with kingship (rex, raj, reign, *reich*, *roi*, regent, and so on), with behavioural analogies of straightness or order (such as right, *droit*, *recht*, regime, erect, rectitude, correct, regiment, regular), and words for straight edges (the Latin *regula*, or French *regle*, for example). Thus in English today we have the word 'ruler' which means both a straight edge and king or leader. 'Direction' can mean either a spatial indication or an order. Early peoples seem to have associated the straight line with the movements of spirits (the feng shui geomants of China were just one group who avoided straight lines leading to a habitation, in order to prevent poltergeist activity). Hierarchical societies reserved the spirit lines for the king or emperor, who literally 'ruled the land'; it was a form of occult rule. The Inca seem to have used the *ceques* in this way, too.[19]

Unravelling the mystery of the meaning of the straight line in the archaic landscape (and mind) is a major aim of modern geomantic researchers.

Another important element in the placing of some ancient sacred places seems to have been the proximity of certain geological features, especially fault lines (fissures within the Earth's crust). In Iceland, for example, the main national site, the tenth-century AD Althing, was built not merely on a fault, but on the rift formed between the North American and Eurasian tectonic plates – an extension of the mid-Atlantic ridge. In Ohio, in the United States, the 2,000-year-old Serpent Mound, an inexplicable earthwork a quarter of a mile long, was built over a geological site unique in that country: due to volcanic action or meteoric impact it is a highly compressed area of intensive faulting. Clearly, the association of such important sites with such distinctive geological features would not have happened by chance.

Other sites rely on faulting for their very existence. At Bath, in England, hot springs that were considered sacred from the early Neolithic period through to the Romano-British era rise on a fault; and a similar site in Greece, the Delphic oracle at Mount Parnassus, relied on mind-altering fumes arising from a fault.

The greatest megalithic complex in the world, around Carnac in Brittany, France, is hemmed in by fault systems, and occupies France's most volatile tectonic region.[20] Geochemist Paul McCartney, acting on an earlier observation by John Michell,[21] confirmed that in England and Wales, at least, all stone circles are situated within a mile of a surface fault or an associated tectonic intrusion (such as a granite upland like Dartmoor).[22] Even stone circles outside the general distribution of such sites, of which the lone Rollright circle near Oxford is an example, have a fault nearby. Anasazi pueblos at Wuptaki, Arizona, are built around the extraordinary 'blow holes' that exhale and inhale air over 24-hour periods and are related to fault systems. There is little doubt that many more ancient sacred sites await to be identified as being associated with geological faulting.

It is certain that early peoples knew their geology: they could find and mine rich sources of flint and other stones for their implements during the Stone Age, and could locate mineral veins during the Bronze and Iron Ages. But why should they identify faults and build holy places on or near them? The basic answer has to be related to the special energetic effects that can occur in their vicinity. Because faulting represents places in the Earth's crust where tremendous geological forces have been at play, many different minerals are often jumbled together relatively near the surface. This causes local electromagnetic anomalies, alterations in ground-water levels and sometimes gravity variations. Faulting also represents weak points in the terrain, which are liable to movement under tectonic stress and strain. This only occasionally results in earthquakes, as the lithosphere is regularly contracting and relaxing. It certainly produces shifting electromagnetic fields: great masses of rock crushing up against one another sometimes produce piezoelectricity, which is an electrical charge produced by pressure on quartz or quartz-bearing rocks. Such tectonic activity can also release radioactive radon gas, and other chemicals and gases, into spring water rising in such regions. Fault zones are thus areas of special energy.

These regions also tend to harbour another kind of energy phenomenon – strange lights. In the eighteenth century it was recorded that miners had for hundreds of years used the appearance of balls of light issuing from the ground as one means of locating copper and tin veins.[23] In parts of Wales there is still a tradition that blue lights occasionally seen rising from certain hills disclose the presence of mineral deposits. Officially, such phenomena do not exist, and those who think they do generally interpret them in terms of UFOs, which, in turn, are usually considered to be extraterrestrial spacecraft. There are a small number of researchers, however, who are quite sure that such energy displays do actually occur, and that they are a novel form of electromagnetism or an unknown, exotic energy form, which originates in fault zones, emerging from processes occurring within the lithosphere (possibly in conjunction with atmospheric conditions). Considerable evidence[24,25,26,27,28] now exists to support this view, but the nature of the lights and the exact mechanisms by which they manifest themselves are unknown at this time, although some useful theories have been put forward. The phenomena are widely reported, have been photographed, and are being studied by individual scientists and other researchers. There are specific geographical regions in the United States, Britain, Scandinavia and Australia where the lights are now known to have a history of regular occurrence. The lights are undoubtedly terrain related.

All three of the authors of this book have seen anomalous light phenomena, and in 1973 David Kubrin even managed to photograph a lightform that appeared over the Pinnacles National Monument in California, virtually over the Pinnacles Fault and very close to the great San Andreas Fault. Paradoxically, the light alternately gave the appearance of having mass and being weightless. It finally rotated and dissipated into the air.

These 'earth lights' must always have been around, and just as the standard cultural view of them today is that they are alien space machinery (imagery, coincidentally, very much in keeping with our own state of development), in the past many traditional societies around the world incorporated them into their worldview, seeing them as spirits, fairies, entrances to the other world, or as phenomena to be used for divination. It may well be that our contemporary attitudes towards the lights – that they are extraterrestrial or simply do not exist – are yet further expressions of our mental estrangement from Earth and the more subtle aspects of natural processes.

The lights could turn out to be an important clue in the attempt to understand the nature of what might be our living, sentient planet, and in Part Three we will look at them again in more detail. For now, it is enough for us to note that these earth lights exist, that they tend to haunt the sort of landscapes often favoured by the ancients for certain types of shrines and monuments, and that they have been directly witnessed occurring above or in the immediate vicinity of megalithic sites, holy wells and holy hills or mountains.[29]

Light phenomena are thus related to another branch of research that has to be climbed when studying a sacred place, particularly a megalithic monument: does the site have a history of unusual energy effects? The folklore record relating to a monument may hint that it does. Further, there may be modern reports of people who have encountered unusual effects there. Perhaps a sensation like an electric shock has been obtained off a stone (a quite common experience at British megalithic sites); or maybe someone saw a strange light phenomenon, heard an odd sound, or saw a 'ghost'. There could be accounts of unexplained electrical breakdowns in vehicles passing the spot on an adjacent road or of someone measuring anomalous geophysical effects there. The rumour that there are special forces at some of these old places has flared to great heights since the 1960s.

The Earth Mysteries investigator will employ both direct sensing (psychic or dowsing) methods and physical monitoring using instrumentation to study the possible energetic aspects of a site. Of all the areas of research incorporated in the holistic, or systems, study of old sacred monuments, this is the most controversial. But the modern geomantic researcher knows that only by this multifaceted approach will all the information a site can offer be comprehended, and our geomantic amnesia accordingly healed.

THE DRAGON PROJECT

In an attempt to sort out what might be real within the rumour of site energies, the Dragon Project was set up in Britain in 1977. Founding director was Paul Devereux; John Steele was a founding co-ordinator for eight years. The project utilized two modes of investigation: 'psychic archaeology' employing psychics, sensitives and dowsers, and physical measurement and monitoring of sites. The research has been carried out by a core group of individuals with scientific, technical and geomantic skills, accompanied by a shifting population of field volunteers, consultants, and other supporters. Two books have been written dealing with aspects of the research,[30,31] numerous articles have appeared in specialist and large-circulation magazines, and radio and television items and interviews have been broadcast intermittently. In 1988, the project became the Dragon Project Trust.[32]

The psychic archaeological work has proceeded sporadically over the research period, producing what are so far unclear results. Since the 1930s, when dowsing work was carried out in France, most dowsers have agreed that megalithic and some other types of ancient site are usually situated over the crossing of underground streams. In recent years there has been the development of a new kind of dowsing called 'energy dowsing', in which dowsable forces around and between old stones are claimed. This work has not yet developed much beyond belief-system status, and awaits the spirit of genuine research. Different kinds of psychics have been used on site, and it is hoped that this line of work will prove fruitful when methods of quantifying the findings can be perfected.

The only scientific work on possible energy anomalies at prehistoric sites up to the inception of the Dragon Project had been carried out in the mid-1970s by Dr Eduardo Balanovski, then of Imperial College, London, and Professor John Taylor of King's College, London, at a Welsh standing stone near Crickhowell. Their investigations with a magnetometer revealed small-scale but unexpected magnetic anomalies within the huge megalith.[33] Due to its limited resources, the Dragon Project's policy has been to look at certain basic forces, such as natural magnetism and radiation, and also to use anecdotes of unusual experiences at sites to suggest other possible avenues of physical investigation. In this manner we have gained some insight into the nature of site energies, although even more questions have been raised. A summary of our physical energy findings is given here to show that this research is leading into areas germane to the idea of the living Earth, and that it is one form of the recollection that is taking place.

SIGNALS AT THE STONES

One example of an anecdote that lead to field research was supplied by a zoologist who happened to pick up unexpected signals one dawn on his wide-band ultrasound receiver or 'bat detector' while studying bat behaviour on an English country estate. (Bats, like dolphins and some other creatures, produce ultrasound for echolocation purposes. Ultrasound is sound at frequencies higher than those normally detectable by the human ear.) The signals were coming from an ancient site on the estate and the zoologist could not find any explanation for them.

In consequence, the Dragon Project began monitoring for ultrasound at its main fieldbase site – the Rollright Stones, 20 miles (32 kilometres) northwest of Oxford – and other sites around the British Isles. Test or control locations were also monitored so that they could be compared with actual sites. Over the years a variety of wide-band instruments did sometimes pick up inexplicable signals. These were almost always around dawn, although round-the-clock monitoring revealed very occasional, isolated signals at other times. The first set of monitoring sessions happened to coincide with lunar phases, and there was the tantalizing hint, still not followed up, that the signals would appear earlier at the time of full moon than at new moon. Ultrasound receivers set at specific, narrow frequencies never registered the signal. The signals were picked up at Rollright and a handful of other megalithic locations around Britain, but never at the test locations. The signals did not appear on a consistent basis. Peak effects seemed to be around February and March, with less activity in the autumn and virtually none during summer months. For several years the source of the signals could not be identified; they would fade in one part of the Rollright complex, for example, and suddenly appear in another. Sometimes they would be detectable in only very small areas a few yards across, while at other (rare) times they would be detectable in the countryside all around the site.

Because the presence of ultrasound could not be explained, debate has continued about the nature of these signals. Accidental production of ultrasound (the rustle of modern fabrics, the jangle of keys in a pocket) was definitely ruled out, but concern has been expressed about the possibility of the circuitry of the various items of equipment producing a false effect. Expert analysis did show that some instruments had room for design improvements, but none were shown to be faulty. Another suggestion was that the transducers in the receivers might be picking up stray radio signals (even though they were screened against them). A laborious test for this was made on one occasion when an instrument was registering an anomalous signal, and normal radio interference was shown not to be the cause.

In January 1987 a particular part of a single stone within the Rollright circle was found to be emitting a signal that affected a wide-band ultrasound detector. This was the first time a definite emission point had been identified. The receiver was set at 37 kHz (37 thousand cycles a second). Electronic consultants on the Dragon Project team were still unsure if the signals were truly ultrasound, but no one could explain the phenomenon, whatever it was. As the received signal on the instrument involved could be brought down into the audible range, a tape recording was made of the signal. The matter remains enigmatic and unresolved at the time of writing.

Odd radio signals definitely were picked up at Rollright, however, and also at Bronze Age cairns in the Wicklow Hills, Ireland. Specialized radio receivers picked up isolated patches of signals, a few feet across, at ground level and up to a few feet above it. These were distinct from normal radio chatter, and did not seem to adhere to the normal patterns of radio propagation. This effect, too, has been tape-recorded, and studied on an oscilloscope. In the opinion of Rodney Hale, the project's chief electronics consultant, the signal seems to be man-made. It is its behaviour around old stone monuments rather than its nature which is the most burning question for investigators. The signals come and go, and never seem to occur in quite the same place. Of course, the energy environment is vastly different to what it was when the megalithic builders put up their monuments thousands of years ago, and what may be happening in cases like this is the observation of modern communications signals, probably military. But their odd behaviour in the vicinity of the monuments may still be highly instructive.

Other anomalies have been noted during Dragon Project research. Infrared photographs taken at dawn on two occasions in 1979 showed an apparent glow or haze around the top of the Kingstone, an outlying standing stone of the Rollright circle. Professional analysis of the pictures seemed unable to provide an explanation. The following year another photographer using infrared film captured the image of a curious 'cloud' hovering about 15 feet (4.5 metres) above the ground between the Kingstone and the circle. The cloud had been invisible to the naked eye, as had a similar effect photographed in infrared by yet another researcher as it apparently floated over Kit's Coty House, a megalithic site in Kent. No explanations were forthcoming, and debate has centred around whether the photographs show some genuine anomaly or are in some way spurious, even though professional scrutiny and processes have been involved.

Other areas of enquiry, such as the monitoring of electric fields at sites and the scanning of standing stones, have so far proved even more inconclusive. Much more work will have to be done in these fields. In addition, there are many other aspects to be explored. For example, project volunteers on site for prolonged periods have noted some curious, recurring phenomena, such as sounds from stones or the ground around them; soft, subtle light phenomena; and strange happenings like quartz wristwatches and alarm clocks malfunctioning. The behaviour of animals at sites, such as their refusal to go near certain megaliths at particular times while being happy to do so on other occasions, has also proved intriguing.

MIND–MINERAL INTERACTIONS

There have also been a few tantalizing glimpses of human interaction with stones during the Dragon Project in which instrumental monitoring has been involved, and which show promise for further research.

In one set of circumstances it was the human being who was monitored. The late Maxwell Cade came on site at Rollright for the Dragon Project on several occasions. Cade was well known for his pioneering work with biofeedback techniques. The instrument used was the 'Mind Mirror', a sophisticated device that shows a subject's brain rhythms (see Chapter 3) from both sides of the brain simultaneously. The project had dowsers and sensitives connected to the device at various times, with electrodes on their scalps linked by cable or radio to a viewing monitor console. At Rollright, Cade was able to make the preliminary observation that deep theta and delta brain rhythms seemed to be triggered in some people when in the vicinity of standing stones. Unfortunately, Cade died before further examination of this interesting observation could be made. Subsequent Mind Mirror work with volunteers at the prehistoric stone rows on Dartmoor, Devon, similarly produced examples of changed brainwave activity as the subjects crisscrossed the lines of stone. But much more detailed work under expert guidance still awaits to be done.

There were also two instances of human interaction during project sessions at Rollright, one with a crystal and the other with the tallest stone in the circle, where measurable effects in the mineral were obtained. In the case of the crystal, a clairvoyant and healer was repeatedly able to affect the molecular resonance in a piece of quartz that had been brought on site. He did this by visualizing a white beam of energy flowing from his hand to the crystal, just as he would in a healing session. He never touched the piece of crystal. In the other experiment, a master dowser and healer was repeatedly able to change the voltage in the tallest stone in the circle by laying his hands on what he called an 'energy node' on the stone. In both cases, explanations involving interference from equipment were ruled out, and others present could not reproduce the effects. Although these instances do not categorically prove anything as far as sceptics are concerned, they are real evidence of real effects that deserve proper attention and require a great deal of further study.

Meanwhile, work on magnetism and radiation has already started to yield valuable insights, both into the way the megalith builders may have harnessed subtle, natural energies, and how we may be able to use their stone instruments again, to connect our consciousness with the energy fields of Earth.

MAGNETIC EFFECTS AT SACRED SITES

The first project work in the area of magnetism involved biosensing experiments using magnetically-sensitive brine shrimps at the Rollright Stones. The tentative result of this experimentation was that there did seem to be changes in magnetic fields around the old stones that creatures sensitive to such fields noticeably responded to. But the catalyst to further work came in 1983 when a report of a magnetic study of the Rollright circle was published in *New Scientist* by an independent researcher, Charles Brooker.[34]

Brooker reported finding unusual configurations of magnetism within the ring of stones. Overall, however, he claimed that the geomagnetic levels within the circle were significantly lower than those in the surrounding countryside. He also discovered that two of the stones on the western side of the circle were magnetically 'pulsing'. The Dragon Project soon contacted Brooker to check with him in greater detail. Having arranged the loan of a magnetometer from Birkbeck College, London, a project monitoring session was set up at the Rollright circle in July 1983 and it was confirmed that one of the stones studied *was* magnetically fluctuating – a phenomenon that none of the experts present could explain. Other stones checked at the same session did not show unusual variations, and neither did control readings at a distance from the site. The fluctuating stone returned to normal readings after a few hours. It was confirmed that this stone was not one of those that Brooker had previously found to be pulsing. The observed changes in magnetism were at a low level, but were definitely taking place.

Subsequently, the project obtained its own magnetometers, and these have been used at a number of sites. Usually, nothing abnormal is found, but noteworthy effects are registered on occasion. Although research is a long way from explaining what is actually happening, it is now certain that unexpected, low-level magnetic variations do seem to occur within standing stones at some megalithic sacred sites some of the time.

In 1987 a new twist took the magnetic work beyond the rarified areas requiring specialized, sensitive measuring devices. A local newspaper story broke in Wales about a woman who had experienced curious body sensations while being driven close to the jagged peak of Carn Ingli in the Preseli hills.[35] It seemed to her that 'something' was emanating from the peak itself. Keith Stevenson, the journalist who followed up the story, climbed Carn Ingli and found that his compass behaved erratically there. He contacted Devereux, feeling that an 'earth mystery' had been encountered. Further work confirmed that full compass deflections could be obtained at points on and immediately around the peak – the compass needle would rotate 180 degrees and point south. This happened both on the surface of some of the Carn Ingli rocks, and also at points in mid-air. Checks with numerous other peaks along the Preseli ridge failed to produce similar findings.

Magnetic rocks such as those which form Carn Ingli come about because they contain iron-bearing minerals that have a measurable magnetization induced in them by the Earth's present-day magnetic field. In addition, when the rocks were formed hundreds of millions of years ago, the minerals trapped in them took on the imprint of the geomagnetic fields prevailing at the time. This fossil or 'remanent' magnetism has allowed geologists to learn that the magnetic poles of the Earth have reversed themselves at various irregular intervals over the epochs. Stones with this sort of complex magnetic history can cause startling effects on compasses, such as those noted by Keith Stevenson. So the effect is not paranormal, but it is special and interesting, particularly in the case of Carn Ingli because the peak was also an ancient site, selected as important by people in prehistory and draped with necklaces of stone walling which can still be perceived today. Moreover, the peak was used by a sixth-century holy man, St Brynach. He spent long periods on the peak, where he prayed and fasted and, it is said, spoke with angels. This is remembered by the name Carn Ingli, which means the hill or peak of angels. Now we have the report of the woman's reaction to it, and subsequently another woman has heard apparently paranormal sounds on the hill slopes. Also, a group of reliable witnesses have observed a rainbow-like effect over the peak – *but at night*.[36] Could the unusual magnetic conditions on Carn Ingli be connected with the ancient importance bestowed on it, and the unusual phenomena experienced around it?

In 1988, alerted by the Carn Ingli case, Devereux started the long process of compass-checking prehistoric sites for such effects, and it has already become clear that the megalith builders in Britain did make specific use of magnetic stones in the construction of some of their sacred monuments. Sites have now been identified where just one stone out of many others is able to scramble a compass; it has been placed at a cardinal position in a circle, or else is an outlier from a circle, sometimes also indicating key astronomical events.

This magnetic factor has recently been noted at sites outside Britain. In the United States there is an outcrop of serpentine on the southern side of Mount Tamalpais which rises above San Francisco. This outcrop has been identified as an Indian holy place or power spot. Devereux discovered in 1986 that it is, in fact, an area with magnetic anomalies, due to magnetized minerals in the serpentine. And in Kenya, American archaeological researcher Mark Lynch has noted that compasses start spinning in the vicinity of alignments of stones in the megalithic complex known as Namoratunga II near Lake Turkana.

The Belgian researcher Pierre Méreaux has made a remarkable

magnetic discovery at the Carnac stone rows in Brittany. Apart from confirming a fault connection with the Carnac complex, and finding gravity variations amongst the stones, Méreaux has also discovered that the great stone alignment groupings – complexes sometimes comprising several lines of standing stones running for miles – show a 'precise frontier' between the generally stable geomagnetic field in the area and a zone of disturbed magnetism. Méreaux writes that 'the field begins to be disturbed in the middle of the field of menhirs, where the variations already reach 200 to 250 gammas'.[37] At three alignment groups, Kermario, Kerlescan and Le Menec, Méreaux noted that 'the disturbances vary between – 400 and + 1100 gammas'.

STONES OF POWER

Before considering the possible significance of the magnetic factor at ancient sites, we must look at an equally relevant feature – natural radioactivity. It is difficult to discuss this subject without the spectres of Three Mile Island, Chernobyl, Sellafield and atomic weaponry being conjured up. But nuclear energy plants and weapons use artificially high levels of radiation. Natural radioactivity is one of the fundamental forces of the universe; it has always been present. On Earth, we experience it from radioactive material scattered through the rocks in the Earth's crust, and from the heavens in the form of cosmic ray bombardment – charged particles from the Sun and galactic sources. Such background radiation is thus always present to some degree. In Britian the National Radiological Protection Board estimates that gamma rays from the ground account for 16 per cent of the total average dose received by a person, while cosmic rays account for 13 per cent. Radioactive radon gas which issues from the ground as a result of uranium decay accounts for a huge 33 per cent.[38]

Radon gas has caused a storm of controversy in recent years in the United States, Britain and other countries, since it was found that the gas can accumulate in modern, well-sealed buildings. Long-term exposure to the gas is thought to encourage lung cancer. It is estimated that up to eight million homes in the United States and at least 20,000 in Britain may have radiation levels above the accepted safety limits. This gas is almost certainly one aspect of what the old Chinese feng shui geomants would have called *sha*, or 'bad breath' from the ground. So now modern society can start counting the cost of the lack of geomantic awareness in contemporary building practices!

Thousands of geiger counter and scintillometer readings have been taken as part of the Dragon Project and by Devereux and colleagues in separate research efforts at numerous ancient sites and test locations, in a wide range of landscapes in Britain, the United States and the Middle East. The first Dragon Project radiation monitoring was at the Rollright Stones. Over the years, most readings showed the circle to have the same range of geiger counts as the surrounding environment, but on odd occasions flares of readings, up to three times above the norm, were registered within the ring of stones.[39] At the time when these occurred, the project did not have the capacity to monitor the site and its environment simultaneously, so it was not known if the increased periods of radioactivity, which lasted only a few minutes, were due to some common source, such as a cosmic ray shower, affecting the whole region. Work conducted in 1987, however, indicated that we may be looking at a site-specific phenomenon.

On 29 September of that year, American Dragon Project volunteers Cosimo and Ann Favaloro made a study of the Scottish stone circle known as Easter Aquorthies. By this time the project had the equipment to monitor background radiation at a site and its surrounding landscape simultaneously. The Favaloros chose this date because archaeologist Aubrey Burl had suggested that Easter Aquorthies is one of a number of Scottish stone circles that has a stone aligned to the Moon during a particular period of the Metonic cycle known as the 'major lunar standstill'. On 29 September an important moonset was due to take place. Taking readings continuously through a 12-hour period, the Favaloros made two noteworthy findings. At one point in the late afternoon the readings within the circle soared way above the normal site readings for a few minutes, while the environment readings remained constant. The second finding was that at the precise moment of moonset, at nine o'clock in the evening, the level of radiation readings in the environment edged above those for the stone circle for the only time in the whole monitoring period. It seems there was some kind of geophysics taking place which we are a long way from understanding.

Some healing and holy wells have been found to be naturally

radioactive. This is true of two of the most famous and ancient holy wells in Britain: the Chalice Well at Glastonbury and the sacred waters of the springs at Bath. But less well-known wells, such as that of Sancreed, in Cornwall, can also yield surprisingly high natural radiation counts at water level.

Another way in which radiation is connected with ancient sites is in the use of granite by megalith builders. Granite is a particularly radioactive rock, and it is in granite regions especially that radon gas tends to be a hazard. Of all the counties in England, granitic Cornwall has the highest incidence of domestic radon; it also has the highest concentration of megalithic sites. Other granite zones include Dartmoor in Devon and the Aberdeen area of Scotland, both of which are also notable focuses for megalithic monuments. And the world's greatest concentration of megaliths, around Carnac, is similarly in a granite landscape.

Granite uprights at some stone circles in Britain have been found to have small areas on them which emit radiation almost continuously, although measured overall their radiation count is simply that of high-energy granite. But the most interesting use of granite by the builders of prehistoric sacred structures was in the creation of enclosed spaces. In Europe these took the form of dolmens – stone uprights with a flat capstone forming a sort of stone box – and underground passages or chambers. These subterranean features are known as fogous in Cornwall but usually as souterrains elsewhere. In the British Isles they are found in northeast Scotland, on the islands of Orkney off the northern tip of Scotland, and in Ireland in addition to Cornwall. Similar features also occur in Brittany. The geology of the Irish sites has not been determined by alternative researchers as yet, but the French, Cornish and Scottish examples are all in granite country, and uranium is known to be present on Orkney.[40]

The souterrains resemble the Indian kivas of the American southwest, which is also an area of uranium deposits – indeed, some regions have been threatened with becoming 'national sacrifice areas' for the extraction of such minerals. The kivas were designed for ritual and ceremonial purposes, and at least some versions of the European souterrains almost certainly had a similar function.

Radiation monitoring took place at a number of the Cornish fogous and dolmens during 1988. Readings within them varied, but all were high, some two to three times higher than the already above-average background readings outside.

The King's Chamber inside Egypt's Great Pyramid at Giza is also constructed from granite. In this case, the stone was shipped from Aswan hundreds of miles to the south to be used in the limestone edifice. It is said that to the ancient Egyptians limestone symbolized materiality while granite represented spirit.[41] This may be a significant factor in the arguments which have been raised about the nature of the King's Chamber: was it simply a tomb, or was it an initiation chamber? The fact that air channels lead to the chamber – constructed on all sides from meticulously worked granite blocks, creating a space conforming to specific geometrical ratios – and that no wall inscriptions, body or burial goods were ever found in it, has led many people to suppose that it was indeed for magical or mystical use. Radiation counts taken of the air in the centre of this dark, brooding chamber were in fact higher than on the surface of the granite walls, presumably as a consequence of radon being emitted from all sides and being unable to dissipate readily. These readings were very similar to those taken in several of the Cornish megalithic interiors, and in a few cases were virtually identical.[42]

ALTERED STATES, HEALING AND SITE ENERGIES

If some sacred sites were identified and chosen, or deliberately constructed, to take advantage of naturally occurring radiation in concentrated form or of special magnetism in rocks, what could the purposes have been? And how would the ancients have known about these properties?

To take the last question first, Chapter 3 has shown us how there is little problem in accepting that human beings may well have had the ability to sense magnetic variations around stones. Although the levels of magnetism we are considering are low, they are quite substantial compared to some of the minute strengths discussed in the previous chapter. In any event, magnetic qualities in rocks could have been detected instrumentally at any point in prehistory by means of the lodestone, a piece of naturally occurring magnetic mineral called magnetite. It is certain that magnetism was known from at least the time of the ancient Greeks. The word 'magnet' is derived, it is said, from the term *Magnes Lithos* or Magnesian Stone, as the Greeks knew that magnetite was to be found in an area of Anatolia called Magnesia. There is also said to be a first-century reference to its use in France.[43] In his *History of Magic* (1854), Joseph Ennemoser claims that magnets were also known to the ancient Egyptians; they were used in temples to suspend images of deities. If there was knowledge of magnetism in this period, there is no reason to assume it was not known before. Certainly, magnets were a part of the stock in trade of magicians, healers and alchemists.

So one way or another, magnetic properties in stone could have been readily identified by early peoples the world over. But how about radiation? We all know only too well of the terrible damage radioactivity can wreak on living tissue, but here we are considering low doses of natural radiation which do not show any obvious effects (for relatively short periods of exposure at any rate). Orthodox science states that ionizing radiation cannot be directly detected by human senses. While this may be true of the five senses as such, there is some evidence that gamma radiation, at least, can be indirectly sensed by living organisms. For instance, in a paper published in 1963, Frank Brown described how he was able to show that flatworms were aware of very weak gamma radiation being emitted by a sample of the mineral caesium-137. In 1966, in a paper entitled 'Diurnal Variation in Organismic Response to Very Weak Gamma Radiation', Brown and colleagues Y. Park and J. Zeno were able to describe how a mouse responded. Z.J. Harvalik has observed in his work with dowsers that some of these people can prove more sensitive to weak radioactivity than geiger counters, a finding also reached in German research. It seems that a general rule of thumb would be that living organisms are able to sense or respond to all the natural fields in which life on Earth has developed, even if many of these sensitivities are below the threshold of conscious awareness, or have changed or even atrophied as environmental circumstances have altered over the ages. Orthodox science tends always to underestimate the sensitivity of living organisms to weak energies.

There is another, more amazing, way in which the megalith builders may have identified energy associated with granite. The builders of the sacred stone edifices of the ancient world had total mastery and knowledge of their medium. One only has to look at the handling of stone at Stonehenge, Machu Picchu in Peru or the Egyptian Great Pyramid to realize this. There would be no property of stone that the ancients would have failed to notice. A curious phenomenon that seems to occur inside the high natural radiation environments provided by structures such as dolmens and fogous has only recently (1988) come to the attention of researchers. While measuring radiation levels at some of these features in Cornwall, Devereux came across accounts describing the appearance of light phenomena within them.

One example was provided by archaeologist Dr John Barnatt, who had observed inexplicable lights while inside the Cornish dolmen called Chûn Quoit. It happened in July 1979, when Barnatt was engaged on weeks of fieldwork studying the Cornish ceremonial monuments. At the end of a long day's work, he and his photographer Brian Larkman camped alongside Chûn Quoit, and after dinner went over to the dolmen to 'look round and just generally relax'. He squeezed inside the stone structure, and, sitting in the darkness, suddenly became aware that on the underside of the capstone above his head there were 'periodic short bursts of multicoloured light' which 'flashed across the stone's surface in short linear bands'.[44] This went on intermittently for about half an hour. The quoit – a colloquial term for dolmen – is located on a remote stretch of moorland; it was night-time, and there was no identifiable source of light to account for the phenomenon. The effect was confirmed by Larkman, who sat inside and also saw lights flickering on the capstone's underside. He could detect no colours, but they were 'a real phenomenon taking place inside the tomb'.[45]

It was later discovered that in June 1988, also in totally dark conditions, former university research psychologist Jo May had witnessed what seems to be an indentical phenomenon, but this time inside Boleigh fogou. Inside this subterranean granite chamber May clearly observed 'thin spirallic filaments swirling . . . around the main capping lintels of the passage'. He made checks to ensure that he was not experiencing some form of optical illusion. Soon he found he was able to attune his eyes to the effect. Although the lights were subtle, he commented that they were clearly 'there'; they were objective phenomena. The swirling filaments 'closely resembled the whorls on fingertips, but lots of them, interlaced and moving gently'. He also noted that they were accompanied by 'hundreds of tiny pricks of light, like stars, again moving gently, with the occasional streak as if some of them were shooting stars'.[46]

It so happens that these two sites gave the highest radiation readings of any granite enclosure sites monitored in Cornwall during the 1988 session.

Obviously, ancient peoples would not think of magnetic or radiation phenomena in terms of geophysics, but as evidence of spirits or magical power (which is not to say such interpretations were necessarily any less valid than those of modern science). But whatever terms they were seen in, energetic stones, whether magnetic or radioactive, would have been noted and used, probably as aids to healing and the production of altered states, almost certainly in conjunction with ritual activities and the ingestion of psychoactive herbs, plants or fungi.

We have already noted in the previous chapter how low-level magnetism can be used as a healing agent, and it is possible the 'magical' magnetic stones were similarly used at sites; this may, indeed, be the original source of the traditional belief relating to healing stones. In addition, the shaman, in a state of ecstasy, may have used such stones in direct body contact to help trigger mind change, or to help direct the experience. Magnetic stones seem to have been modified to accommodate such usage. Gors Fawr in Wales is one of several stone circles recently identified as having a magnetic stone associated with it. The site comprises a ring, 72–foot (22 metres) in diameter, formed by 16 fairly low stones, with two much taller outliers a few hundred feet to the northeast. None of the stones is magnetic, except for the outlier furthest from the circle. The two outliers were found by Thom to create an alignment marking the midsummer sunrise. The magnetic stone has a curious shape that allows it to form a seat; using this to sit on the stone, one's head leans back on precisely that part of the outlier which most affects a compass. It is not beyond the bounds of possibility that if one is in a certain mental state, engendered by fasting, dancing or hallucinogenics, the placing of the head, and thus the brain, in the stone's magnetic fields may trigger or enhance visionary or spiritual experiences, the hippocampus being suitably massaged by the magnetism. Perhaps the moment of dawn at midsummer was a particularly good time for this activity to be carried out. Similarly, the serpentine outcrop on Mount Tamalpais has a smooth cleft that acts as a perfect seat, although here it is the base of the spine which is pressed in close contact with the magnetic rock.

While magnetism can be fairly readily associated with healing and effects on the brain, the ability of heightened natural radiation to do either is less obvious. Nevertheless, research is producing evidence to suggest that it may have such roles to play. Healing with low-level radiation may seem a bizarre notion, yet some people claim just this. Around the turn of the century, Americans used to visit radioactive caves in Colorado in much the same way as Europeans would visit spas (some of which, as we have noted, have mildy radioactive waters). A few decades ago, radon kits were sold as supposed healing aids: canisters containing the radioactive gas were sniffed. Even at the present time, people visit old gold and uranium mines, such as those at Boulder, Montana, and swear that they have experienced significant healing of conditions such as crippling arthritis, diabetes, and so on.[47] These people are exposed to the radon in the old mines for strictly timed periods. Perhaps a 'homeopathic' dose of low-level natural radiation can in some cases act as a healing agent, while too much causes harm. As the sixteenth-century alchemist Paracelsus put it: 'The poison is the dose.'

The mind-changing potential of certain levels of natural radiation was first noted on the Dragon Project, although by accident. The area around the Rollright Stones came in for a good deal of monitoring attention of all kinds over the years, and it was soon realized that the country lane running immediately past the circle had an abnormally high geiger count rate for a few hundred yards of its length at its closest approach to the stones. Dosimetric tests of the road surface materials showed nothing unusual. For a time it was thought that the road might simply be running over a small uranium deposit. John Steele observed that the land rights issues with the Indians in the United States and the Aborigines in Australia revolved around the fact that some indigenous sacred sites had been found to be in locations rich in minerals, especially uranium. Dribs and drabs of other evidence came to the project's attention supporting this apparent link between some sacred sites and uranium deposits. The French writer Marc Dem noticed that the areas of France with the highest uranium deposits coincided with the greatest concentrations of megalithic sites.[48] Swiss researcher

Blanche Mertz has measured high natural radiation levels at a number of important Tibetan monasteries.[49] It is also claimed that there are uranium deposits around Serpent Mound in Ohio. And Mount Harney in South Dakota, subsequently found to contain uranium, figured prominently in the Great Vision of the Oglala Sioux holy man, Black Elk.[50]

Nevertheless, project personnel were to be disappointed. Intensive radiation monitoring in 1988 showed that the increased levels of radioactivity were so tightly correlated with the width of the road that it could only be assumed that material in the road's foundation must be the culprit. But this was still natural radioactivity, and because of the project activity at the site, a highly instructive coincidence came to light in 1980. Within two weeks of each other, two highly reliable witnesses, one a surveyor and the other a scientist, observed strange phenomena on the same stretch of the lane, in the middle of the radioactive zone.

In the first incident, the surveyor observed the apparent disappearance on the road of a car with two occupants. Only three explanations proved possible: the witness had blacked out for a few seconds while walking along carrying out a task; he had hallucinated; or the image of an apparently normal, solid vehicle had actually flashed into sight for a few moments.

In the second incident, the scientist observed the momentary appearance of a huge dog-like animal by the side of the road next to the circle. He saw every detail of the creature's grey, coarse fur.

Eighteen months later, another member of the project witnessed the appearance of an old-fashioned, horse-drawn gypsy caravan for a few moments. It was going away from her, yet nothing had passed her on the road.

In all three cases, the witnesses and the imagery observed were on the radioactive length of road. Two and possibly all three of the incidents could be interpreted in terms of 'time slip' phenomena, in that somehow or other the observers fleetingly gained access to a moment of other time on the roadway. Reports of the three experiences were quietly and individually handed in to Devereux as director of the project, and for a long time each of the percipients were unaware of the other reported events; they are not, and never have been, in touch with one another socially.

By chance, it seemed, the existence of a phenomenon apparently associated with localized zones of high background radiation had been brought to the attention of the Dragon Project. Could such zones really help to trigger altered states? It seemed unscientific to dismiss such reports from people of known reliability, or to consider the radiation link as coincidental. It is not an area where there is much scope for anecdotal information to become available, but accounts have come to researchers' attention from time to time. For example, because Boleigh fogou is in the grounds of the Centre for Alternative Education and Research (CAER), a number of experiences in this souterrain have been recorded. In one case, a woman standing alone in the pitch darkness of the fogou suddenly found herself in a vivid 'waking dream' in which she was in bright daylight near a church witnessing a wedding. She was simultaneously conscious of standing upright in the dark fogou while observing every detail of the church scene. Other instances of altered states and the appearance of a 'white lady' have also been reported at the same site, and another Cornish fogou (Pendeen Vau) has a long-standing legend relating to a white lady.

In the Chûn Quoit incidents recounted above, Brian Larkman, in addition to observing the light phenomena on the underside of the capstone, also saw a curious 'reflection' of his own figure on one of the supporting upright stones. While he was sure the lights were an objective energy of some kind, he has continued to struggle mentally with the memory of the 'reflection' – was it some bizarre paranormal event, or some ultimately explainable retinal illusion?

In her home at Sao Jôse do Rio Prêto, northwest of São Paulo, Brazil, Cynthia Newby Luce has witnessed phenomena typical of those becoming associated with radiation zones; this could be because her house is perched on a whole mountain of granite. On one occasion she was suddenly aware that an antique marble-topped butcher's table was not present in its usual corner. After a few seconds it reappeared. During the incident she noticed 'a slight shift in the quality of the light'. On numerous occasions human figures and animals have appeared 'like subliminal flashes'.[51] Light balls are sporadically seen in the grounds of the house, and are well known to the locals as *Mae de Ouro* (Mother of Gold).

Clearly, such reports do not yet amount to rock-hard evidence, but they do indicate a fresh and potentially informative line of enquiry.

That is why research is now under way to study possible mind-change effects at sites possessing special magnetic or high background radiation characteristics. (Interestingly, sites so far studied do not seem to possess both together.) This work involves research into the curious interior light phenomena of enclosed granite monuments, brain rhythm studies of subjects in contact with magnetic stones, and direct experiential work with mind-change techniques at magnetic or radioactive sites and stones at particular times of the day and year. Researchers have also found some evidence that holy wells and springs where there is a radiation factor may help induce quiescent states, a special kind of languor, that correlate with alpha brainwave conditions.

Exploration along these lines will obviously take time, but it represents the first real modern usage of these ancient places. Ecopagans, New Agers and others visit such sites, of course, and that is beneficial in itself as suggested earlier in this chapter, but the invented rituals they perform at these places are little more than theatrics; they have little knowledge of the aspects of the sites being discussed here. If one wants to dream at a site, for instance, it is helpful to know which stone was designed for that purpose, and which may give the hippocampus a small boost!

This kind of investigation is going on in difficult circumstances. Conventional science dismisses the reality of paranormal or *psi* phenomena, and altered states are generally seen in terms of pathology or antisocial behaviour. On the other hand, serious researchers from a variety of disciplines and backgrounds are indeed studying aspects of altered states – psychoactive substances, myth, shamanic traditions, psychological therapy, ESP, and so on – but there is little evidence in the papers and literature resulting from these studies of an awareness of the importance of place, of geophysical conditions, as they related to traditional mind-change practices, and thus by implication, to possibly recoverable techniques that could be explored today. So it is that an expert in consciousness studies on the west coast of the United States, for instance, tends to have difficulty relating such work to the geomantic studies going on elsewhere, or is even completely ignorant of it. In consequence, the link between the human mind and the Earth, especially at places marked by people from remote times, is not being perceived.

It is important for us to try to comprehend the geomantic

understanding of traditional societies. The ancient sites are a form of memory bank whereby we may be able to recollect something of this. We need to know the role of geophysics in mind-change activities. What is the radiation count in, for example, a shaman's cave? What geophysical characteristics has a place of power, a megalithic monument, a sacred peak? As we learn this, we will 'remember' much about ourselves, our planetary environment and our relationship to it, and thus grow to realize how we may properly utilize the old places once more.

We may discover that altered states at sites with special properties allow entry to highly specialized orders of consciousness which give direct access to the energy body of Earth – a line of thinking we will explore further in Part Three. It may not be accidental that St Brynach chose a magnetic peak to talk with angels. It may be that alpha, theta and delta states, induced by physical contact at a specific time with a naturally magnetic stone implanted in the ground, could allow us to key directly into the great electromagnetic rhythms of the planet described in the previous chapter, and allow our consciousness to resonate at global levels.

We must not allow the attitudes and fragmentation of our times, the consequence of our cultural amnesia, to dissuade us from following these avenues of investigation. The recollections obtained may allow us to build a new geomancy from the information left encoded in the sites of sanctity on the Earth's body by those who lived long before us.

CHAPTER FIVE

GAIA AGAIN

During the course of the twentieth century the ancient idea that the Earth is alive has once more entered our consciousness. It has crept in through the mystic, visionary and scientific modes of our thinking, now so fragmented, and has been exemplified in the writings of three acknowledged figures in those spheres. We need to listen to them all.

THE IRISH SEER

The Irish nature mystic George William Russell, or 'AE', was born in 1867. As well as exploring with careful analysis his spiritual self, he was an agricultural reformer, political writer, journal editor, poet and painter. When he left school he pursued his artistic development at evening classes in Dublin, where he met W.B. Yeats, a fellow student. It was also during this period that Russell 'became aware of a mysterious life quickening within my life'. Through Yeats, he was introduced to Theosophy, an inclusive, non-sectarian approach to ancient occult wisdom developed by H.P. Blavatsky and others, and along with Yeats and other leading Irish intellectuals, writers and artists, he supported the formation of a Dublin lodge of the society in 1886.

To support himself while he attended the evening classes, Russell worked as a clerk at various businesses including a drapery firm called Pim's, where he was described as 'wild-looking, but very businesslike'. He stayed at Pim's for several years while the inner life of visions, ESP episodes and mystic transports continued to develop within him. His powerful intellect strove to comprehend the experiences he was undergoing, and he found that a useful framework was provided by the wide range of occult literature, especially ancient Indian scripture, made accessible by his theosophical connections. He also had strong sympathies with the old Celtic legends and myths of Ireland, which were haunting the thinking of people such as Yeats and the other Celtic revivalists of the time.

Russell wrote poems and allegories, and also attempted to depict his visions in startling paintings throughout this whole blossoming of his mystical genius. In one of his earlier works, he attempted to depict the appearance of Primal Man in the Divine Mind. Although some of his paintings were 'only the fancies of a boy', this picture seemed to result from 'something ancient and eternal'. He was excited by the painting and lay awake at night wondering what he could call it. 'While I was preternaturally dilated and intent,' Russell recalled decades later in *The Candle of Vision*, 'something whispered to me, "Call it the Birth of Aeon."'

The evocative sound of the word 'Aeon' thrilled the young Russell, even though he did not know what it meant. In his imagination, this Aeon descended from heaven 'into the chaos, weaving out of the wild elements a mansion for its spirit. That mansion was our earth, and that Aeon was the God of our world'.

About a fortnight later, when Russell was in the library at Leinster House, he noticed an open book lying on the desk. His eye was caught by the word 'Aeon' on one of its pages. Feverishly scanning the lines associated with the word, he discovered it was the term the Gnostics had used to refer to the first created beings. 'I was certain I had never heard the word before,' Russell declared, 'and there rushed into my mind the thought of pre-existence and that this was memory of the past.' This made such an impression on Russell that he signed one of his subsequent articles 'AEON'. A proofreader was unable to decipher the whole word, so only the first two letters were printed. Russell took this as a sign, and thereafter wrote under the pseudonym of AE.

In 1897, Russell became an organizer for Sir Horace Plunkett's Irish Agricultural Organization Society, which was formed to establish rural co-operatives among farmers, in order to help rebuild Irish agriculture, devasted after the Great Famine. Irish writer Michael Sayers recalled:

'The desolation of Ireland was the destruction of the Irish peasantry. . . . We had no sense of seasons because we had no harvest . . . a few black-faced sheep, cattle and race horses for the English, which they bred there – we had nothing. I grew up in it. AE started the modern dairy industry with his co-operative movement. So he had that side to him, which also relates him to the earth. AE had a tough, political side to him.'[1]

Russell went on to advise the Danes on the development of their agricultural policy, and was frequently consulted on rural policy by the United States Department of Agriculture. From 1905 onwards, Russell edited *The Irish Homestead* and its successor *The Irish Statesman*, and he continued to write poems, articles and pamphlets. He painted, read or visited the countryside at weekends.

Although concerned and involved with the Irish political issues of the day, Russell saw such problems against a cosmic backdrop. He had a strong sense of vast cycles of time, which he expressed through the concept of yugas, ancient Hindu and Tantric ideas filtered through to him via the Theosophical Society. Yugas are epochs lasting hundreds of thousands of years, and there are four of them: the Golden, Silver, Bronze and Black or Iron ages. We are in the Black or Iron age now – the Kali Yuga. This is the most materialistic, violent, darkened epoch, most removed from the spiritual values and the vast, aeonic sense of time experienced by earlier peoples. According to this teaching, humanity has to go through these cycles during each of its manifestations as a race, of which there are several during humanity's evolution. The Kali Yuga of this cycle supposedly commenced at the death of Krishna in 3102 BC, and Russell poetically described that moment in an allegorical story, based on one of his own visions, in which he states:

'The earth and the air around it seemed to tingle with anguish . . . within me I heard as from far away a note of deeper anguish, like a horn blown out of the heart of the ancient Mother.'[2]

But Russell felt that Ireland was potentially a place where the ancient sense of the sacred could be resurrected:

'. . . this spirit of the modern, with which we [in Ireland] are so little in touch, is one which tends to lead man further and further from nature. She is no more to him the Great Mother so reverently named long ago, but merely an adjunct to his life, the distant supplier of his needs. What to the average dweller in cities are stars and skies and mountains? . . . The Holy Breath from the past communes no more with him . . . .

'. . . we might do worse than turn back to that ideal Paganism of the past. . . .'[3]

To Russell, the heroes and gods of Celtic Ireland were but references of a particular period to archetypal beings who may have existed in the remote antiquity of an earlier cycle, but who also eternally co-existed with us in another order of time and consciousness; an idea very much in keeping with the Australian Aboriginal concept of the Dreamtime. Although Russell's visionary talents allowed him to perceive beings and primal landscapes co-existing with our normal, terrestrial surroundings, he was also acutely aware that these were representative of different levels of consciousness, which allowed the planet to be observed in other ways. The Celtic Land of Youth, Tir-na-nog, is simultaneously a myth, a state of consciousness and 'a name for the soul of earth, the enchantress and mother of all'. Although humanity as a whole may take literally ages to return to the more refined levels of being beyond the Kali Yuga, individuals could gain access to them at any time if they worked at the mental disciplines that enabled this to be achieved.

Russell and Yeats began to drift apart in 1898 when Russell left the Theosophical Society after they objected to him combining Theosphy with rural economics[4] and were concerned at his political involvements. Also, Yeats had joined the Hermetic Order of the Golden Dawn and Russell was uneasy with ritual magic, preferring to follow the way which 'gives wisdom rather than that which gives power'.[5] Nevertheless, they kept in touch over the years.

Russell used meditation to ensure that the outer clamour of his life did not prevent the continued pursuit of his understanding of his altered states. These came to him spontaneously, and were also cultivated by him. One form of meditation he used was retrospective, tracing back through the days, months and years of his life. Not only did he recall events and actions, but also his visions, moods and intimations; ceaselessly he tried to trace them to their source, which took him to sublime heights of insight. As a by-product of this line of enquiry, Russell became interested in studying the basic sounds, the phonemes, behind language, suspecting that there was some primordial set of sounds out of which certain words had their genesis – a language of the gods. In short, his methods and interests centred around memory at many levels.

'The physical explanation of memory itself breaks down even as the material explanation of imagination breaks down,' Russell stated. He wondered how the simple act of will could bring about the appearance of figures or scenes in imagination, or their apparently autonomous, complex appearance in dreams. 'If they are human memories merely,' he argued, 'vibrations of stored-up sunlight fixed in some way in the brain as a photograph is fixed, the alteration of these by a simple wish involves incredibilities. . . .'[6]

He analysed the texture, motion and composition of mental imagery. Where does the light come from for these images? Where does the light come from in a dream? He observed that as one persevered in meditation, although inner darkness might prevail for weeks or months at first, 'our faculties readjust themselves. . . . The dark caverns of the brain begin to grow luminous. We are creating our own light'. Russell found that his concentrated meditation produced 'a growing luminousness in my brain as if I had unsealed in the body a fountain of interior light'. This luminous quality gradually became a normal part of his meditations and 'at times . . . there broke in on me an almost intolerable lustre of light, pure and shining faces, dazzling processions of figures, most ancient, ancient places and peoples, and landscapes lovely as the lost Eden'.

The Irish seer felt that artists and poets were insufficiently curious about the source and nature of their images and inspiration, and that psychologists likewise did not sufficiently consider the mechanics and nature of mental imagery. Everything was too easily dismissed by modern thinking.

> 'The moment we close our eyes and are alone with our thoughts and the pictures of dream, we are alone with mystery and miracle. Or are we alone? Are we secure there from intrusion? Are we not nearer the thronged highways of existence where gods, demons, men and goblins all are psychic visitors?'[7]

As he sifted the images which entered his mind, Russell began to determine that various sources were involved. He was convinced that when he was in certain moods some autonomous sympathetic action caused his psyche to coincide with someone else on Earth who was on the same mental frequency at that moment, and he was able, fleetingly, to see out of that person's eyes, observe people and scenes he did not know, and feel what was in that person's heart. The people concerned were usually unknown to him so proof was impossible, but on one occasion, when thinking about a friend, he suddenly saw night-time views of the Great Pyramid and the Sphinx. He did not know it at the time, but the friend was in Egypt and spent a night at the pyramids. He described this kind of experience as intersecting with someone else's consciousness, rather than telepathy. But some images were certainly due to telepathic intrusion, as he proved to himself while working at Pim's. One day he pressed his face into his hands during an idle interval. He immediately saw images of a small shop in which there was a red-haired girl and an old man behind the counter fumbling with some papers. He discovered that his office companion was writing a letter home at that precise moment, and the images Russell had seen were in every detail those of the man's home and relatives. Russell had been 'in a vacant mood' when his companion's thoughts spilled over into his mind. Such a state, as we noted in Chapter 3, would nowadays be recognized as being associated with alpha rhythm brainwave activity. (Russell felt that in deep dreamless sleep we tuned into universal consciousness. Delta rhythms occur in such sleep states, and are also associated with higher levels of consciousness.) Alerted by this incident, Russell wondered 'how many thousand times are we invaded by such images and there is no speculation over them?'

Other images came from spiritual memory. Sometimes this was symbolic material, memories relating to the individual refashioned with added content in dreams or imagination by the interior architect, who Russell identified as the ancient self, the oversoul, the immortal strand of being that linked many separate lifetimes, the umbilical cord that linked each person with the infinite, eternal godhead. This allowed 'a revelation of the self to the self'. Other images were from the remote past of earlier lifetimes experienced by this immortal spirit within the individual, or as some might now speculate, from a kind of cellular memory. Certainly the idea of a cellular memory was not an alien concept to Russell:

'In that acorn which lies at my feet there is a tiny cell which has in it a memory of the oak from the beginning of earth, and a power coiled in it which can beget from itself the full majestic being of oak. From that tiny fountain by some miracle can spring another cell, and cell after cell will be born, will go on dividing, begetting, building up from each other unnumbered myriads of cells, all controlled by some mysterious power latent in the first. . . . There is nothing incredible in the assumption that every cell in the body is wrapped about with myriad memories.'[8]

What more articulate exposition of Sheldrake's hypothesis of formative causation (Chapter 3) could there be than this? Mystic and scientist can come to similar conclusions. In *Song and its Fountains* Russell similarly showed he could anticipate recent developments such as 'chaos' physics (where the study of fractal patterns and interlinking systems in nature shows that there can be an almost endless redistribution of energy through, effectively, the structure of chaos, so that in theory the fluttering of a butterfly's wings may eventually contribute to a distant hurricane). Russell wrote:

'There is as great a mystery about our least motion as there is about our whole being. We are affected by the whole cosmos. Emanations from most distant planets pour on us and through us. Everything is related to everything else.'

This also foreshadows the sort of interactions described in Chapter 3, while the knowledge of 'connectedness' is, as we have seen, the foundation of ancient, traditional wisdom.

Spiritual memory can hold transpersonal images too, relating to collective human memories of incalculable antiquity, Russell came to understand. It could go back to the time when the Many emanated from the One, the spiritual equivalent of the physicist's 'big bang' at the commencement of the universe.

'This memory of the spirit is the real basis of imagination,' Russell declared. Imagination in Russell's terminology, like that of Blake and other mystics and magicians, is a profound creative state greatly superior to the weak version most people experience in normal waking consciousness, although images arising even from that, Russell argued, cannot be explained.

EARTH MEMORY

All the kinds of imagery referred to in the preceding paragraphs could burst in on Russell's consciousness anywhere, any time: in town or country, in meditation, in sleep and reverie, in waking consciousness – even when walking down a street or corridor. But Russell also had another range of mystical and visionary experiences:

> 'I was made certain that the images which populate the brain have not always been there, nor are refashioned from things seen. I know that with the pictures of memory mingle pictures which come to us, sometimes from the minds of others, sometimes are glimpses of distant countries, sometimes are reflections of happenings in regions invisible to the outer eyes; and as meditation grows more exalted, the forms traceable to memory tend to disappear and we have access to a memory greater than our own, the treasure-house of august memories in the innumerable being of Earth.'[9]

This last type of vision Russell referred to variously as 'the memory of the Earth', 'the Earth breath' or, sometimes, 'the memory of nature', and he would talk in terms of an 'Earth spirit' or *anima mundi*. He said the Earth was 'many-coloured', by which he meant it had many layers, and novel aspects of the landscape around us could be revealed in certain states of consciousness in which other beings, or images of people or objects from the past could be seen. Russell often called these subtler levels of the countryside 'supernature'.

It was this type of perception of nature that was Russell's mystical hallmark and makes him so relevant to the theme of this book. As a child he had a few brief intimations of this ability to see into his natural surroundings, but in general 'I was not conscious in my boyhood of any heaven lying about me'. He was 16 or 17 years old when he began to be 'astonished':

> 'Walking along country roads, intense and passionate imaginations of another world . . . began to overpower me . . . my senses were expectant of some unveiling about to take place. . . . The tinted air glowed before me with intelligible significance like a face, a voice. The visible world became like a tapestry blown

and stirred by winds behind it . . . I said of the earth [in poetry] that we and all things were her dreams. . . .'[10]

So similar to what the Kalahari Bushmen told Laurens Van der Post! Russell recalled 'the greatest of all wonders' of his boyhood when:

'. . . I lay on the hill of Kilmasheogue and Earth revealed itself to me as a living being, and rock and clay were made transparent so that I saw lovlier and lordlier beings than I had known before, and was made partner in memory of mighty things, happenings in ages long sunken behind time.'[11]

We dismiss such experiences at great peril to our understanding of the nature of our planet. Russell's thoughts:

'. . . turned more and more to the spiritual life of Earth. All the needles of being pointed to it. I felt instinctively that all I saw in vision was part of the life of Earth which is a court where there are many starry palaces. There the Planetary Spirit was King, and that Spirit manifesting through the substance of Earth, the Mighty Mother, was, I felt, the being I groped after as God. The love I had for nature as garment of that deity grew deeper. . . .

'I believe that most of what was said of God was in reality said of that Spirit whose body is Earth.'[12]

Russell recognized that to be made a partner in Earth's memory involved a geographical factor. In an interview with the great American scholar W.Y. Evans-Wentz, he stated:

'I have seen them [the visions of supernature] most frequently after being away from a city or town for a few days. The whole west coast of Ireland from Donegal to Kerry seems charged with a magical power, and I find it easiest to see while I am there. I have always found it comparatively easy to see visions while at ancient monuments like New Grange and Dowth, because I think such places are naturally charged with psychical forces, and were for that reason made use of long ago as sacred places.'[13]

Indeed, Russell was distinctly aware that the Earth's body did have special places where the landscape would 'suddenly blaze . . . with supernatural light in some lonely spot' marking 'a place that is holy ground'. This subject, the geographical dimension of altered states, almost completely overlooked in modern consciousness studies, is returned to again in Part Three.

As soon as the expansion of his consciousness began, Russell got away whenever he could to the mountains and countryside.

'Sometimes lying on the hillside with the eyes of the body shut as in sleep I could see valleys and hills, lustrous as a jewel . . . in that land I saw . . . shining folk who . . . were, I believe, those who in the ancient world gave birth to legends of nymph and dryad. . . . Sometimes I wondered if they had any individualised life at all, for they moved as if in some orchestration of their being. If one looked up, all looked up. If one moved . . . many bent in rhythm. I wondered were their thoughts all another's, one who lived within them, guardian or oversoul to their tribe?'[14]

He likened such beings to a hive of bees – 'a single organism with disconnected cells'. It is fascinating to compare Russell's accounts of these particular denizens of supernature with the description given by Whitley Strieber in *Communion* of the entities he encountered in his alleged abduction experience:

'. . . If I was seeing real beings, then what was most striking about them was that they appeared to be moving to a sort of choreography . . . as if every action on the part of each independent being were decided elsewhere and then transmitted to the individual.

'I return to the thought that they may be a sort of hive.'[15]

These modern abductions have usually been interpreted in terms of action by extraterrestrials in UFOs. This may, indeed, be simply another sign of how far the modern psyche has estranged itself from Earth. To be fair to Strieber, he does say in his book that there was no reason to believe that his 'visitors' were from another planet, and that we may 'have a relationship with our planet that we do not understand at all, and the old gods, the fairy, and the modern visitors are side effects of it'.

Russell's glimpses of other levels of Earth included other kinds of beings, god-like as well as elemental creatures. On a couple of occasions he also saw 'airships', glittering with lights, floating over a valley. He did not know if he was seeing something from some previous cycle of civilization, or from some point in the future. The objects were, of course, remarkably similar to today's reported cigar-shaped UFOs. At other times he saw directly into the past. Once he was waiting for someone at the ruins of an old chapel, when he was suddenly flooded with images of how the building had looked in its prime, and even saw people at worship there.

To Russell the 'Earth seemed . . . bathed in an aether of deity' and 'to touch the Earth was to feel the influx of power as with one who had touched the mantle of the Lord'. His ability to tap the Earth's memory was not 'what people call imagination', Russell insisted. It was 'an act of vision, or perception of images already existing breathed on some ethereal medium which in no way differs from the medium which holds for us our memories'. If we modernize that quotation by replacing 'ethereal medium' with 'field', we are not too far removed from some contemporary scientific speculations.

In *The Candle of Vision* Russell wrote:

'These earth memories come to us in various ways. When we are passive, and the ethereal medium which is the keeper of such images, not broken up by thought, is like clear glass or calm water, then there is often a glowing of colour and form upon it, and there is what may be a reflection from some earth memory connected with the place we move in or it may be we have direct vision of that memory. . . .

'. . . I was able at times to evoke deliberately out of the memory of nature pictures of persons or things long past in time, but of which I desired knowledge. . . . The fact that the Earth holds such memories is itself important, for once we discover this imperishable tablet, we are led to speculate whether in the future a training in seership might not lead to a revolution in human knowledge.'

A revamped version of this possibility is something we have already hinted at in the previous chapter, and will look at again in the final section of this book, in the light of both ancient and contemporary information.

If George William Russell was a 'hands on' nature mystic, describing his insights with colourful pen and brush, then Pierre Teilhard de

Chardin was an intellectual visionary, who used more cerebral methods to discuss his belief that the Earth was evolving an extra sphere, a layer of consciousness which he called the 'noosphere' (from *noos*, the Greek word for 'mind').

THE PRIESTLY SCIENTIST

Teilhard's nature was both religious and analytical, and this was expressed in the fact that he became both a priest and a scientist. He was born in France in 1881, and his father, a naturalist, taught him to study the natural environment around the family home in the Auvergne. At ten, Teilhard was sent to a Jesuit boarding school where his subject record was good, except in religious studies. This seems to have been because he thought the images purveyed were ridiculous and childlike. By the age of 17, however, his deep religious leanings led him to join the Jesuit order, and he spent the first years of his membership in the Channel Island of Jersey, in Cairo and in England.

It was while Teilhard was in England that he 'became aware of the universe no longer as an abstract notion, but as a . . . presence'.[16] He was ordained as a priest in 1912 and shortly afterwards went to Paris for formal training in palaeontology (the study of fossils). When war broke out in 1914, Teilhard enlisted as a stretcher-bearer, and he went on to win an award for bravery. Because he was calm under fire, the North African members of his regiment believed he was protected by his *baraka*, an Arabic term for spiritual power. When asked by a fellow soldier how he kept so cool in battle, Teilhard replied that if he was killed he knew he would simply experience a 'change of state', a term he was to use frequently later when he expounded his theory of an evolving terrestrial consciousness field.

In 1916, Teilhard underwent a mystical experience. He was meditating on a picture of Christ in a church, when the outlines of the holy figure suddenly seemed to melt, and a vibrating atmosphere developed around the image. This was 'shot through by what appeared to be phosphorescent trails, tracing a continuous path of light as far as the outermost spheres of matter, making a sort of network of nerves thoughout all the substance. *The whole universe vibrated* – and yet every *thing* in the universe remained clearly defined, its individuality still preserved. . . .'[17]

After the war, Teilhard went back to Paris to continue his studies in palaeontology, geology and prehistory. In 1922 he took his doctorate, having already become a professor of geology at the Catholic Institute of Paris. He began to envisage evolution as a process involving matter, biological processes and consciousness in linked stages, and started to lecture on his ideas, which were far more advanced than both the theological and scientific thinking of his day. These talks created great interest amongst his students. In 1923, Teilhard went on a palaeontological mission to China. While he was away, word of his lectures got around, and on his return to Paris a year later he was accused of unorthodoxy by his religious superiors who forbade him to continue teaching.

Virtually an exile, Teilhard returned to China in 1926 and became a scientific adviser to the Geological Survey. He met leading palaeontologists of many nations, and his own reputation grew within scientific circles. In 1938 he was appointed director of a leading French geological and palaeontological laboratory, but the outbreak of World War II prevented his return to France for six years. During his time in China, the Jesuit palaeontologist developed his ideas on evolution; he wrote essays and occasional articles in the scientific press, gave lectures at specialist conferences and addressed small groups. He also completed the manuscript of his major book, *The Phenomenon of Man* (*Le Phénomène Humain*), in 1938, but the Vatican banned its publication, and that of all his philosophical writings, during his lifetime. A few copies of his manuscripts were passed around amongst friends, but otherwise they remained unknown.

Although offered compensatory forms of recognition in France, Teilhard spent the final years of his life in the United States. Renée Haynes, who met the priest during this period, described him as 'quiet, but [he] seemed to have a strong sense of humor: I remember gray eyes and a thin figure . . . an "atmosphere" (what Hindus call the *durshan*) . . . came with him'.[18]

Teilhard saw himself as a 'geobiologist' and 'a pilgrim of the future on the way back from a journey made entirely in the past'. He always wanted to die on an Easter Sunday, the Day of Resurrection. His wish was to be fulfilled. On Easter morning 1955, he attended mass at New York's St Patrick's Cathedral, took a walk in Central Park, had lunch with Jesuit colleagues and said he had never had such a lovely Easter before. While with friends that afternoon, however, he suddenly collapsed. He regained consciousness, asked 'What's happened – where am I?', and in minutes was gone.

Shortly after his death *The Phenomenon of Man* was published in France, and more than 70,000 copies were sold of the first edition alone. An English-language version was published in 1959 and was hailed by some as one of the century's outstanding intellectual events – although others complained that it was neither theology nor science. Other books and collections of essays by Teilhard were published in the following years.

Teilhard de Chardin's vision centred around a somewhat specialized idea of evolution. He saw the development of the material universe as an outer phenomenon accompanied by an inner counterpart – 'a *within* of things'. As human beings, we could see ourselves outwardly as biological organisms, but we also knew that 'within' us consciousness was at work. Teilhard wrote:

'The apparent restriction of the phenomenon of consciousness to the higher forms of life has long served science as an excuse for eliminating it from its models of the universe. A queer exception, an aberrant function, an epiphenomenon – thought was classed under one or other of these heads in order to get rid of it . . . consciousness, in order to be integrated into a world-system, necessitates consideration of the existence of a new aspect or dimension in the stuff of the universe. . . .

'It is impossible to deny that, deep within ourselves, an "interior" appears at the heart of beings. . . . This is enough to ensure that, in one degree or another, this "interior" should obtrude itself as existing everywhere in nature from all time. Since the stuff of the universe has an inner aspect at one point of itself, there is necessarily a *double aspect to its structure*, that is to say in every region of space and time . . . *co-extensive with their Without, there is a Within to things.*'[19]

Teilhard considered that 'everything in nature is basically living, or at least pre-living'. Indeed, he was sure that the cosmos in general was 'fundamentally and primarily living'. Otherwise, how could life arise from matter at all? He noted that 'biology, in forming theories, has scarcely noticed, scarcely studied the "evolution of consciousness"'.[20]

Teilhard envisioned an ascending ladder of complexity: out of the elementary particles of the universe stars were born; from their relatively simple constitutions arose the planets, through some agency or other, where more complex elemental structures emerged, creating geology. Again through some unknown agency, macromolecules emerged, at least on Earth, and from them simple cells, then simple plant life, then more complex vegetation and more complex cells culminating in the higher forms of life.

In living things, the Frenchman realized, increasing levels of complexity corresponded to higher levels of consciousness, until in human beings a crucial development of consciousness took place – it became self-reflective, it could perceive itself. We can think about thinking. As Teilhard put it: 'We know that we know.' Other creatures know, but do not know that they know (although some of us may have suspicions regarding mammals such as dolphins and other members of the whale family). Life had become turned in on itself through the agency of the human being, it could observe its own development, its own history. It could question where it was going. Whereas lower creatures were stuck in a behavioural groove, humans had been dealt a 'wild card'. Humanity therefore was the apex of evolution on Earth (Teilhard accepted that the process might also be going on elsewhere). Assembled out of the base elements of the universe, via star, planet, geology and biology, the human mind had become the spearhead of evolution, in Teilhard's scheme.

The Jesuit thinker emphasized the nature of complexity. He pointed out that 'there are something like a hundred billion cells in an average mammal, and hundreds of millions of atoms to each cell!'[21] But complexity is not just quantity: a pile of sand, for instance, is not complex, it is merely an aggregate of tiny grains. 'The actual number of atoms contained in complex units is of minor importance compared with the number and quality of the *links* established between the atoms,' Teilhard wrote in *The Future of Man*. It is the interlinking, the connections between parts that denote complexity. And the greater the complexity, the greater the consciousness that occurs 'within' the form. The more 'formidable [the] edifice of atoms and varied mechanisms which is found to exist in living creatures, *the more living they are*', Teilhard observed with revelatory fervour. The implication of this is that the atoms themselves must hold the key to consciousness.

In his concern with complexity, Teilhard was simply expressing, in his own idiosyncratic way, the age-old wisdom of the interconnectedness of all things. Out of 'the veil of the biosphere' emerged living structures of increasing complexity, thus of increasing consciousness, in just the way that the biosphere had emerged from the lithosphere. He felt that the 'juvenile earth' possessed a 'quantum of consciousness' which it had passed on to the biosphere. The process had gone on until the appearance of self-reflective consciousness in human beings, whereupon the thrust of evolution had turned back on itself; consciousness became conscious of itself.

There was only one entity on Earth, Teilhard stated, and that was life itself. Mind and matter were two energies within evolution, and together they formed life. Life 'compels us increasingly to view it as an underlying current in the flow of which matter tends to order itself upon itself with the emergence of consciousness', Teilhard argued. If an extraterrestrial being could have watched life developing on Earth through a special telescope which showed up consciousness as luminescence, Teilhard pictured, there would first have appeared very dull glows in patches on the Earth's surface; these would have gradually grown in size and become a little brighter. As the ages passed, these patches would have extended, contacted one another and grown more brilliant. By the twentieth century the world would be girdled with a blinding phosphorescence.

The French sage thought the fact that the world was round was of crucial significance; life emerging on a flat plane would have spread out remorselessly and faded away, but on the enclosed surface of our globe it was bound to keep meeting itself, creating ever more complex links and interactions – with which came increasing consciousness. This happened with the biosphere as a whole, but was particularly the case with humanity. Teilhard called it the planetization of humanity (a process which he felt really commenced in earnest in the Neolithic era):

'The first phase was the formation of proteins up to the stage of the cell. In the second phase individual cellular complexes were formed, up to and including Man. We are now at the beginning of a third phase, the formation of an organico-social super-complex, which, as may easily be demonstrated, *can only occur* in the case of *reflective, personalized elements* . . . the *planetization* of Mankind. . . . Mankind . . . coming gradually to form around its earthly matrix a single, major organic unity, enclosed upon itself; a single hyper-complex . . . hyper-conscious arch molecule, co-extensive with the heavenly body on which it was born.'[22]

To Teilhard, an aircraft carrying people from one continent to another was simply the global-scale equivalent of the wind carrying the seeds of a plant to other locations. The 'seeds' in this case were those of consciousness. Out of the biosphere was emerging the noosphere: the 'within' of the biosphere, the terrestrial sphere of mind, a layer of global-scale consciousness. The noosphere was the 'spirit of the Earth'.

'We find ourselves in the presence, in actual possession, of the super-organism we have been seeking, of whose existence we were intuitively aware,' Teilhard stated.[23] We were moving towards a 'state change' even more significant than that which occurred with the appearance of self-reflective consciousness – 'all of us together, and each of us separately', in the way the cells of the body have their own level of existence but combine to produce something greater than its parts. 'No doubt everything proceeds from the individual and in the first instance depends on the individual,' Teilhard commented, 'but it is on a higher level than the individual that everything achieves its fulfilment.' What was going on around us in human society was not disordered movement, but 'something purposefully stirring, as in a living being'.

Teilhard insisted that the noosphere was real, as real as the atmosphere, not an abstract concept. It was a 'stupendous thinking machine'; it was a 'brain of brains'. What amounts 'on the *exterior* to the gradual establishment of a vast nervous system . . . corresponds on the *interior* to the installation of a psychic state on the very dimensions of the earth'.[24] Humanity was pumping ever increasing amounts of energy into the noosphere with its ceaselessly expanding physical interconnections, its remorseless production of machinery which increased the ability of consciousness to explore and act, and its endlessly growing abilities in rapid global communication. At the same time its educational systems, libraries, museums, and other data storage banks were forming a burgeoning 'collective memory'. This expanding activity was causing an increase of psychic energy within the noosphere, which was 'irresistibly . . . accumulating an ever-increasing tension', leading perhaps to a crucial outcome:

> 'Until now we have never seen mind manifest itself on the planet except in separated groups and in the static state. What sort of current will be opened up, when the circuit is suddenly completed?
>
> 'I believe that what is now being shaped in the bosom of planetized humanity is essentially a rebounding of evolution upon itself. . . . Life is preparing at this moment to accomplish the supreme, ultimate leap. . . . Who can say what forces will be released, what radiations. . . .'[25]

Teilhard felt there was a possibility that 'one day, by means of chemical quantitative analyses or by the discovery of some vital radiation', science might 'succeed in measuring the power released in the course of psychic events' on the scale he was conceiving them.[26] Indeed, he increasingly suspected that the growth of the noosphere might release new faculties and consciousness within us, that 'the secret that lies at the heart of metaphysics' would come to be understood.[27] The 'extraordinary network of radio and television communications' was perhaps anticipating 'the direct syntonization of brains through the mysterious power of telepathy' which, as telecommunications already did to an extent, would 'link us all in a sort of "etherised" universal consciousness'. He wondered:

> ' . . . is it not possible that by the direct converging of its members it [planetized humanity] will be able, as though by resonance, to release psychic powers whose existence is still unsuspected? . . . the entire complex of inter-human and inter-cosmic relations will become charged with an immediacy, an intimacy and a realism such as has long been dreamed of and apprehended by certain spirits particularly endowed with the "sense of the universal", but which has never been *collectively applied*. And it is in the depths and by grace of this new inward sphere, the attribute of planetized Life, that an event seems possible which has hitherto been incapable of realization: I mean

the pervasion of the human mass by the power of sympathy. It may in part be a passive sympathy, a communication of mind and spirit that will make the phenomenon of telepathy, still sporadic and haphazard, both general and normal. But above all it will be a state of active sympathy in which each separate human element, breaking out of its insulated state under the impulse of the high tensions generated in the Noosphere, will emerge into a field of prodigious affinities, which we may already conjecture in theory. For if the power of attraction between simple atoms is so great, what may we not expect if similar bonds are contracted between human molecules? Humanity . . . is building its composite brain beneath our eyes. May it not be that tomorrow, through the logical and biological deepening of the movement drawing it together, it will find its *heart*, without which the ultimate wholeness of its powers of unification can never be fully achieved?'[28]

The priestly scientist also tentatively envisaged a time when the 'living planet' might reach out in what today are considered paranormal ways to contact other planets that had also awakened as conscious entities.

Teilhard saw such noospheric events happening during the evolutionary rush of consciousness to 'the ultimate, noospherical point of Reflection', to which he gave the name point Omega. He perceived this entity as a supreme attractor, pulling consciousness towards it. At the Omega point, at the culmination of its space-time evolution, consciousness would achieve its final flowering. Teilhard felt that the radiations emanating from point Omega were love – love considered as an actual force, as real as gravity (which might, indeed, be its 'outer' expression). But although ahead of humanity in linear time, and the focal point of its evolutionary destiny, 'to be supremely attractive, Omega must be supremely present'. Because its nature was both transcendental and of space-time, Omega was not only ahead of us, it was eternally accessible. So the 'radiation' of love, although emanating from a point ahead in linear time, was already with us because of the time-transcending properties of its source.

These ideas were not all that far removed from AE's idea of a constantly accessible state of Earth consciousness – like the Aboriginal Dreamtime – which also had a place in linear time. If it had a transcendental characteristic, Omega must also be found at the beginning too: Alpha and Omega. It was in this area, particularly, that Teilhard de Chardin tried to forge links with Christian concepts. But his attempts to reconcile his Christian beliefs with his overwhelming personal vision were barely possible in the simplistic terms of orthodoxy; it is easy to see how such heady stuff alienated most of his religious superiors, and at the same time drew the fire of many scientists. (Even some of his scientific friends and supporters such as Sir Julian Huxley found it 'impossible to follow him all the way'.)[29]

At the Omega point humanity would cease in a space-time sense, graduating from the 'Ultra-Human' to the 'Trans-Human at the ultimate heart of things'; not death but a state change of ultimate proportions. But point Omega was aeons ahead of us in normal time; the 'totalization' of human consciousness within the noosphere, creating a sort of global brain, was much nearer, Teilhard reckoned. In previous evolutionary changes millions of years had been involved, but with the increase of psychic energy and the present rapid planetization of humanity, he felt this noospheric state change could occur much more quickly, although it seems he was still thinking in terms of thousands of years. For this reason he counselled against despair at the state of modern international affairs. Nevertheless, Teilhard's rose-tinted glasses did have a few cracks in them; he warned that 'something will explode if we persist in trying to squeeze into our old tumble-down huts the material and spiritual forces that are henceforward on the scale of a world'.[30] He recognized that since the 'eighteenth century . . . despite our occasional obstinacy in pretending that we are the same, we have in fact entered a different world'.

GAIAFIELD

In 1982, Peter Russell's *The Awakening Earth*[31] (*The Global Brain* in the United States) was published, and this was to an extent an update on the ideas of Teilhard de Chardin. Peter Russell felt that Teilhard's 'state change' into fully activated noospheric consciousness could happen much more rapidly than the Frenchman envisaged. Russell noted the rapid development of information technology. It was merely in its infancy in Teilhard's last years, and although the Jesuit seer had correctly anticipated its growth, this was on such a scale that even he would have been surprised. Teilhard would surely have considered it ironic that it had been accelerated by humanity's leap off its home planet, although he would readily have understood the psychically energizing effect of the image of Earth from space being transmitted into the planetized consciousness of our species.

Russell records how the worldwide telecommunications network of 1975:

'. . . was no more complex than a region of the brain the size of a pea. But overall data-processing capacity is doubling every two and half years, and if this rate of increase is sustained the global telecommunications network could equal the brain in complexity by the year 2000 – if this seems an unbelievably short time ahead, it is probably because few of us can really grasp just how fast the growth is.

'The changes that this will bring will be so great that their full impact may well be beyond our imagination. No longer will we perceive ourselves to be isolated individuals; we will know ourselves to be part of a rapidly integrating global network, the nerve cells of an awakening global brain.'

Russell observes that Marshall McLuhan's vision of the 'global village' is already with us, and cites how he can telephone Fiji from a cottage in an English forest 'and it takes the same amount of time for my voice to reach Fiji down the telephone line as it does for my brain to tell my finger to touch the dial'. Indeed, Russell might have pointed out that it is in our language, and therefore a conceptual reality to us, to refer to the act of telephoning as 'calling'; we can call around the world. Planetized humanity is at that level of close interaction right now.

Russell likens Teilhard's concept of the noosphere with the mystic Sri Aurobindo's 'Supermind'. Such planetary consciousness could be viewed as 'a completely new level of evolution, as different from consciousness as consciousness is from life, and life from matter', Russell suggests. This stage of evolution would not be happening to humanity, but at a planetary level, to the Earth itself. Russell puts forward the term 'Gaiafield' for this state of planetary consciousness 'since we do not yet have an adequate term [for it] in our vocabulary'. The Gaiafield 'would possess entirely new characteristics incomprehensible to consciousness' in Russell's view.

He incorporated the term 'Gaia' because of its earlier use by Professor James Lovelock in the naming of a hypothesis that brings the Goddess, the living Earth, into the modern laboratory.

THE GAIA HYPOTHESIS

Lovelock, a radical English scientist, has revolutionized the Earth sciences with the Gaia hypothesis which states that the Earth is a living organism. Lovelock is an independent scientist and natural historian unattached to any university or research institute. His range of investigation is as wide as his planetary subject: chemistry, biology, medicine, cybernetics, physiology, geophysics and climatology. At the National Institute of Medical Research he spent 15 years 'browsing across all the scientific divisions without noticing whether there were any fences or not'.[32] His interdisciplinary explorations were rewarded in 1974 by membership of The Royal Society, the equivalent of the National Academy of Sciences in America.

Lovelock is a visionary maverick who has had a profound effect not only on science, but also in the fields of philosophy, psychology and religion. With the help of his principal collaborator, biologist Lynn Margulis, he has reanimated the Earth as a vital, urgent topic of concern which transcends all national borders. His vision of Gaia is timely, for it is evident that the Earth is being recklessly polluted and ravaged. *Time* magazine recently devoted an entire issue[33] to 'The Planet of the Year', subtitled the 'Endangered Earth', which analysed the gamut of our environmental ills.

Now in his seventies, Lovelock lives in an isolated country cottage in the southwest corner of England. On the white front gate to the property there is a sign that reads 'Coombe Mill Experimental Station'. This is his concession to scientific propriety. In front of the house stands a white statue of a Greek goddess, which is undoubtedly the embodiment of Gaia, the Earth.

Modern science has impoverished itself, Lovelock believes, by having no place for the individual thinker. Furthermore, he remarks that 'this lack of individuals with time and opportunity to wonder about and explore the world, has grievously weakened our understanding of the natural environment'.[34] The inclination to wonder is an open invitation to discovery. It precedes the testing and development of scientific theories. Often in his writing he states that his hypothesis is heuristic – from the Greek verb *heuriskein*, to discover or invent – meaning that it is not an end in itself. It does not matter if it is right or wrong; the important thing is that it should serve as a springboard towards an increasingly coherent explanation of how nature works. In this context it is interesting to note that the word 'eureka', with its scientific-breakthrough associations, is derived from the same verb.

Lovelock is a first-rate inventor. In fact, some 30 years ago one of his inventions, the palm-sized electron capture detector, was instrumental in starting the environmental movement. This astonishingly sensitive device provided the data base for pesticides, such as DDT, that were building up to toxic levels in foods, animals and people around the world. 'This data,' wrote Lovelock, 'enabled Rachel Carson to write her seminal book *Silent Spring* and warn the world of the ultimate consequences if these chemicals continued to be improperly used by farmers.'[35] This same device was subsequently used to monitor the eroding of the Earth's atmospheric ozone layer by chloroflurocarbons from spray cans and refrigerants.

In 1965 he was invited to be an experimenter at the Jet Propulsion Laboratory in California on NASA's first lunar instrument mission. It was not long before he was given the opportunity to design sensitive devices to measure planetary soil and atmospheres. The first question was, 'How is life recognized on another planet?' After hearing about the biologists' attempts to detect life on Mars, he thought that biology had gone seriously astray. No one on the NASA Viking team had a clear idea of how to define life. Lovelock's insight was to envisage a planet's atmosphere as a conveyor belt for raw materials and waste products of life processes. Along with Dian Hitchcock, a philosopher employed by NASA, Lovelock concluded that the key was not to look for life abstracted from its environment, but rather to compare the near equilibrium atmosphere of a dead planet, such as Mars or Venus, with the vibrant, far from equilibrium atmosphere of a living planet, such as the Earth. He then asked himself another question: 'What if the difference in atmospheric composition between the Earth and its neighbours, Mars and Venus, is a consequence of the fact that the Earth alone bears life?'[36]

Having ascertained that Mars and Venus were lifeless, Lovelock was curious to see what a telescope on Mars would show of our home planet. Infrared telescopes can determine the chemical composition of atmospheres across the immensity of space. The telescope revealed what Lovelock called the 'song of life'.[37] It disclosed that the Earth's atmosphere was remarkably unusual, in fact downright improbable: highly reactive gases, such as methane and oxygen, were coexisting without reacting. Normally, these gases would strongly react and then cease to exist when the atmosphere reached equilibrium, with the consequent death of any life forms. Surprisingly, there was no decline towards equilibrium in the Earth's atmosphere. This could never have happened by chance on a lifeless planet. These ideas were first presented to his scientific peers in a brief article, 'Gaia as seen through the atmosphere', published in 1972.[38]

It was evident that the disequilibrium of the atmosphere, a constant cycling of unstable gases, was indicative of life on planet Earth. 'It represents a violation of the rules of chemistry to be measured in tens of orders of magnitude,' Lovelock wrote.[39] Furthermore, there was evidence of several other regulatory mechanisms at work: temperature, oxygen, nitrogen, methane, ammonia and salinity were all amazingly maintained in ranges that were optimal for life over millions of years. He deduced that there must be a super-regulatory organism co-ordinating all the other regulatory mechanisms. At the suggestion of novelist William Golding, Lovelock called it Gaia 'after the Greek Earth Goddess, also known as Ge, from which root the sciences of geography and geology derive their names'.[40] *Gaia – A New Look at Life on Earth* was published in 1979. Lovelock saw Gaia as 'a complex entity involving the Earth's biosphere, from whales to viruses and from oaks to algae, atmosphere, oceans, and soil; the totality constituting a feedback or cybernetic system which seeks an optimal physical and chemical environment for life on this planet. The maintenance of relatively constant conditions by active control may be conveniently described by the term "homeostasis".'[41] It implies an internal stability in organisms which automatically compensates for environmental variations, such as temperature.

Far from resting on his laurels, Lovelock and his colleagues have been continually expanding his original thesis. At the Camelford Conference on the Implications of the Gaia Hypothesis in 1987 Lovelock remarked to his scientific peers: 'I say "the Earth is alive, the Earth is an organism", I admit a little provocatively because I think that my colleagues need a bit of provoking; they have been sitting on their chairs a bit too long.'[42] In his most recent work, *The Ages of Gaia* (1988), he speaks of the elusive boundaries between the animate and inanimate domains in a way that is sure to agitate orthodox biologists: 'There is no clear distinction anywhere on Earth's surface between living and non-living matter. There is merely a hierarchy of intensity going from the "material" environment of the rocks and the atmosphere to the living cells.'[43]

Gaia is such an awesome subject that it is difficult to comprehend her history. If the big bang that generated the universe occurred 15 billion years ago, 'she is a quarter as old as time itself'.[44] In the style of a consummate raconteur, Lovelock tells us the scientific version of Gaia's Greek mythic birth from Chaos:

'At some time early in the Earth's history, before life existed, the solid Earth, the atmosphere, and the oceans were still evolving by the laws of physics and chemistry alone. It was careering, downhill, to the lifeless steady state of a planet almost at equilibrium. Briefly, in its headlong flight through the ranges of chemical and physical states, it entered a stage favourable for life. At some special time in that stage, the newly formed living cells grew until their presence so affected the Earth's environment as to halt the headlong dive towards equilibrium. At that instant, the living things, the rocks, the air, and the oceans merged to form the new entity, Gaia. Just as when the sperm merges with the egg, new life was conceived.'[45]

After writing his first book, *Gaia*, Lovelock came across the work of another Englishman, James Hutton, who was known as the father of geology. Hutton was deeply influenced by William Harvey's research on the circulation of the blood through the body. He used this physiological system as a metaphor to describe both the cycle of life sustaining elements in the soil and the hydrological cycle in which water falls as rain, collects in rivers and oceans, and subsequently evaporates back to the atmosphere. In 1785 Hutton presented a paper to the Royal Society of Edinburgh. In an extraordinary statement he declared, 'I consider the Earth to be a super organism and its proper study should be by physiology.'[46] This holistic view of a dynamic living

Earth was virtually forgotten or repressed in the zealous scientific reductionism of the nineteenth century.

From his own studies in medicine and cybernetics, Lovelock knew that physiology was a transdisciplinary science which embodied general principles that were applicable to a broad spectrum of natural processes. Incorporating Hutton's physiological insights, Lovelock's second book introduced a union of the Earth and life sciences in the new science of geophysiology. He rhetorically asks the question, 'Why run the Earth and life sciences together? I would ask, why have they been torn apart by the ruthless dissection of science into separate and blinkered disciplines? Geologists have tried to persuade us that the Earth is just a ball of rock, moistened by the oceans; and that life is merely an accident, a quiet passenger that happens to have hitched a ride. . . . Biologists have been no better. They have asserted that living organisms are so adaptable that they have been fit for any material changes that have occurred during the Earth's history.'[47]

Throughout his writings, Lovelock draws attention to this 'scientific apartheid of Victorian biology and geology'.[48] In addition, he deplores the way in which each discipline is subdivided into numerous small enclaves which do not communicate with each other. 'There are thirty different branches of biology now,' Lovelock says. 'The practitioners of each branch are quite proud that they know nothing of the other branches. If you talk to a molecular biologist about theories in population biology, he will say "I'm not interested in that kind of stuff"; you ask a botanist and he will say much the same thing.'[49] In a sense, the separation of these sciences into isolated scientific domains contains seeds of geomantic amnesia.

Geophysiology, however, is a single evolutionary science which 'describes the history of the whole planet. The evolution of the species and the evolution of their environment are tightly coupled together as a single inseparable process'.[50] Self-regulation of essential Gaian processes, such as climate and chemical formation of the soil, are a direct result of this seamless evolutionary process. Such a tightly coupled living system is sufficiently complex to produce emergent behaviour unpredicted by the sum of its parts.

Instead of being circumscribed by the Gaia hypothesis, Lovelock remains open to criticism which he knows can only improve and refine his theory. Perhaps the most persuasive critique was expressed by

Ford Doolittle, a Canadian molecular biologist. Doolittle suggested that planetary self-regulation would require foresight and planning by a 'Council of Life'.[51] He reasoned that committees of species would have to meet regularly to determine how to alter the climate, for example, in order to produce the optimal conditions for life. Doolittle thought that this was nonsense. Competing species could not possibly communicate with each other, let alone come to consensus decisions on planetary regulation. Forecasting on the part of plant and animal life smacked of purpose. From a reductionist biological perspective, it was inconceivable that such a super organism could exist.

Lovelock puzzled over Doolittle's objection to purposeful species behaviour. Richard Dawkins, a sociobiologist, made a similar objection on the grounds of an implied planetary altruism on the part of organisms.[52] After a year of contemplation on these problems, Lovelock came up with the Daisyworld model to illustrate how Gaia might evolve without planning:

> 'It pictured an imaginary world that spun like the Earth as it circled and was warmed by a star that was an identical twin of our own Sun. On this world, the competition for territory between two species of daisies, one dark and one light in colour, led to the accurate regulation of planetary temperature close to that comfortable for plants like daisies. No foresight, planning, or purpose was invoked.'[53]

What stabilized this system? In Daisyworld one species can never grow unchecked. If the population of one type of daisy suddenly expands, the environment becomes adverse and growth is restricted. Correspondingly, while the daisies grow, the environment is not able to move towards unfavourable states. The reactive growth of the relevant-coloured daisy prohibits it. 'It is the close coupling of the relationships which constrain both daisy growth and planetary temperature that makes the model behave,' Lovelock suggests.[54]

Subsequently, Lovelock did extensive computer modelling of Daisyworld, first adding a grey daisy, then 20 different coloured daisies, then rabbits grazing on the flowers, then foxes eating the rabbits, and finally subjecting Daisyworld to periodic catastrophes such as plagues. 'The generality you obtain from such models,' said Lovelock, 'is that the more species and the more interactions you put into the system the more stable it becomes.'[55] Daisyworld is a model based on cybernetics, derived from the Greek word *kybernetes*, meaning the helmsman of a ship. Also known as control theory in engineering, it is used by physiologists to understand biological feedback processes, such as breathing.

In *The Ages of Gaia* Lovelock takes the reader on an extraordinary geophysiological history of Gaia beginning with the first cyanobacteria 3.8 billion years ago. These blue-green bacteria, which still run the planet, were the first organisms to excrete oxygen as a photosynthetic waste product. In turn he analyses in fascinating detail the probable evolutionary development of, for example, oxygen, calcium carbonate, salinity and carbon dioxide.[56] Lovelock points out that just as the organisms and their environment are tightly coupled, so too are the chemical elements in their evolution.

Although carbon dioxide has decreased during the Earth's history, in the last hundred years it has virtually doubled in concentration, from 180 to 350 parts per million.[57] A by-product of burning fossil fuels, carbon dioxide acts as a heat trap (the 'greenhouse' effect) that could result in the melting of the Polar ice caps, which in turn would dramatically raise the sea level.[58] Lovelock estimates that sometime in the twenty-first century the change of climate may be as great as that from the last ice age, 12,000 years ago. This change 'would make winter spring, spring summer, and summer always as hot as the hottest summer you can recall. . . . Will Boston, London, Venice and the Netherlands vanish beneath the sea? Will the Sahara extend across the equator? The answers to these questions are likely to come from direct experience. There are no experts able to forecast the future global climate'.[59]

We have learned, however, that Gaia adjusts to environmental changes, and since 1971 Lovelock has been researching into another geophysiological mechanism related to carbon dioxide regulation. Along with his colleagues, Lovelock argues that marine algae give off dimethyl sulphide gas, which is the greatest if not the sole source of the nuclei on which cloud droplets form. In turn, cloud density affects world climate by reflecting sunlight that might have been absorbed by the dark oceans, perhaps offsetting the potentially alarming temperature rise due to the heat trapping capacity of carbon dioxide.[60] Lovelock recently reported that 'independent observers have noted that marine algae density of the Pacific Ocean has increased by 100 per cent over the last decade. At the same time, cloud cover and windiness have been increasing worldwide. These are the types of system responses that you would expect if the system was able to respond to greenhouse warming'.[61]

The cutting down of the rain forests has even more serious implications, Lovelock believes, than the greenhouse effect. He points out that each year we burn away an area of tropical rain forest the size of Britain.[62] This destruction incapacitates the vast water vapour evaporation/cloud formation/sunshield/rain cycle that keeps these regions from becoming deserts. And this is only one of the many environmental maladies that we face. Using the metaphor of a doctor and a patient, Lovelock suggests 'the need for a new profession: planetary medicine, a general practice for the diagnosis and treatment of planetary ailments'[63] with geophysiology as its scientific advisor.

There is no doubt that Lovelock has touched a sensitive nerve in the community of his scientific peers. At the American Geophysical Union Chapman Conference on the Gaia hypothesis in March 1988, he said 'the biologists hate it, the climatologists and geophysicists like it and the geologists and the geochemists are sitting on the fence'.[64] In particular, the molecular biologists who follow Jacques Monod's reductionist theme of chance and necessity in evolution dislike Gaia because they believe it implies purpose. On the other hand, Lynn Margulis, the distinguished microbiologist who has helped Lovelock expand the Gaia hypothesis wrote, 'The history of science is full of the Wegeners and Galileos and Harveys whose observations were rejected because their phenomena, at first, had no mechanistic explanations. Mechanisms for Gaia will emerge as they are further sought.'[65] Another microbiologist, Penelope Boston, suggested that 'Lovelock's theory, if valid, is to evolution what Einsteinian physics is to Newtonian physics, that is, an adjunct and expansion which analyzes phenomena at a different level. Relativity does not invalidate Newtonian physics within the framework of its operation, it merely transcends it'.[66]

The general public has also been profoundly affected by the Gaia hypothesis. Two out of every three letters that Lovelock has received address religious ramifications of the subject. Lovelock's panoramic vision is unique. He fits physicist Brian Swimme's description of the scientist who 'has returned to the larger culture with stories, awesome and frightening, but stories that serve to mediate ultimate reality to the larger culture. The scientist, in this transcientific role, has assumed a function that has been carried out in previous eras of humanity by the shaman or the contemplative recluse'.[67] Lovelock told environmental psychologist Jim Swan that 'he draws a good deal of inspiration for his work from visits to a nearby, ancient, volcanically formed peak named Brentor, on top of which sits a church'.[68] Lovelock said that sometimes when he climbs the hill, he senses a 'presence' and feels as though he attains a fleeting contact with some entity larger than and outside his own mind.

In his first book Lovelock hardly mentions the feminine qualities of the Earth. In the sequel, however, responding to the recent resurgence of interest in Goddess scholarship and consciousness, he acknowledges that in ancient cultures the Earth was worshipped both as a living being and as a Goddess. In a passage of remarkable candour he explains:

> 'Those millions of Christians who make a special place in their hearts for the Virgin Mary possibly respond as I do. The concept of Jahweh [Jehovah] as remote, all-powerful, all-seeing, is either frightening or unapproachable. Even the presence of a more contemporary God, a still, small voice within, may not be enough for those who need to communicate with someone outside. Mary is close and can be talked to. She is believable and manageable. It could be that the importance of the Virgin Mary in faith is something of this kind, but there may be more to it. What if Mary is another name for Gaia? . . . Any living organism that is a quarter as old as the Universe itself and still full of vigour is as near immortal as we ever need to know. She is of this Universe and, conceivably, a part of God. On Earth she is the source of life everlasting and is alive now; she gave birth to humankind and we are part of her.'[69]

Lovelock also recognizes that as well as being the fertile, nurturing and compassionate great mother, the Goddess is also the resolute dispenser of justice, dissolution and death. 'If you broke the rules of the old Goddess you were zapped,' said Lovelock, 'and strangely the Gaia theory says much the same thing. You can make models that demonstrate this. They show that any species that adversely affects its environment is eliminated. If we continue to corrupt, pollute and rip the skin off the Earth by deforestation, then we may be eliminated, but of course, life will go on.'[70] Lovelock points out that Gaia is not antihuman, but unless we change our ways and start behaving as part of a whole planetary system, rather than treating the world as if it was there purely for our benefit, we will become part of history – just another uncoupled species that forgot how to relate to our planet.

There is a compelling parallel between Lovelock's geophysiological modelling of natural processes and Neolithic Goddess beliefs in cycles of birth, life, death and regeneration. They both recognize the life cycles of Gaia, one through science and the other through religion. They both reveal deep insights into the details and dynamics of each successive state as well as a cross-state perception of how each phase is integral to the whole cycle.

In his later work Lovelock repeatedly disclaims that foreordained design is part of his argument for planetary regulation. For example, he states that he is 'happy with the thought that the Universe has properties that make the emergence of life and Gaia inevitable. But I react to the assertion that it was created with this purpose. It might have been; but how the Universe and life began are ineffable questions'.[71] For Lovelock, that which is ineffable is unmanageable. Yet he maintains a delicate balance between an insistent rejection of purpose and an open acceptance of emergent phenomena.

Lovelock considers himself to be a positive agnostic 'too deeply committed to science for undiluted faith; equally unacceptable to me spiritually is the materialist world of undiluted fact. That Gaia can be both spiritual and scientific is, for me, deeply satisfying'.[72] He has also remarked that 'in the old days, theology was a science and I would like to see it reintegrated into science'.[73] Lovelock is one of those rare individuals who can bridge several disciplines. It is not an easy task, for he is held accountable by science, theology and psychology. Inevitably, there are tensions and unresolved issues, but as Lovelock would be the first to admit, these issues are bound to open up further creative explorations.

In August 1985 a symposium entitled 'Is the Earth a Living Organism?', sponsored by the National Audubon Society, was held at the University of Massachusetts. Serving as chairperson for an academic panel which questioned Lovelock after his presentation,

Steele posed the question: 'If we can agree that the Earth is a living organism, what can we say about its awareness and memory?' Lovelock replied that this was the most difficult question of the day and left it at that. However, in *Gaia* he does define memory in a cybernetic system as the capacity to store, recall and compare information in order to self-correct and self-direct the system.[74] Memory is the self-referencing capacity of a system, its identity. How does memory arise? One way is by interaction with another system. If this interaction leads to the coupling of a species and an environment, then the memory of each system will be incorporated in an enriched, higher order memory resulting from the combination. Conversely, when they uncouple, the memory of both the species and the environment will be disengaged and impoverished. Uncoupling represents a cybernetic disarray, a loss of systemic memory which can threaten the survival of both the species and the environment. It indicates that life is out of balance. When humanity and Gaia uncouple, the result is an out of control, runaway system.

Perhaps there is another clue regarding the memory of Gaia in the work of the anthropologist Gregory Bateson. In 1969 Bateson formulated an early version of tightly coupled systems when he wrote, 'The unit of survival is the organism plus the environment. We are learning by bitter experience that the organism which destroys its environment destroys itself.'[75] Both Lovelock and Bateson were deeply influenced by cybernetic models in their respective fields. 'The simplest cybernetic circuit,' remarked Bateson, 'can be said to have memory of a dynamic kind – not based upon static storage but upon the travel of information around the circuit.'[76] For example, the dimethyl sulphide cycle described earlier has a dynamic system memory,[77] as does every geophysiological cycle. Thus the memory of Gaia could be envisaged as the dynamic system produced by all the geophysiological cycles of the Earth, including its atmosphere and biosphere.

In conclusion, what can we say about Gaia? According to Lovelock, Gaia is alive and 'her unconscious goal is a planet fit for life'.[78] He maintains 'that God and Gaia, theology and science, even physics and biology are not separate but a single way of thought'.[79] But he also states that 'in no way do I see Gaia as a sentient being, a surrogate God'.[80] Following this line of reasoning, Gaia is not capable of purposeful behaviour; she is a colossal dynamic system memory. Finally, Lovelock also considers Gaia to be akin to a Goddess in the guise of Mary or Kali[81] 'and, conceivably, a part of God'.

'If we are a part of Gaia,' conjectures Lovelock, 'it becomes interesting to ask: "To what extent is our collective intelligence also a part of Gaia? Do we as a species constitute a Gaian nervous system and a brain which can consciously anticipate environmental changes?"'[82] He believes that our communications networks have 'vastly increased Gaia's range of perception. She is now through us awake and aware of herself. She has seen the reflection of her fair face through the eyes of astronauts and the television cameras of orbiting spacecraft'.[83] The focus here is on the scientific extension of Gaia's intelligence and senses through humanity, rather than a communion with the planet, which is reminiscent of Teilhard de Chardin's viewpoint.

The Gaia hypothesis is the scientific foundation of a global awakening from geomantic amnesia. Although Lovelock has concluded that Gaia is 'intelligent', he does not directly address the question of an Earth 'mind'. He does, however, quote Bateson, who wrote that 'there is a larger mind of which the individual mind is only a subsystem'.[84] This larger mind, Bateson says, is comparable to God and is perhaps what some people mean by God, but it is embodied in the social and ecological fabric of this planet. It is this larger mind that is explored in the final part of this book.

PART THREE

RE-MEMBERING

We last saw our metaphorical amnesiac trying to assemble all the fragments of memories of his former life into some sort of coherent picture. He has come to realize that time is short and that he must make sense of the pieces because they add up to information that will help him assess his current situation. Too many of the pieces are missing for the information to be perfectly remembered, but he is sure that enough of the helpful, positive aspects of his existence prior to his amnesia can be salvaged and used to allay his present predicament. He looks at the photograph he recently encountered that jolted his memory and stirred his emotions; it is, he is sure, the picture of an old friend. He fears for his own safety, and, because of deep feelings he is only just beginning to articulate, for that of his friend in the photograph. Can he remember in time?

We have to leave our imaginary fellow in that cliffhanging situation, because the last part of the story has not yet been written! Just as our amnesiac has to try to put all his fragmented memories together, so must we dig back into our past to find a way forward. Some new ways of thinking have to be fashioned that use as a foundation perennial principles inherent in traditional worldviews. We have to remember, both in the sense of recalling, and in the sense of putting back together – literally re-membering.

The concept of the Earth as a living thing must not be fudged. Either we mean it, or we do not. And if we mean it, we must face up to the main implication, which is that our world is a being. If it is alive, how can we picture its consciousness? If it has consciousness, can we contact it directly? The final section of this book attempts to outline some prototype answers. Inevitably, this is the most speculative part of our adventure, but it is only such attempts at re-membrance that will forge the perspectives required for our future here on Earth. Such attempts need not be hopelessly abstract; they can identify specific courses of action, as will be shown. As Robin Williamson sings in 'The Circle is Unbroken':

Come let us build the ship of
  the future
In an ancient pattern that
  journeys far.

CHAPTER SIX

TOWARDS EARTHMIND

We have seen that ancient peoples believed the world to be alive, to pulse with energies, to have a soul, to dream. While we have charted how we have fallen away from that view, we have also observed that modern research is showing or reminding us that life and its planetary environment are interlinked on levels beyond the visible, obvious ways; these links certainly involve electromagnetism and perhaps more subtle forces. We have noted, too, that influential thinkers in primary modes of human awareness – scientific, mystical and visionary – have, each in their own way, re-introduced the idea of the living Earth during the course of the twentieth century. The question now is: how can we proceed from here with that idea?

This challenge has two aspects which have to be addressed: what conceptual model can we fashion regarding the sentience of our planet, and, assuming such planetary consciousness exists, are there any practical ways in which human intelligence can attempt to contact or consciously integrate with it?

While any suggestions offered for use in grappling with the ancient theme of the living Earth are bound to be contentious to the modern mind, at least for the foreseeable future, the methods put forward here for consideration regarding the possible contact with the consciousness of Earth are pragmatic, being accessible to direct experience and, ultimately, even amenable to objective testing in some instances. But while the two aspects of the challenge are ultimately related, they need to be dealt with as separate issues for the time being.

ANIMA MUNDI

How can we envisage a terrestrial, planetary consciousness? Some people in our culture become quite angry when asked such a question.

They point to rock, to soil, to the ocean, to the landscape and snort: 'How can these things possibly add up to anything living?'

It is initially a problem of recognition. If the Earth has a consciousness, it will be on a planetary scale – a scale that renders it virtually invisible to our awareness, just as a flea on an animal cannot perceive the totality of its 'host'. But a further point is immediately raised: who could identify the nature or location of *human* consciousness? Some may try to evade this crucial issue by saying that consciousness is manifested in the behaviour of human beings. But we know that Earth, too, behaves as if it were a living organism. Lovelock has shown how terrestrial systems check and balance one another, how optimum conditions are constantly maintained, and how the Earth regenerates itself. All these are characteristics of life and, indeed, awareness. Earth is self-organizing. Furthermore, as Peter Russell points out, one branch of General Systems Theory deals with living systems, and a pioneer of this, James Miller, found that all living systems 'are composed of . . . nineteen critical subsystems that seem to characterize living systems. . . . It is very difficult to find examples of non-living systems which both possess the nineteen critical subsystems and are self-organizing. . . . Gaia appears to satisfy both criteria'.[1]

If evasion merely lands the sceptic in hot water, tackling the question of human consciousness directly is no less troublesome. To most people nowadays the seat of personal identity seems to rest inside the head at a point between and slightly above the eyebrows. But if one were to pry into that portion of the head, only bone, tissues and liquids would be found. The brain, indeed the whole body, could be taken apart cell by cell, and no trace of consciousness would be discovered. The sense of location for personal identity is like the 'ghost speaker' between two stereo loudspeakers; it is a mirage. Given the requisite stimulus – mental illness (which is uncontrollable mechanical disorder in the brain), traumatic shock, a near death experience, hallucinogenic substances, a powerful aesthetic or emotional catalyst, ritual or yogic exercise – the location of our consciousness can wander all over the place. It can seem to hover above the head; it can move to any part of the body; it can leave the body altogether (shamanic ecstasy or Western out-of-the-body experience); or it can merge into something in the environment.

Devereux recalls a delightful episode many years ago when, in a state of altered consciousness, he directly and powerfully participated in the primal-level awareness of a flower – a daffodil as it happened. He quite unintentionally developed an interactive relationship with the flower – it caught his eye and 'showed itself' to him. As if with X-ray vision, Devereux saw tiny beads of water rising within the stem, and then the petals moved as if in time-lapse photography. This speeded-up time effect was clearly and analytically observed. Then his own awareness slipped into that of the daffodil. His sense of 'self' was maintained, but became 'soft-edged' and could merge into the object under study. The feeling created by the light falling on the daffodil's petals was like a ray of sunlight on the first dawn in Eden – continuously.

The normal social sense of personal identity is simply a co-ordinate of time and space; in transcendental experience, when what we normally understand as time and space are surpassed, the co-ordinates slip and slide, eventually causing the event known as 'ego death'. Similarly, on return, the co-ordinates re-establish themselves, although usually at a jaunty new angle and, for a while at least, in a more fragile relationship. This is the initiatory experience of death-rebirth sought by shamans and mystics throughout human history.

The same problem of location affects specific elements of human consciousness. For example, in the United States brain researcher Karl Lashley spent 30 years cutting away portions of brains trying to pin down the seat of memory storage, but was forced to the conclusion that 'it is not possible to demonstrate the isolated localization of the memory trace anywhere within the nervous system'. Theories purporting to explain this difficulty abound, but on the whole have little or no supporting evidence. One theory, that memory is somehow produced by shimmering electrical reverberation in the brain, may possibly account for very short-term memory, but does not solve the problem of long-term and complex memories. Another suggestion that memory is encoded in molecules of RNA (ribonucleic acid) in the brain may possibly explain some forms of simple learning, but does not begin to explain the complex memories of human beings. And while there is no need to doubt that networks of nerve cells or neurons can form in response to experiental input, and that parts of the brain such as the hippocampus seem implicated in memory function, such mechanisms are not in themselves memories. That the mechanism is not the memory is a fact, in the same way that a doorway is not the room.

However deep we dig we cannot find the physical seat of human memory. The mind is indeed a ghost in the machine of the physical brain, as Arthur Koestler observed. Likewise, perhaps there is a ghost within the physicality of the Earth – AE's Earth spirit, or the *anima mundi* of antiquity – the soul of the world. If we cannot grasp the nature of human memory or consciousness, small wonder we have difficulty in doing so at a planetary level. But unless we come to understand the nature of consciousness, we will not be able to perceive its association with either the human being or the planet.

The prevailing orthodox view on consciousness is that it is a transient phenomenon manifested by the electrochemical processes of the brain. It is difficult for anyone who has experienced, whether deliberately or involuntarily, significant expansion of their own consciousness to understand how anyone can hold such a view. However, researchers such as Rupert Sheldrake are urging their biologist colleagues to take an approach more in keeping with the newer attitudes of physicists – to embrace more readily the concept of fields discussed in Chapter 3. If Sheldrake's species memory fields exist, then consciousness as a whole must exist in field form. In fact, we can see the whole of existence as interacting field phenomena, at various levels. This phantasmagoria of 'states of space', of fields, is probably what is observed by people experiencing profoundly heightened consciousness levels. This 'delicate sacred gossamer web . . . this shimmering mosaic'.[2] From this perspective, AE's 'ethereal medium' or Earth memory and Teilhard's 'noosphere' would both exist, interacting with one another, just as the individual human mind field would interact with that of the Earth and of all things in the environment. Everything is connected.

As we have noted, when a person undergoes a mind-changing experience one of the first sensations registered is the alteration in the perception of time and space. Such changed perceptions can be triggered by many factors other than psychotic episodes or the ingestion of psychoactive material – many people have experienced an apparent slowing down of time during a car accident or similar *in extremis* situation, for example. Yet these two most fundamental aspects of our existence, time and space, cannot in themselves be seen, touched or apprehended by any of our senses, even though we register them indirectly in a variety of ways. These aspects, which embrace everything else in the universe, are nothingness from the point of view of our senses, as is that which contemplates them – consciousness. If time and space change when consciousness alters, it may be that consciousness relates to, or, more probably, *is* an aspect of space-time, which is a way of describing the geometry of the physical universe according to Einstein's special theory of relativity, in which space and time are considered together as a kind of single entity.

Space-time is scientifically explored and studied by means of specialized mathematics. There are as yet no mathematics of consciousness as such, but space-time is known to behave in certain ways that might provide clues regarding the nature of a planetary consciousness field, or at least give us an indication of how to start thinking of such a thing.

We now know, from Einstein's general theory of relativity and more recent experimental evidence, that the presence of mass distorts the geometry of space in its vicinity – 'gravity' is experienced. Gravity is an expression of curved space; the more space is curved by a mass, the stronger gravity is felt to be. Human beings live within the Earth's curved space – and within its time, because space curvature automatically affects time, as both are part of the same substratum of existence of space-time. However, because of varying geological factors, there are gravity anomalies over the Earth's surface. Variations in the thickness of the Earth's crust, variable distribution of masses of minerals in it, height from sea level – all these factors affect the force of gravity, and the stronger it is, the slower time passes. This effect, although tiny, is large enough to be measured, but it requires the incredible accuracy of atomic clocks to do so. An atomic clock sent into orbit above the Earth, for example, where gravity is weaker than at ground level, will show a different elapsed time from one left on the ground, even though they were synchronized before take-off. Similarly, the rate of a clock taken from low-lying Washington DC to the city of Denver, a mile above sea level, would differ; the inhabitants of Washington DC age less rapidly (by a very small degree) than those in Denver. . . .[3]

Maps exist which show gravity variations over sections of the Earth's surface; contours on these maps cluster in some areas and spread wide apart in others. Such a map is also, in effect, showing contours of time on the landscape. The space-time fluctuations across the countryside are, of course, very minor indeed, but small forces can have a surprising effect on living things, as we clearly saw in Chapter 3. Since the variations we are considering here have been measured by instruments, there is every possibility that living things can also register such changes, even if it is below the threshold of conscious awareness. Dr Cyril Smith of Salford University in England emphasizes that 'the sensitivity and precision with which living systems make use of physical quantities should not be underestimated'.[4]

With regard to gravity waves, biologist Lyall Watson commented in 1973 that:

'. . . nobody has yet been able to demonstrate that life is aware of them. The best evidence so far comes from a Swiss biologist working on little flying beetles with the interesting name of cockchafers. He put swarms of the beetles into an opaque container and found that they responded to the invisible approach of a lump of lead outside. When lead weighing more than eighty pounds was moved closer to their container, the beetles gathered on the side farthest from it. They could not see the lead, and the experiment seems to have been designed to eliminate all other clues, so we must assume that these insects at least are aware, by a change in gravity, of the distribution of masses around them.'[5]

Measurements of gravity have so far been only by means of its effects; no one has measured gravity waves (undulations of the curvature of space) directly, although their existence has been confirmed by detailed astronomical studies.

Gravity is the weakest of the four scientifically recognized energy types in the universe (the other three being electromagnetism and the 'strong and weak' nuclear forces), so it is exceptionally difficult to find ways of detecting it directly. Nevertheless, nature may already have perfected its own way of doing this, as has so often been found with other energy effects. The nature of that detection may register in consciousness. Perhaps, as Dr Arnold Lieber has speculated:

'. . . we shall discover there are "gravoceptors" within the human body. They might be located along nervous pathways and in the walls of blood vessels. Gravoceptors, picking up the immediate thrust of gravitational force, could mediate sudden shifts of nervous and vascular functioning.'[6]

Gravity may be weak, but it is strong in terms of the distance over which its presence is effective from a given source. The observation of the push and pull of tides against a coastline is a simple example. Gravity is certainly a candidate for being the most fundamental of the physical forces in the universe, and perhaps subtle would be a better description than weak. It is a subtle force that results from – indeed is – the geometry of curved space. If consciousness, too, is an aspect of space-time, then perhaps effects analogous to those of gravity similarly occur. If a mass can distort space and give rise to gravity, perhaps it can also effect what we call consciousness. If cockchafers can sense a lump of lead, surely humans can sense and respond to huge mineral deposits in the Earth's crust, subterranean water, great ridges of rock or mountains of iron? (Interestingly, the poet Robert Graves once claimed that the major religions had been cradled in areas with major iron deposits.) It should not be beyond the wit of science to find ways of testing this possibility, at least indirectly through mass studies of brain rhythms in a variety of locations, for instance.

It could be that the tiny time variations corresponding to gravity anomalies over the Earth's crust do subtly affect consciousness. For instance, we have all had the experience of certain landscapes or places creating particular feelings within us for no apparent reason. If consciousness is an aspect of space-time, then mass must have an effect. In theory, this would mean that a contour map of consciousness for a given landscape could be drawn up, just as gravity anomaly maps exist today. Perhaps this was just what the old systems of geomancy were all about. The Chinese feng shui practitioner, for example, would observe the magnetic properties of a place, consider the lie of the land, then rush helter-skelter down slopes[7] to sense from the way his body moved over the surface in which direction the subtle energy of the Earth, its *chi*, was flowing. Depending on the topography of the site, and the wealth of his client, the feng shui geomant might sometimes have large-scale changes made to the shape of surrounding hills or ridges, and might even alter the course of rivers. He would divine the balance of the terrestrial and atmospheric *chi* and the relationship between the polarities of yin (soft, negative) and yang (angular, positive) at a location. All this was done to produce optimum conditions for human habitation; to create harmony, good luck and happiness. If we strip this procedure of its colourful symbols and expressions, we may be looking at what were essentially archaic methods of manipulating the contours of consciousness.

Einstein failed in his attempt to formulate a unified field theory that would combine gravity and the three other fundamental forces in terms of the geometry of space-time. But the search goes on in a variety of ways for that old 'holy grail' – a universal force or medium. In the 1980s the talk has been of a fifth force or 'hypercharge', and other unknown forms of gravity. Physicist Michael Nieto at Los Alamos has predicted that three kinds of gravity will ultimately be discovered.

Somewhat beyond the pale of even this esoteric scientific quest have been the findings of Australian medical scientist Bevan Reid and physicist Sergei Barsamian. They believe they have experimental evidence suggesting the existence of a 'low-level' energy field that pervades the whole universe. This universal field has a memory and carries information. Most of their findings result from the study of crystal growth. In one set of experiments in 1984 Reid and colleague H.E. Anderson crystallized sodium chloride in the presence of proteins. The usual crystal forms are cube-shaped. However, when various actions were carried out concurrently at distances ranging from a few inches to 98 feet (30 metres) from the crystallization location, marked changes in the crystal growth patterns were noted. In one test, lumps of lead placed 8 inches (20 centimetres) away caused distinct changes in crystallization patterns. The effect was repeatable. Different weights of lead did not change the disturbed type of crystallization pattern produced. In other tests, various chemical reactions taking place at distances of 15 to 50 feet (5 to 15 metres) disturbed the crystallization rate and pattern of the sodium chloride. In one of these tests, there was a brick wall between the crystallization process and the chemical reactions. Several of the tests were carried out with the crystallization process taking place in an electrically shielded environment, to rule out electromagnetic interference. Evidence of some of the action-at-a-distance being associated with ambient oxygen was found, but the rest of the effects were considered to demonstrate unknown aspects of the 'structure and other properties of space'.[8]

In other experiments, polymer coatings on slides took on the image of bacteria in culture medium placed 2.5 feet (75 centimetres) away, and revealed vortex patterns when placed over lead weights. Lead seems to concentrate the force that Reid and his colleagues claim to be detecting; this would seem to suggest that, like gravity, it is somehow associated with the distortion of space.

Perhaps science has difficulty in perceiving and understanding the universal field because that which is attempting to study it, human consciousness, is actually an expression of it. It is a little like trying to pick oneself up with one's own bootstraps.

In Chapter 1 we came across just a few of the traditional names other cultures had for the universal life force; it is significant that today we do not have a word for it. That is because we have a blind spot concerning it; we have no word because we have no concept requiring it. We either draw on ancient terms such as *chi*, or we use the fragmented terminology of modern science – and it is that fragmentation that prevents the matter from being clearly seen, like an image in a shattered mirror.

But whatever the actual nature, mechanisms and name involved, if we are really to think of the Earth as a living, sentient being, we will have to view its consciousness as some kind of field effect. It may be structured at many different levels, but it would add up to a whole superfield, an Earth field or Gaiafield, a vast conscious entity quite invisible to its constituent parts. Gaia, thinking the thoughts of a planet, sensitive to the life forms existing within her, sensing the push and pull of her lunar companion, the planets and the Sun, acknowledging the welling energies within her lithosphere, feeling the breeze of cosmic rays rippling her magnetosphere and atmosphere, and perhaps listening in to the tinkling of distant star fields as we might hear the chimes of church bells across the countryside. Gaia, with the memory of aeons.

Although such an Earth field would have to be subtle and all-pervading, it could nevertheless interact with other fields, known and unknown. Mass and electromagnetism might affect this consciousness field.

The implications of humanity being unaware of such a field are enormous. Consider the effect our cities, for example, would have on such a hypothesized field. Because modern cities are maelstroms of mass and energy, they have their own fields which might distort the Earth field. Cities could be considered to have their own microclimate of consciousness. This is precisely the experience of living in a large city; many people sense it, yet the reality of an Earth field still eludes modern acceptance. The realization of its existence would mean that geomancy, instead of being considered a quaint old superstition, would become a matter of concern. In the light of conditions on Earth today, a new geomancy would need to be developed. The scale, orientation and materials of buildings would become crucial matters. How natural and artificial conditions would interact would be fundamental considerations in the siting of buildings and new towns. The generation and use of electricity, the propagation of radio, microwaves and so on, would pose geomantic problems the old systems never had to deal with.

This is not simply fanciful. We already have geomantic problems that are noted by modern society but not seen in that context: the effects of high-tension cables and microwave transmitters on the health of those living in their vicinity; the radon gas scare; the apartment blocks that seem to foster delinquency; the health problems of office workers exposed to banks of electronic apparatus; the mysterious incidence of leukemia around nuclear power stations (and there is a whole geomantic can of worms waiting to be opened about the presently inexplicable nature of geographical concentrations of certain diseases); and the physical and mental illnesses caused by the stress of city life. These are just some of the more obvious areas of concern that almost certainly require a geomantic dimension to be applied to them.

The larger ecological problems besetting our world may also owe more to the type of consciousness engendered in city energy vortices than appears at first glance. Plans for agriculture, for the countryside, for industrial processes, for waste disposal, for the treatment of the rain forests, and virtually everything else, are carried out according to the dictates of thought processes emerging from urban consciousness. City talks to city about world affairs ('Washington responded cautiously today about suggested cuts in European medium-range weapons proposed by Moscow'); it is in city institutions that the abstract invention of world economy has been created and is served. Urban humanity is now effectively like a colony of astronauts sitting in a base-bubble on some alien planet. It is the view from this urban bubble that creates an economic logic that allows, even encourages, the destruction of rain forests, and can permit mass starvation in one part of the world while elsewhere food rots because of overproduction. The state of mind produced in the urban microclimates of consciousness is essentially unwholesome. It is at odds with the wisdom of the natural, planetary consciousness field that it unwittingly disrupts.

Having created this unhealthy state of affairs, we have to look hopefully towards some sense of balance, some deep change of mind and heart in mainstream culture that could modify the situation to manageable proportions. A major step in such a colossal process has to be the acceptance of the idea that the Earth is alive – only such a simple, direct image can hope to move people's feelings on a scale sufficient to allow the enormous realignment of our attitudes and relationship to the planet now becoming essential. The key to this vital step is to accept the idea of the planet being, in some way, conscious. In turn, such a concept will ultimately have to spring from a reappraisal of the nature of consciousness itself.

It is being suggested here that the adoption of the idea of a consciousness field is the crucial hurdle. Those who are prepared to study closely the workings of their own minds, to become more sensitive to the variations of consciousness that take place within them, as AE did, for example, will soon realize that the brain is simply an organ that is processing something that comes from 'outside'. Just as the eyes process but do not create light, the ears process but do not produce sound, the respiratory organs process but do not directly produce the air we breathe, so too does the brain process but not produce consciousness. We accept that the brain processes stimuli provided from outside the skull through the known windows of the senses, but there the acceptance seems to stop. The brain is surely more like a television receiver, if such a crude analogy is permissible; it tunes in to the field of consciousness as the television receiver tunes in to the electromagnetic field. The brain selects 'channels' from the field, what Aldous Huxley called 'Mind-at-Large', and their processing can be determined by mechanistic biology. But it does not actually produce the field – not directly, at any rate. Certainly, personal material is added to the information drawn from the 'Mind-at-Large' as it is processed by the individual, in the same way that other bodily organs modify the material passing through them, but just as an attempt to find the little man on the television screen by cutting into the set will fail, so will the attempt to find consciousness within the physical circuitry of the brain. The television presenter seen on the screen is in a studio far away; fiddling with the set may affect the reception of the channel (the signal), but it does not affect anything going on in the studio.

The brain's circuitry is a mechanism enabling reception of the consciousness field, and, almost certainly, enabling transmission through that field. Evidence of this transmission ability is surely shown in the work of people such as Persinger (see Chapter 3). The consciousness field may have a close resonance with the natural ELF fields pulsing to the rhythm of Earth and living brains, or it may even be partially composed of them.

The acceptance of consciousness as a field phenomenon as opposed to a skull-centred effect would lead to a breakthrough in understanding at all levels of human activity – physical, psychological, parapsychological, social, ecological, economic. It would be useful and perhaps surprisingly effective for us today to picture consciousness as an environmental effect, to invest the landscape with the mindscape, to use Steele's terminology (Chapter 1). Can Western culture ever summon up the courage to let consciousness out of the skull? Dare we let the genie out of the lamp?

THE MIND-GATES OF GAIA

Assuming, for the sake of argument, the existence of some kind of planetary consciousness field, are there ways we can attempt to interact with it? Traditional peoples did so through a softer-edged, less ego-centred state of mind to that possessed by us today. As Teilhard de Chardin repeatedly pointed out, we are developing an increasingly self-reflective level of awareness. This may arguably have some evolutionary function, but it certainly tends to separate us from the natural environment, as we have noted. While traditional peoples integrated mentally (and thus in terms of social behaviour) with their surroundings in an unselfconscious way, modern human beings will have to be consciously aware of the process. We will have to learn to commune with the Earth field in our own way, but we will have to combine aspects of the ancient wisdom with our current understanding. In the final analysis it may transpire that this is indeed an evolutionary step, and that although we have run a dangerous course, it may have been a journey we had to undertake so that we could become poised for a more complete, more far-reaching integration with the *anima mundi* than that achieved before.

So how do we set about interacting with the Earth field? To use the analogy of the human body, even though the whole person is suffused with life, we have to communicate with that person through particular channels, usually the five senses. Correspondingly, although the whole planet may be suffused with consciousness, we will need to identify the channels that will enable us to communicate with the Earth field. In Chapter 5 we saw that AE was aware that geographical factors, particularly ancient sites, could play a part in his altered states. Raynor C. Johnson recalled that when Dr Monk Gibbon asked him why this should be so, AE answered that 'just as a human soul using a body has special senses in the latter, so the body of Earth had special regions through which the traffic of perception seemed most clearly to take place'.[9]

In the less safe analogy of a computer, we know we can interface with it through a keyboard, a microphone and other methods. So what interfaces does the planet have for its spirit?

Naturally occurring electromagnetism in certain contexts is undoubtedly one interface. The ELF fields would seem to comprise a global interface with planetary-scale processes. It seems that these could indeed link the human mind directly with planetary rhythms (Chapter 3).

In Chapter 4 we saw there was apparently deliberate usage of stone with magnetic and radioactive properties at some ancient sacred sites. Also, it was noted, numerous sites around the world seem to have been situated in relationship to geological factors such as fault lines and mineral deposits, where electromagnetic effects, among others, are likely to have been involved.

Gravity, or some aspect of this little-understood force, may also provide a 'window' or interface in particular circumstances. Again as we saw in Chapter 4, Pierre Méreaux has claimed to have discovered gravity anomalies amongst the stone row complexes at Carnac, and there has been some American research indicating both magnetic and gravity anomalies at springs. Faulting, too, sometimes marks changes in local gravity values. But all this is virgin territory, and much more will need to be known before gravity can be seriously considered as an interface.

Rocks or minerals may in themselves be a kind of interface; certainly Orphan Boy (Chapter 1) would have agreed. In his *Stalking the Wild Pendulum*[10] Itzhak Bentov wrote, 'We know that matter is consciousness (or, if you prefer, *contains* consciousness). This consciousness, if there is enough of it (a critical mass), will develop a dim awareness of self. Over millions of years this dim awareness may be strengthened into a sharper identity, possibly through interaction with other creatures.'

To make his point, Bentov envisaged a rock in a cleft of which an animal finds refuge. The animal feels grateful to the rock, and the rock registers that appreciation. Later, a bird makes its nest there, laying eggs and starting new life, and this boosts the rock's ego considerably, increasing its consciousness quotient. 'Sooner or later,' Bentov observed, 'the consciousness of the rock will evolve into a "spirit of the rock".' More and more creatures become attracted to the rock and its consciousness increases. When at last a human being encounters the rock, that person will sense something special about the place. More and more people will come to the rock. Before long 'there is a cult going. This boosts the ego of the "spirit of the rock" immensely because the thoughts of the people who concentrate on him add to his power . . . he is stimulated by the level of energy produced by the human nervous system. . . . Eventually, the "spirit of the rock", which started out as a vague, dim awareness in a mass of matter, develops into a powerful spirit or a tribal god'.

Bentov points out that we can now measure the energy produced by thought in the brain outside of the head (Chapter 3) and that the energy involved in thought is therefore broadcast. In his model of the rock spirit, Bentov saw the mineral structure actually absorbing and integrating that frequency of energy.

Scottish biochemist A.G. Cairns-Smith has argued that aeons before the 'high-tech' cell appeared on Earth there must have been a 'low-tech' precursor structure, possibly some form of crystal. Referring to Cairns-Smith's ideas, J.T. Fraser writes:

'The idea that the earliest forms of life were crystal-like is not in itself new. It has been known that between the realms of the living and the non-living, crystals represent the highest degree of stable organization. Inorganic matter is not able to create more ordered, stable systems than those found in crystals. . . .

'Cairns-Smith, a specialist in clay chemistry, postulated that early life inherited at its core a solid-state crystalline structure but replaced its chemistry with what later became the DNA-RNA-protein system of "modern" life. Two and a half billion years modern. During the last fifteen years, he and NASA scientists . . . have carried these ideas further and . . . began to paint an increasingly plausible picture of life's crystalline origins. . . .

'Perhaps our most distant ancestors were molecular noodles floating in a primordial broth, perhaps crystals rhythmically shivering in wet clay.'[11]

Robert O. Becker has likewise drawn parallels between crystals and living organisms. He lists the 'bare minimum' definitions of the processes that must occur before an entity can be called living: there must be some way of receiving, processing and storing environmental data – 'in other words, a sort of crude consciousness and memory must be present from the first'; there must be an ability to sense damage and repair itself; and, finally, a form of cyclic activity must be present. He goes on:

'The funny thing is that all of these criteria are met by the activities of semiconducting crystals. . . . The idea of certain rocks, in the course of a billion years or so, gradually becoming responsive to their surroundings, growing, learning to "hurt" when a lava flow or sulfuric rain ate away part of a vertex, slowly rebuilding, pulsing with, well, life, even developing to a liquid crystal stage and climbing free of their stony nests . . . all this may seem a bit bizarre. Yet it's really no more strange than imagining the same transformation from droplets of [primordial] broth. The change happened somehow.'[12]

Crystals and gems have for centuries, and probably millennia, been associated with esoteric traditions and healing properties in many cultures around the world. Precious stones with certain properties were worn in ancient Egypt, for instance, and rock crystal or quartz – 'solidified light' – was a key feature in Australian Aboriginal initiation ceremonies; crystals could be ground up and drunk in water, or inserted directly into the skin of the initiatory candidate.[13] In medieval Europe, certain crystals were supposed to have particular properties, and these ideas linger even today. In recent years crystals have experienced a revival in New Age circles. Perhaps because of their piezoelectric property – the turning of physical pressure into electrical charge and vice versa – it is generally believed by some groups today that quartz crystals can store signals put into them by the human mind; these can be thoughts, feelings or healing energies. By the same token, such stored information is said to be accessible by certain procedures. Dragon Project experiments were described in Chapter 4 in which human interaction with minerals produced measurable changes in the stones involved.

There is an undoubted crystal component to many megalithic sites. For example, at Callanish, a group of stone circles on the remote Isle of Lewis off Scotland's west coast, one is hard put to find a standing stone amongst the dozens there which does not have a piece of hornblende, quartz or feldspar embedded in it. And in Cornwall the Duloe circle is composed of huge monoliths of pure white quartz. A great many of the stone circles contain, or used to contain, some crystal element within their structure. In Ireland, the huge chambered mound of Newgrange is faced with white quartz on the eastern side (facing the rising sun). It is clear that the megalith builders had some reason for using crystals at their sites. It may not be scientific, but it is certainly tempting to daydream about what might be stored in the crystals at these ancient sites, if the information they possibly contain could only be decoded.

Another aspect of rock, mentioned in Chapter 4, is the now reliably observed light phenomena occurring on granite in darkened, radon-rich enclosures such as dolmens and fogous. We have also seen that certain terrains, especially faulted ones where particular classes of ancient monuments tend to be located, seem to produce earth light phenomena – anomalous balls of light. Both of these fascinating and complex phenomena will be discussed again later on, in terms of their possible interface value. It is possible that earth lights may be the most direct interface of all with the Earth field.

One of the prime potential interfaces where an 'Earthmind' state could be created has to be the most abundant chemical substance in the Earth's crust – water. It is so obvious an interface that it is easily overlooked. Surely, one thinks at first, water is too common and too ordinary for such an exalted role? On the contrary, water is a good interface candidate precisely because of its ubiquity, and its nature is in fact mysterious and complex, as a few basic facts about it reveal.

Roughly three-quarters of the Earth's surface is made up of water, which matches the approximate proportion to be found in living things (the proportion in humans is about 65 per cent). Vast volumes are to be found within the lithosphere as ground water, on the Earth's surface as oceans, lakes, rivers and icecaps, in the atmosphere as water vapour, and within the cells and tissues of the biosphere. Water resists heating more than most substances, and is most easily warmed between 35° and 40°C – a narrow range encompassing the preferred body temperature of around 37°C displayed by mammals, including, of course, human beings. It is more dense as a liquid than as a solid, unlike nearly all other substances; as its temperature lowers to 4°C it starts to become lighter in weight because it is expanding rather than contracting as other materials do, and by zero degrees it has increased its volume by around ten per cent (this is why unprotected water pipes tend to burst in freezing conditions).

Water is rare in that it can act as both acid and base, so that under appropriate conditions it can react with itself – it is not an inert [...] vent, able to erode rock [...] the molecules of water [...] cular structure of almost [...] water pulls material out [...] ution of something. The [...] f the glass in a very short [...] ter makes it both strong [...] rogen bonds within it is [...] er together or forms on [...] urface tension'. Water [...] ly with other surfaces – [...] ey also contain a great [...] t on a greater scale than

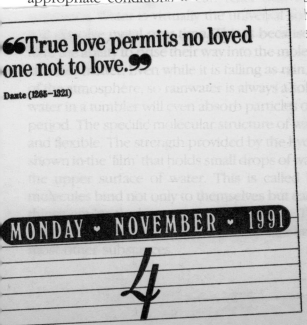

66True love permits no loved one not to love.99

Dante (1265–1321)

MONDAY · NOVEMBER · 1991

4

Ice is the most perfectly bonded hydrogen structure known, with precise crystalline lattices which persist even into the liquid state. As Lyall Watson puts it:

> 'Melted ice may look clear, but actually contains short-lived regions of crystals that form and dissolve many millions of times a second. It is as though liquid water remembers the form of ice from which it most recently came by repeating the formula over and over again to itself, ready to change back at a moment's notice. If one could take a photograph with a short enough exposure, it would probably show ice-like areas even in a glass of hot water.'[14]

The receptive or impressionable qualities of water are clearly expressed in its nature. Water reflects. It is also incredibly sensitive to minute environmental stimuli, as Italian scientist Giorgio Piccardi discovered in the 1930s. Piccardi found that the rate of chemical reactions taking place in water solutions could be mysteriously affected by cosmic influences, such as the lunar and sunspot cycles, solar eruptions, or sudden cosmic ray showers. As Michel Gauquelin has put it, water is 'subject to major changes as a result of even very low energy influence. . . . Water studied in the laboratory is as sensitive to very slight changes in electric or magnetic fields as the animals Brown [Chapter 3] studied'.[15]

Because water makes up so much of our bodies, these subtle influences must also occur within our own cells and tissues. Water therefore links us in a profound way to both the terrestrial and the extraterrestrial environment.

Theodor Schwenk, a German engineer, has likened water's sensitivity to that of the human ear. He considers water to be 'a receptive "sense organ" . . . the impressionable medium *par excellence*'. In one experiment he had a number of identically prepared bottles of water mechanically shaken at short periods before, during and after a total solar eclipse. He then placed a set number of wheat grains in each bottle and let them germinate. The wheat blades emerging from the water shaken at the time of the eclipse were significantly stunted compared to those emerging from the other samples shaken before and after the event. Schwenk concluded that water and its structures such as vortices were effectively 'sense organs open to the cosmos', able to *pass on* impressions. As Lyall Watson remarks: 'It is a fascinating and provocative thought that a body of water deserves to be considered as an organism in its own right.'[16]

The question of a memory function in water has taken some remarkable turns in the latter part of the 1980s. In 1988 French immunologist Jacques Benveniste and colleagues had a paper published in the British science journal *Nature*[17] – but with 'editorial reservation'. This was because Benveniste and his associates found that they could affect white cells in the blood with antibody solutions so diluted that not a single molecule of antibody could possibly be present in the water. They suggested that possibly water could act as a 'template' for the basic molecule of the antibody, and were convinced that 'transmission of the information depended on vigorous agitation, possibly inducing a sub-molecular organization of water'.

The findings of the team were obviously uncomfortably close to the scientifically derided principle operative in homeopathy, where incredibly diluted solutions of appropriate substances (a process using agitation, interestingly) are believed to be effective in the healing of diseases, the symptoms of which are provoked by large amounts of the very substances that are diluted. The editorial of that issue of *Nature* made it clear why the results reached by Benveniste *et al* were unlikely to be accepted; they were 'startling not merely because they point to a novel phenomenon, but because they strike at the roots of two centuries of observation and rationalization of physical phenomena.'[18]

Over the years others have, however, come up with similar findings to those of Benveniste and colleagues. Amongst the more interesting research has been that carried out by Dr C.W. Smith of Salford University, with Drs Jean Monro and Ray Choy of the Allergy Unit at the Nightingale Hospital, London. Monro and Choy had been using a method of working with multiple allergy patients developed in America by Dr J. Miller. In this, an allergen is diluted in water in a series of dilutions. By dilution 34 there is no chemical left of the allergen, yet the series goes on to further dilution. These sets of diluted allergens are used on the skin of a patient, until a dilution is reached at which the patient undergoes a maximum reaction. It should not work, as the levels are beyond those at which any chemical factor can be involved. But it does work, as careful tests have confirmed. The fact that some multiple-allergy patients are incredibly hypersensitive to electricity[19] provided the clue that set the London doctors working with Smith.

Smith discovered that an electrical rather than a chemical effect was involved, and the researchers found they could induce a patient's symptoms by means of transmitting electrical fields of varying frequencies to a patient. It was further discovered that water exposed to electrical fields somehow remembered the frequencies applied.[20]

Physicist Fred Alan Wolf has suggested that water may possess an even more esoteric memory ability, by invoking quantum physics. He has boldly proposed that memory is recorded on a molecular or atomic scale in water occurring 'at the synapses or connections between neurons in the brain'.[21] If this is true, then water is certainly one medium that holds memory.

Water also seems to be responsive to sound. In Bavaria, for example, there is the old tradition of *Tonsingen* or tone singing. Towards evening each day in the growing season the farmers sing ascending notes as they stir a little clay into a bucket of water in an anticlockwise motion and descending notes as they swish the mixture around in a clockwise direction.[22] The buckets are then left overnight in the dark and the contents sprinkled over the crops early next day.

Marcel Vogel, a former IBM research scientist who has done a great deal of work with crystals, has confirmed that the beating of a shaman's drum can affect the structure of water, especially, it seems, if a crystal has been immersed in the water. He claims that if water is spun round a crystal, the liquid draws charge from the mineral which can be measured. This echoes a similar practice in ancient Tibet, where certain gemstones were put in water which the patient then drank. American researcher Pat Flanagan has confirmed that crystals placed in water do affect its surface tension for a short period.

Vogel also claims that when he has studied water 'from various sacred locales, I find a structure in that water which is unique from the bulk water. I got a sample from a sacred spring in Hungary, and it exhibits an energy level that transcends anything I have seen anywhere'.[23]

Water clearly varies in quality and nature. Spring water, and water subject to vigorous motion as in mountain streams and babbling brooks, is more 'alive' than tap water or stored water. As has been shown by doctors seeking allergen-free water for consumption by patients with extreme allergy problems, bottles of spring water buried in the ground for a few days take on special, purifying properties. In the light of this discovery, what remarkable qualities might spring water bubbling up through the strata from the geological depths possess? And if there is such a thing as primary water – water produced deep within the Earth rather than collected from rainwater percolating through the crust – might that too have particular properties? The sources of water are important, and affect its character.

As well as its source, the agitation water is subjected to seems important. Schwenk, Vogel, the Benveniste team, homeopaths and the *Tonsingen* tradition all comment on the value of water that has been agitated. The German mystic and scholar Rudolph Steiner also recommended the swirling of water for agricultural purposes; he had precise procedures for this. And Pat Flanagan found that spiralling water could produce electric potentials of up to 20,000 volts.[24]

In addition to all these mysteries and marvels, though probably related to them in some way, water may exhibit even more subtle and profound qualities. This seems indicated by the traditional belief that certain springs produced water able to impart special healing or visionary powers, and by the insistence of people such as the feng shui geomants that water could conduct *chi*, the universal energy field. Rapidly flowing and straight watercourses at a location would tend to drain off the *chi* and were to be avoided. On the other hand, ponds or tanks fed with fresh water could mitigate the effects of bad feng shui or '*sha*' at a site, and 'slow, sinuous, deep watercourses' were 'conducive to the accumulation of *chi*', especially if they formed a pool in front of a house or tomb.[25]

So water may attract or directly resonate with the Earth field. Its field may have a special relationship with that of the planet, making it one of the chief interfaces with, or sense organs of, the *anima mundi*. The sense of holy wells and springs being interfaces with the Earth field is inherent in the Celtic tradition of water, as can be gleaned from this description by the scholar J.C. Cooper:

'The waters, lakes, sacred wells . . . have magical properties and are the dwelling place of supernatural beings . . . they also give access to the other world, and the powers of the waters represent other-world wisdom and the foreknowledge of the gods. Tir-nan-og, the Celtic paradise, the land of the ever-young, is either beyond, or under, the waters.'[26]

EARTH DREAMING

It is to ancient sacred sites that we must now turn to seek ways in which we may actually use these potential interfaces, channels or planetary senses. As we can deduce from Chapter 4, ancient sites are places likely to contain one or more of the interfaces with the Earth field, having been selected or constructed for such a purpose. The survival of many of these sites provides us with ancient knowledge to use in our modern quest. By telling us where our base of operations needs to be, they provide us with step one.

The second step is to understand the old places of power. Again in Chapter 4 we saw how modern research is attempting to do this, and we noted that a few aspects are just beginning to become clear. If one wants to dream the dream of Earth at a stone circle, for example, it is necessary to know which stone one needs to be in contact with in order to dream. If the specific magnetic or radioactive stone is unknown, the site – the ancient instrument – is not being properly used.

Step three is to learn in what ways the interfaces, the old mind-gates, are to be operated. Once more we must take our cue from ancient wisdom, which tells us that altered states are required. The ancient site is the geophysical arena in which consciousness is to be changed. We can change consciousness anywhere, of course, but these sacred spots, these sense organs of Gaia, act as 'wave guides' for the consciousness loosened in the altered state. A qualitative difference can be expected between an altered state in a fogou and in a city room, for example.

An altered state can be achieved in various ways; some are probably more appropriate at certain sites than others, and, indeed, vary in acceptability from one person to another. Fasting is a reliable method of making consciousness more mobile, as is meditation. Obviously it is necessary to begin fasting a day or two before visiting a site, but meditation has to be carried out *in situ.* These methods are probably most effective when they are combined. A more active approach is the use of ritual drumming and movement – dancing. Flickering light enhances this process because its strobing effect can alter brain rhythms. Traditionally, this was produced by a fire (now to be highly discouraged at sites), although certain American Indian groups would use pieces of quartz shaken in a kind of rattle (quartz pieces in friction can produce a surprising amount of light when viewed in appropriately dark conditions). Today, one could use a flashlight, although this would preclude the production of consciousness-affecting air ions (charged particles) which the other methods create in addition to flickering light.

Another method that might be more appealing to many is dreaming. Psychologists have long known the value of dreams as a diagnostic tool, and many people have learned to use the mysterious process as a means of self-discovery. It can, however, be an even more potent tool, leading to contact with transpersonal levels of the consciousness field, including what AE called the memory of the Earth or 'supernature'.

Ritual dreaming was practised in the ancient world, usually in two particular contexts. One was the initiatory dream of the shamanic candidate, the other was the divinatory dream, used especially in connection with healing, and it is this type of dream that is appropriate for the new shamanism envisaged here.

The dreaming Temple of Epidaurus in Greece is probably the best known of its type, but there were hundreds of such sites in the Mediterranean countries, including Egypt, during Graeco-Roman times. Ritual dreaming (dream incubation) at holy places goes back thousands of years before ancient Greece in fact, and versions of the practice were doubtlessly used throughout the world.

The basic procedure of 'temple sleep' involved certain preparations, usually sexual abstinence, fasting, offerings to the god to be invoked (usually Aesculapius, the god of healing in the Graeco-Roman world), ritual bathing and sometimes copious drinking of the water emerging at the dream site (the prophetess at the Temple of Apollo at Delphi, for instance, would drink from the Castalia spring before mounting her tripod seat over the hallucinogenic fumes issuing at the site – some say from a fault or fissure,[27] others from the burning of laurel leaves). The dream candidate would finally go to sleep in a special dream cell. If all went well, the invoked god, or an associated image or spirit, would be expected to appear in the patient's dream. In earlier traditions, the dream itself would have been intrinsically healing, but later it was assumed that a cure had been revealed in the dream, and the message had to be decoded. In the Greek system, temple attendants or *therapeutes* helped the patients to interpret their dreams – this is where the word therapist comes from. Similar methods were used for other types of purposeful dreaming, such as prophecy.

The ruins of a Romano-British dream temple, now in the private grounds of Lydney Park, Gloucestershire, reveal much about the nature of interfaces at a sacred site. The temple was built on a promontory (known as 'Dwarf's Hill') overlooking the River Severn, in the fourth century AD, as the Roman presence in Britain was waning. Inscriptions uncovered during excavations have shown it was dedicated to Nodens, a native British god who had his roots in Ireland. Nodens was a god of hunting and healing; he also had water connections, as the American scholar James Hersh noted, concluding:

> 'His Neptune-like appearance on the bronze plaque found in the temple, the fact that he is surrounded by tritons and a fisherman catching a salmon, the predominance of the baths and their direct access to the hall of incubation . . . the proximity of the entire temple precinct to a potent spring and the fact that the hill overlooks the Severn; all of these facts point to the ancient symbolical connection of water and healing.'[28]

The water connection is further emphasized by a mosaic floor uncovered at the site depicting fishes and a sea serpent. The hill certainly has numerous springs on it, and it also contains something else: iron. In fact, the temple-bath complex was built directly over a prehistoric iron mine. In addition, the hill is faulted, as the builders of the temple soon discovered; it is evident that soon after it was completed one of the pillars collapsed into an unnoticed geological fault in the bedrock, making repairs and alterations necessary. Preliminary checks by the Dragon Project in February 1989 suggested that there may be a magnetic anomaly near the centre of the hilltop, and that the temple was built in an area yielding double the radiation count obtained at peripheral points around the hill.

Another major technique for achieving altered states of consciousness is the use of psychoactive plants. This method poses research difficulties, however, as the present cultural conditioning against altered states has allowed hallucinogens to be confused with dangerous narcotics and similarly legislated against. The result has been a limiting of genuine consciousness research.

In traditional cultures hallucinogenic substances were considered sacred, beneficial, and an essential part of the religious belief system of a society or tribe. Natural hallucinogens have been used by traditional peoples around the world for countless generations. There are hundreds, possibly thousands, of plants, cacti, tree barks, resins and leaves possessing psychoactive properties, and all have been used by people at one time or another, somewhere or other, to alter their consciousness. The use of hallucinogens goes back to prehistory. In the New World, for example, pre-Columbian wall paintings discovered in the Kuaua kiva in New Mexico show a figure holding jimson weed, a hallucinogen. In the Old World, a man buried in a cave fifty thousand years ago, in what is now northern Iraq, was accompanied by a range of flowers[29] which have been shown to have been psychoactive.[30] Prehistoric rock paintings in the Tessali, southern Algeria, show figures with sacred mushrooms.[31]

Indigenous peoples have always used the experiences vouchsafed by such substances to get in touch with the roots of the natural world, and with the memory of the planet. The Amazonian Yebamasa, for instance, take caji; under its influence they meet the mythical heroes, gods and demons who take them through the universe to study its secrets. Again, the South American Tukano use yajé and 'the flow of time is, as it were, reversed: one . . . returns to and re-experiences the beginnings of mankind and the origin of the universe'.[32] The Huichol Indians of Mexico chew peyote or mescal and 'as they do so time assumes a mythical duration'.[33] Maria Sabina, a Mazatec Indian shamaness of Central America, says that when she eats the sacred mushroom she can 'look down to the very beginning. I can go to where the world is born'.

American psychologist Alberto Villoldo took part in a journey along the mysterious Nasca lines in Peru. These dead straight lines, interspersed with images of creatures and geometric forms, were incised for unknown purposes on the pampas above the town of Nasca one to two millennia ago. The group, led by the shaman Don Eduardo Calderon, took an infusion based on the highly hal-lucinogenic San Pedro cactus. They saw visions all right – collectively. To give an example, one member of the group 'seemed to be followed by an older woman and a child with a dog, which almost everyone appeared to see. The shaman asked the man to identify this older woman and child. He replied that it was his mother, who had died the previous year, and that the child was himself, walking with a pet he had owned in his youth'.[34] This kind of evidence of the field concept of consciousness should not be ignored.

Shamans have used such drugs for centuries not only for learning about the history of the world, the workings of nature and the spiritual condition of humanity, but also for healing purposes, clairvoyance and other *psi* functions, especially the classic shamanic flight or ecstasy – out-of-the-body experience. In this way they can travel great distances and see faraway places, people and events. The ethnologist Kenneth Kensinger was told by six out of nine people engaged in a ceremony involving the use of the hallucinogen ayahuasca that they had seen the death of his grandfather, an event which was only confirmed two days later by the researcher's field radio. Such cases are further evidence that consciousness is not skull-centred.

How 'primitive' peoples of the rain forests and other remote locations obtained their sophisticated knowledge of hallucinogens and healing herbs is a source of mystery to modern pharmacologists. What is not realized is that people who can contact nature directly through psychoactive plants are receiving the best geology, history, prehistory, botany, biology and psychology lessons available on Earth. That is because they are given by Earth.

The highly respected mycologist R. Gordon Wasson suggested that sacred mushrooms could have been responsible for the genesis of religion and also for the level of consciousness in humans that distinguishes them from the animals – self-reflectiveness. Terence McKenna reinforces this view. He refers to experiments with chimpanzees that show they will respond to arrangements that reward them with the hallucinogen DMT (which occurs in many different plant species) in preference to those that supply them with food and drink. If early protohumans were similarly drawn to such substances over generations, McKenna argues, distinct developments in consciousness may have been brought about which would not otherwise have occurred, or not so relatively rapidly as they seem to have done. He refers to Henry Munn (*The Mushrooms of Language*, 1973) who argues that the ingestion of psychoactive mushrooms can act as a stimulus to language activity. Even more dramatically, as was mentioned in Chapter 1, McKenna suggests:

'One view of plant hallucinogens is to see them as interspecies messages or exopheremones. Pheremones are chemical compounds exuded by an organism for the purpose of carrying messages between organisms of the same species. . . .

'If hallucinogens are operating as exopheremones, then the dynamic symbiotic relationship between primate and hallucinogenic plant is actually a transfer of information from one species to another.'[35]

The German ethnopsychologist Holger Kalweit sums up the power of hallucinogens as used in the sort of disciplined, mythical framework found in traditional cultures as allowing the 'communication between species, contacts with suprapersonal beings . . . as well as with cosmic entities and archetypal formations'.[36]

Obviously, natural hallucinogens have to be viewed as another interface, literally a mind-gate, with the *anima mundi*, but because of their particularly powerful effect on human consciousness, it is perhaps best to think of them as enabling agents to be used in conjunction with the other channels.

Although hallucinogens can operate anywhere, there may be geographical connections between the growing places of hallucinogenic vegetation and the situation of sacred sites. At present such links have barely been researched, but preliminary study by British researcher Paul Bennett at ten stone circles in northern England has revealed two particular types of natural hallucinogen growing near each of the sites. This could be indicative of the sort of hallucinogens originally used at the circles. If this pattern is borne out by further botanical examination it could be significant, since traditional peoples treated such plants as if they had a sentience of their own. The spirit of the plant, fungus, cactus or whatever it was, could appear in a vision seen by the person taking the substance. Permission would be sought from the plant spirit before the hallucinogen was used, and where such things grew would be treated with veneration. So there could well have been a connection between the placing of certain types of site and local botany.

For this reason, only naturally occurring and site-specific hallucinogens can be said to be suitable tools for mind change in the context being considered in this chapter. However, this particular method of achieving altered states cannot be recommended here because the use of such substances in the present cultural climate is in most cases illegal, and the selection of natural hallucinogens could be extremely dangerous, possibly lethal, without expert guidance ensuring the correct identification and dosage of the various plants, fungi and so on.

There can be little doubt that of all the methods of producing altered states mentioned above dreaming is the most practical and effective. Two types of site are likely to be most appropriate for this method: magnetic stones at stone circles – or rock outcrops at non-engineered places of power – and ancient sacred wells.

At a stone circle, the magnetic stone (if present) can be identified[37] by the careful use of a liquid-filled compass. This process is more time-consuming if a peak or rock outcrop considered to be sacred by local lore or surviving indigenous peoples is involved. During the sleep period the head must be in actual contact with the magnetic stone. In some cases, as mentioned in Chapter 4, the stone or outcrop may be fashioned into a sort of crude seat that naturally allows one to sit on it or lie comfortably cradled by it.

That sleeping while in head contact with a 'stone of power' can result in altered states (special dreams) is of course indicated in the biblical account of Jacob (Chapter 1). Similarly, at the Shinto temple at Usa in Japan, the emperor used to incubate dreams while sleeping on an incubation bed known as a *kamudoko*, which was made from polished stone. There are numerous associations of special 'power stones' and kingship. Perhaps the best-known example is the Stone of Scone placed in the Coronation Chair at Westminster Abbey; British monarchs are crowned above it. The Stone of Scone is said to be, in fact, the stone on which Jacob had his dream.

The special problem of the new shaman is how to integrate with or contact the Earth field, the *anima mundi*. In the way that a patient at a healing temple would have invoked a god to appear in the healing dream, the modern shaman needs to quietly, powerfully, invoke the Earth Goddess, Gaia herself, then trust the process that follows in a dream state at an ancient sacred site. A waveguide is a device for channelling electromagnetic energy at a given frequency. We can use the term less technically but with the same general meaning here to suggest that the magnetic stone or area might act as a waveguide for the dreaming consciousness, to allow a very accurate tuning to the Earth field. The rock's magnetism may influence the electromagnetically sensitive hippocampus, the brain feature associated with dreaming. The technique of cross-state retention will need to be developed through practice, so that the special dream can be clearly recalled and, indeed, recorded. It may be that the most significant points of the sleep cycle turn out to be the moments before full sleep commences, the hypnogogic state, and the moments between sleep and full waking, the hypnopompic condition. These two phases typically produce short, sudden bursts of visionary material; physiologically, they are when the brain is producing rhythms in the theta and low alpha frequencies, which, as we noted in Chapter 3, are the same as those of some ELF waves. So in these key threshold states one can be resonating with global rhythms, and they might be the times when the channel of consciousness to the Earth field opens up, tuned by the physical contact with the magnetic stone, which has one end embedded in the ground and the other protruding like an antenna.

Some holy wells seem to provoke a sleepy state, as was briefly mentioned in Chapter 4. For example, at the remarkable and secluded holy well at Sancreed in Cornwall, Devereux has witnessed an almost entire group of about 15 people become languid or fall asleep. The immediate area around the subterranean granite chamber enclosing the crystal clear waters of the well gives the sort of high geiger readings associated with many parts of Cornwall (interestingly, similar readings are obtained in some parts of New Mexico where there are many Indian kivas), and the water surface inside the chamber gives very high readings indeed. Steele, too, has experienced a similar effect at a mildly radioactive spring with legendary associations in North Bimini in the Caribbean; after drinking and bathing there, he and his colleagues were overcome with sleep. (There were other mind-affecting chemicals in the water, too.) Other tentative items of evidence suggest a certain sleepy state (and thus ELF-equivalent brain rhythm frequencies) can be induced by heightened natural radiation.[38]

Natural ionizing radiation may be only a factor in the undoubtedly calming effect experienced at virtually all undisturbed sacred wells; at such places one is close to a powerful body of underground water, and this in itself may have fields which have an effect.

Old holy wells and springs are traditional interfaces with the Earth spirit, and this can usually be almost palpably felt at such places; they are truly sacred locations. It would be a gross violation to carry out noisy or even physically energetic rituals or ceremonial activities at them. Dreaming is ideal for such sites; if the dreams of Earth can be dreamt anywhere, it is at these sacred waters. Drink the water at the spring or well, then curl up and go to sleep near the point of issue, after invoking the *anima mundi*. At these sites more than anywhere else it is appropriate to visualize the Earth spirit as a goddess figure, because, as J.C. Cooper observes, sacred waters are traditionally 'symbolic of the Great Mother, and associated with birth, the feminine principle, the universal womb, the *prima materia*, the waters of fertility and refreshment and the fountain of life'.[39]

It is interesting in this respect to note that many, if not all, of the more reliable instances of Marian visions, the supposed appearances of the Virgin Mary, have been at places associated with water. At Lourdes, in 1858, Bernadette Soubirous was seen on one of the visionary occasions scrabbling in the dirt in the grotto, putting earth in her mouth until she retched. She did this until she found mud rather than soil, then ate some leaves of a nearby plant. The onlookers were mystified, until a spring erupted from the disturbed ground. In two days this water was issuing at the rate of 18 gallons a day, and became the 'Lourdes water' of healing fame. Bernadette explained that the visionary Virgin (whom no one else saw) had pointed at the ground and instructed her to 'Go and drink at the spring and wash yourself in it'. When the mud patch had been found, she had been commanded to 'Go and eat that plant there'.[40] (It would be intriguing to find out if the leaves had hallucinogenic properties.) The grotto itself was also located by a stream. This seems to have been a geographically dependent event where an individual gained direct, interactive communication with the Earth field and obtained specific information.

Another example of water connections with Marian visions comes from La Salette in France. In September 1846 a young girl and boy noticed a bright light near a stream on a rocky hillside. They saw 'a lady in the light' who, after communicating with the children (giving specific prophecies of local significance which were borne out), slowly dissolved from the head downwards leaving just 'a brightness in the air' which soon vanished. Not only did the Virgin appear beside a stream, but after the vision another stream formed from a spring 'that started flowing out of season' and came to be regarded as having healing properties. It is perhaps not without significance that the children had slept prior to the vision, which occurred in the afternoon, following a lunch of rye bread. Rye can be affected by ergot, a powerfully hallucinogenic parasite of the plant, which did get into bread from time to time – in one instance 'turning on' an entire French village!

The 'Blessed Virgin', who is associated with the living spring, the sealed fountain and the sea, is of course a Christianized version of the Great Mother, the Mother Goddess – Gaia.

It must also be noted that the identification of the Virgin Mary in what have become accepted as Marian visions is open to question. At Lourdes, for instance, Bernadette initially claimed that she saw something white which she interpreted as the figure of a woman or girl. At the time she referred to it as 'that thing'. In fact, the first rumour to go around the district was that it was the ghost of a local girl who had recently died. Only later did the vision become settled as the Virgin Mary. Also, at La Salette the children did not give any identification to 'the lady' they saw in the light. White shapes are seen near wells from time to time, and, especially in non-Catholic countries, are usually considered to be ghosts. The majority of the reported spectral figures are female and are often referred to as 'White Lady' ghosts in folklore.

Gaseous, slightly luminous columns – often interpreted as figures by witnesses who are usually frightened and trying to put as much distance as possible between themselves and the phenomena – are quite commonly reported concurrent with outbreaks of light phenomena of the 'earth lights' variety (see Chapter 4), and may well be associated with geological factors such as faulting undergoing mild tectonic stress, as the lights themselves seem to be.[41] There are certainly instances where light phenomena have been seen at wells (which are, of course, frequently associated with faulting) and sometimes both lights and 'ghosts' have been reported at holy well sites. In 1973 a classic case was reported by the vicar and other witnesses at St Mary's, Willesden, in north London. The church was founded in the tenth century and was a major centre of pilgrimage in the Middle Ages, after the Virgin had appeared and caused a spring to flow. In the recent incident, a curious golden radiance which did not cast a shadow appeared within the chapel.

Clearly, holy wells and springs are the very special places of the Goddess, the *anima mundi*, where visions are seen and certain classes of phenomena tend to appear. They are also traditionally associated with dreaming. Francis Hitching has written that in Greece alone more than three hundred early medical centres, where patients experienced healing dreaming, were placed at water sources.[42]

While sacred waters are the perfect type of site for Earth field dreaming, the megalithic enclosures such as dolmens and fogous are less suitable. Enclosures of this sort, it was stated in Chapter 4, if made of granite or located in an appropriate type of geology, can become chambers of concentrated natural radiation. Evidence is beginning to emerge that people who enter such fields tend to have 'time-lapse' experiences, in which people, objects or scenes appear momentarily with complete realism. Although such an environment seems to be highly conducive for tuning into the postulated Earth field, since it gives a springboard to mind-change experience, the prospective shaman needs to choose an altered state in which he is consciously aware. The only suitable kind of dreaming in this situation would be lucid dreaming. Lucid dreaming is when a person becomes conscious within a dream; a certain amount of training is required, but it is not exceptionally difficult. It is a way of achieving out-of-the-body experiences and is also used by occultists to gain access to other levels of consciousness (other frequencies of the field we might say here) and to develop high-level control of their imaginative capabilities.

It has also been mentioned that a hitherto unknown type of light phenomenon has been reliably reported inside sites such as dolmens and fogous. This phenomenon usually takes the form of white pinpoints of light, and moving whorls or strips of soft light on the surface of granite. Light effects such as these might be a result of the heightened background radioactivity in the enclosed spaces; it may be an unfamiliar form of electromagnetism. However, there is some slight evidence (unpublished) to suggest that it may be a totally novel form of energy. Certainly the old megalith builders would have known of this phenomenon and would have considered the lights to be a spirit manifestation. We have to ask ourselves: how do these lights appear when observed in altered states of consciousness? They may, indeed, prove to be a very effective interface with the Earth field once we learn how to use them.

LIGHTS OF THE WORLD

The kind of 'interfacing' work outlined above can only be carried out by an individual or, preferably, small groups of people who may in time produce findings that become applicable on a much broader level. There is, however, a primordial energy aspect to the landscape, one that some ancient sacred places may relate to, that is ready now for the 'big science' approach. This energy is the light phenomena that Earth produces from its body. As we have noted, these 'earth lights' haunt specific terrains: faulted geology, mountain peaks and ridges, bodies of water and areas of mineral deposits.

In the United States, more than a hundred regions have been identified where such lights appear. Often called 'ghostlights', some are definitely misperceptions of distant car headlights, but others are undoubtedly authentic. Around Marfa in southwest Texas, for example, light phenomena centred on the Chinati Mountains have been recorded regularly since the first written account was given of them by a white settler, Robert Ellison, in 1883. Ellison thought he was seeing distant Apache campfires – until they started moving around. The lights skip over the prairie. Geologists have chased them at close quarters in jeeps, people have seen them from the roads in the region, and they have been photographed. They are typically 'baseball sized' (as are most earth lights throughout the world) and white, yellowish or orange in colour. They tend to perform aerobatics and have a playful, almost kittenish nature, typical of earth light behaviour everywhere. Like all earth lights, they can spring into existence suddenly, and can change their shape, merge with one another or split into smaller lights. They either 'go out' suddenly or fade away.

Other locations in the United States include Brown Mountain and Maco Station in North Carolina. Since around 1908 there have been arguments about the nature of the Brown Mountain lights, but the latest research suggests that at least a core of phenomena reported in the faulted location are of an earth light type. A single light was reported at Maco Station in the 1860s, but it was joined by another in its regular night-time jaunts in 1873. Both disappeared after an earthquake in 1886, and it was some time before a light reappeared at the spot.

Chicago-based ghost researcher Dale Kaczmarek has debunked at least one ghostlight case, proving it to be a refraction of distant headlights, but claims that a lightball often occurring near Joplin, Missouri, is the real thing. He has photographed it (as have others) and seen it at close quarters as well as through binoculars. He describes it as being 'a diamond-shaped object with a golden hue and a hollow centre. You could actually see trees and bushes right through it. . . . The area where the light was a second ago still glowed with some kind of luminosity or phosphorescence. The area twinkled with energy'. Terrain-related lights have been seen elsewhere in Missouri, in Oklahoma, Virginia, Colorado, Utah, California, Alaska, in the states of New York and Washington, and in many other areas of the USA. One American research group, called Vestigia, claims that almost all the known ghostlight locations occur at or near fault lines.

The first association between anomalous lights and faulting seems to have been made by French researcher F. Lagarde in the 1960s, although the famous American collector of anomalies, Charles Fort, had noted the curious coincidence between some earthquake activity and the apearance of unusual aerial light phenomena at around the turn of the century, and Italian geoscientist I. Galli had recorded the occurrence of lights at the time of earthquakes even earlier.

It is now widely accepted in scientific circles that the Earth can produce unusual lights in association with some earthquakes (earthquake lights or EQLs) and also in conjunction with some electrical storms (ball lightning). EQLs are similar to the balls, glowing effects and columns of light that are seen from time to time around certain mountains, ridges and hills. Sometimes called 'mountain peak discharge' or MPD, these lights are so far unexplained, and while they have some electrical characteristics they have other properties (such as the ability to pass through metal screens without discharging) that are novel and difficult to explain within the laws of electromagnetism. They are clear evidence that nature can produce variously shaped, multicoloured, mobile bodies of light. These phenomena are close relatives of earth lights, the main distinction being that the terrain-related phenomena do not appear only in conjunction with an earthquake or thunderstorm.

Professor Michael Persinger has suggested[43] that the source of energy producing the earth lights type of phenomenon may be low-level tectonic stress within the Earth's crust at certain points. Fields of this stress may cross certain regions during mild flexing of the local geology at certain times. This may show up as a small or medium-sized earthquake where the crust gives way a little – typically at faulting – but in more resistant parts of the geology powerful electromagnetic fields build up, sometimes resulting in the manifestation of light phenomena. The exact mechanisms whereby this happens are not yet understood, and entirely new areas of geophysics may yet await discovery. Persinger likens the effect to one seen in meteorology: the energy normally dispersed through the atmosphere produces gentle breezes and winds, but given certain circumstances that same energy can build up into the terrific vortex of force we call a tornado. Features typical of earth light zones are faulting, ore deposits, and bodies of water (the lights have long been noted to hover around lakes, reservoirs, and sometimes streams and waterfalls). Often they are places with a history of moderate earthquake activity.

Persinger and John Derr of the US Geological Survey have found this theory to be well borne out by detailed studies of particular areas, such as the Yakima Indian Reservation in Washington State. In the 1970s there were outbreaks of light phenomena[44] at the reservation which took the form of fiery lightballs, glowing effects and flashes, and curious luminescent clouds. Subterranean rumbling was also frequently reported. The lights were well observed by multiple witnesses and photographs were also obtained. The phenomena tended to congregate around the multifaulted Toppenish Ridge, which snakes across the reservation. Moreover, the Yakima Reservation is on the eastern flanks of the Cascades Mountains, near where Kenneth Arnold saw his famous 'flying disks' in 1947, effectively triggering off interest in 'flying saucers' and UFOs. (Arnold never did think his disks were extraterrestrial, incidentally.) The Cascades are of great geological significance. They are on the margin of tectonic plates – great slabs of the Earth's crust floating on semi-molten magma – which are prone to seismic activity. This was shown by the eruption of Mount St Helens in 1980.

Another region studied by Persinger and Derr was the Uintah Basin of northeast Utah. This zone experienced a 'UFO flap' also in the 1970s. Again, balls and ovoids of light were seen, and globes that seemed to have a metallic sheen were observed in daylight. Derr and Persinger made their studies in 1985[45] and found strong evidence to support the tectonic strain hypothesis.

Similar evidence has been forthcoming from work carried out in Britain and Scandinavia. In Britain, earth light zones have been located in parts of the Pennines, around Burton Dassett in Warwickshire, around Helpston in Cambridgeshire, on Dartmoor in Devon, in selected regions of Wales, at specific lochs in Scotland and at many other well-defined locales. In the Pennines a small research group called Project Pennine, headed by David Clarke and Andy Roberts, have unearthed remarkable accounts of phenomena occurring in the same regions over generations. Balls of light have been observed repeatedly, and occasionally in a faulted valley called Longdendale, which contains a chain of reservoirs, a whole hillside lights up! A severe drop in temperature has been noted to coincide with this latter kind of light effect. Local people in the sparsely inhabited Pennines are loath to talk of the phenomena, but it is clear that the parents and grandparents of the present-day farmers and shepherds also saw the lights and viewed them with great superstition and fear. Legends, place names and traditions also record the existence of lights in the areas known to be affected by the phenomena.

In one of these zones, the wild moorlands around Grassington in Yorkshire, many police officers have seen the lights during their night-time patrols, and some extraordinary photographs have been taken. Clarke and Roberts have been able to show correlations between light phenomena, faulting and seismic activity. In Wales, Devereux and colleagues have also been able to correlate certain earth light zones with similar geological factors, and in Scotland seven of the eight lochs involved with light phenomena events have been shown to be on major faulting, the eighth being affected by lesser, local faulting. The British material includes numerous eyewitness accounts of lights that have emerged directly from the ground.

In Norway, the remote valley of Hessdalen near the border with Sweden underwent a tremendous outbreak of lights in the early 1980s (there is also evidence of low-level occurrence of such phenomena in preceding and following years). A brave effort in appalling winter conditions was made by a Norwegian-Swedish UFO research team, and photography, visual observation, and instrumental monitoring of various kinds was achieved during actual occurrence of light phenomena. Several hundred photographs now exist of the Hessdalen phenomena. Hessdalen is faulted, has low-level tremor activity, and has noteworthy mineral deposits. In Sweden, excellent work has been done, notably by Dan Mattsson, in identifying several 'windows' of light phenomena activity.[46,47] Here, too, strong correlations between seismic activity, iron ore and other deposits and faulting have been made.

Research has shown similar earth light zones or windows throughout the world. (Thorough and highly referenced documentation of all the earth lights locations mentioned in this chapter, and many more besides, appears in *Earth Lights Revelation*[48] along with details of research and evidence.) In many countries there are certain areas of valleys, mountains, hills, prairies, deserts or moorlands where over long periods of time curious lights quietly and sporadically pop out of the ground and drift into the air or sputter and dissolve. It is going on somewhere on Earth all the time. Every so often there is a sudden flare-up of activity at one of these spots, or a new one fleetingly appears for a few days, weeks or months, and we have a 'UFO flap'.

It has already been suggested that the modern idea of these things being extraterrestrial may simply be symptomatic of the modern condition, Earth blindness, which is manifesting itself in so many ways. It is only since World War II that we have associated such lights with extraterrestrial sources, an approach significantly coincidental with our own stage of technological development. Prior to that time the frames of reference were different, and we can see interpretations such as unknown foreign aircraft, mystery enemy technology (during periods of war), airships, strange meteors, spirits, portents, signs from God, and so on, depending how far back in time one goes. One of the most enduring interpretations was that the lights were dragons which rose from caverns deep within the earth and flew through the air exhaling fiery breath. This explanation was disputed from at least the thirteenth century, when Albertus Magnius considered the dragon idea to be 'impossible'; he thought the mysterious fiery lights were 'vapours' burning in the air, issuing smoke which was misperceived as dragon wings by 'ignorant people'. In 1590 Christopher Hill felt that the luminous flying dragon was in fact a 'fume kindled'. But as late as 1792 curious aerial lights seen over part of Scotland were considered by the country people to be dragons, according to the diary of a local clergyman.

Today, people tend either to disbelieve in the lights altogether – a subjective view greatly enhanced by not having witnessed one of them – or consider them to be craft from outer space. These polarized attitudes have hopelessly hindered the study of this remarkable energy phenomenon. There is some justification for the sceptical view; most UFO reports originate from mundane objects being misperceived, from hoaxes and from people with psychosocial problems who subconsciously fantasize UFO sightings or more complex encounters. But there is no justification for a total dismissal of the phenomenon, especially now that specific locations have been identified where there is a high incidence of light phenomena.

While there may or may not be extraterrestrial craft visiting us, earth lights definitely do exist. But three aspects of the lights make those preferring UFO explanations feel they cannot accept the terrestrial origin of the phenomena. One is that on some occasions aerial lights are seen to travel for some distance over the landscape (a rarer type of report than one might think). In fact, earth lights are known to do this. To give an example, in April 1905 near Llangollen in Wales, three vicars standing on an acqueduct over the River Dee (close by the Aqueduct Fault) saw blue-white balls of light emerge from the ground; most of the balls flickered and 'burst luridly', but in a few instances the lights stabilized themselves, grew more brilliant, then flew off out of sight.

A second concern of spaceship aficionados is that the earth light idea does not explain 'daylight disks' seemingly made of metal. Seventy per cent or more of all UFO reports in fact refer to light phenomena only, very few to metallic objects. But the nature of the energy forming the lights might well appear metallic in daylight conditions; plasma, for example, can take on the false appearance of a metallic sheen when seen in daylight. Also, refractive effects can occur between a medium and whatever it is suspended in – air bubbles in water, for instance, appear to have silvery surfaces.

Finally, there are the reported cases of what appear to be definite craft, humanoid entities and abductions. These are a tiny minority of all reports, but because of their sensational aspects they are widely discussed in the press. The American UFO researcher John Keel long ago noticed, however, that every craft-like object that is seen at some stage exhibits non-solid characteristics.

Persinger has published a paper[49] on the possible effects that proximity to a light phenomenon might have on the brain-functioning of a witness. Assuming that there is some form of electromagnetic field around the lights, or perhaps in the immediate locale concurrent with the appearance of the lights, he draws on known clinical effects of such fields on the temporal lobe regions of the brain (which include the hippocampus). All the reported effects on close-encounter witnesses – time loss (which is, of course, amnesia), remarkable visions (while the subject is in waking consciousness), externalized voices, bodily sensations (especially round the genital area in certain field conditions), and even sensations of 'floating' (many abductees say they are 'floated' towards the spacecraft) – can be experimentally reproduced. Electromagnetic interference of the hippocampus region can also create minor distortions in recalled memory, both after and just prior to the disturbance itself. The natural electrochemical status of a witness's brain will also be a determining factor in his or her response to the fields surrounding a luminosity. The existence of such experimental, clinical material is virtually unknown to critics of the terrestrial origin of light phenomena. Another powerful clue that close-encounter witnesses have in fact experienced an involuntary altered state is the strong similarity between reports of abduction experiences and those of out-of-the-body and near death episodes. Persinger catalogues the variable mind-change experience of close-encounter witnesses in terms of increasing order of proximity to a light phenomenon. The key factor is that the lights can cause altered states.

It is possible that the image-producing capacity of the lights may account for some close encounter 'fairy' cases, too. The famous occultist W.E. Butler told author Mike Howard that once when he and his wife were walking in Hampshire, in the South of England, they came across an old stone. Butler's wife, a natural psychic, saw a guardian fairy at the rock, while Butler himself saw only a sphere of light.

Some witnesses have come very close to earth lights without seeming to suffer any adverse effects, while others have incurred severe amnesia and even skin burns. This variability may have something to do with the frequency at which the lights are operating. Similar variability has been noted with ball lightning. Certainly, some earth lights have singed or burned the vegetation around where they have appeared.

As we have seen, earth lights have always been viewed through the prevailing conceptual filters of the times, and the modern extraterrestrial notions are no worse (but no better) than many that have gone before. However, there is no reason why those who feel the need to hold on to the extraterrestrial concept cannot at the same time appreciate the importance of terrain-related light phenomena.

Traditional societies have never doubted that the lights are terrestrial, although sometimes of the order that AE referred to as 'supernature'. American Indians of the Cascades area, the Snohomish, claim that the lights are gateways to the 'other world'. Some of the Yakima Indians, whose reservation played host to the considerable light phenomena of the 1970s mentioned above, told researcher Bill Rudersdorf that the lights – their number, colour, direction of flight and so on – are used for divination, in the same way that the Etruscan augurs used bird flight. In California, some Indians have a tradition relating to a ball of light called the 'spirit-eater' – it was not wise to get too close to it. A similar tradition exists around Darjeeling in India, where the lights are thought to be the lanterns of the *chota-admis* or 'little men'. Illness or death will ensue if they are approached too closely. In Malaysia they are called *pennangal* – spectral, disembodied heads. At the turn of the century, a British government official witnessed these lights playing around a hill called Changkat Asah for a whole night. The hill also had a rock on it that lit up at times; the local people called it *bilek hantu* – a 'spirit room'. The *pennangal* flew close to the ground, twirled lazily up in the air to great heights and also darted and swooped. The official said they were round in front and tapered away slightly at the rear. This is a typical 'tadpole' shape often commented on by witnesses around the world. The Japanese had similarly shaped luminous spirits called *shito-darma*. In Hawaii, there are the *Akualele* – flying spirits or gods. The Australian Aborigines have their Min Min lights, which are viewed as spirits of the ancestors or of evil sorcerers. Some Eskimo tribes consider the lights to be sent out by evil magicians. The Lapps thought they were the weapons of rival shamans (and said much the same thing about the aurora borealis). The Penobscot Indians also felt that the lights could be the spirits of shamans, but sometimes they could be *eskuda'hit*, or 'fire creatures'.

In old Europe, folklore reveals that lights could be seen as omens (usually of death), spirits of the dead, or, particularly in Germany and Denmark, as 'treasure lights' – globes of light marking the location of hidden riches. This may come from the tradition noted in Chapter 4 that lights hovering above or emerging from the ground marked the position of substantial veins of metal. This mining belief was widespread and included Britain, where it has been noticed that old lead mines often figure in modern reports of lightball events.

If the lights appear in specific areas because of some association with geological factors present in those places, it might be expected that laboratory evidence of such lights could be achieved. In fact, there is no doubt that odd lights are noted in various experiments where rock samples are placed under stress and fractured, representing on a miniature scale what happens in the actual body of the Earth. For example, during experiments with pieces of granite in a rock-crushing machine, Devereux has witnessed orange balls of light, hazy glowing mists and, on one occasion, a small, glittering blue light executing precise geometrical curves through space.

In the light of the traditional wisdom that life was born of Earth, a paper published in *Nature* in 1986[50] is of great interest. The paper describes how Brian Brady of the US Bureau of Mines, together with Glen Rowell, carried out some sophisticated rock-crushing experiments using image intensifiers and spectroscopes. They noted lights that could be explained as well as light phenomena that could not be so readily identified. The lights occurred in air, in near vacuum conditions, in selected gases and . . . under water. Brady and Rowell noted chemical changes in the water caused by the light phenomena which led them to hint that here could be another energy candidate for biogenesis – the origins of life on Earth. Current theories suggest that the pre-Cambrian soups were energized by lightning causing the formation of amino acid chains, or that bacterial forms may have come to Earth on meteoric or comet fragments. If Brady and Rowell are correct in their suspicion, then it would be the body of the Earth itself, the rocks, which gave birth to life. Mythically, this is the most satisfying theory. The lights, far from being extraterrestrial, may be our own ancestor lights.

It was stated in Chapter 4 that in Britain certain ancient sites have been found to occupy landscapes with the same geological characteristics that produce earth lights. Certainly lights have been observed playing around stone circle sites and at other types of ancient sacred places around the world.[51] To give just a few examples, balls of white light were seen playing above the Castlerigg stone circle in the English Lake District in 1919; lights seen over prehistoric earthworked hills in Ireland are referred to there as fairy lights; luminous phenomena occurring around their burial cairns were called *haug-eldir* by the Vikings; lightballs have been seen encircling Himalayan temples; on the southernmost peak of Wu T'ai Shan in China, a temple was built specially for viewing light phenomena; and lightballs and magnetic anomalies have been noted amongst the mysterious lines on the pampas at Nasca in Peru. Also, many of the holy hills and mountains around the world – Mount Shasta in California, for instance, and Glastonbury Tor in England – produce strange lights.

Although geophysical factors are undoubtedly involved in the manifestation of earth lights, the phenomena are not simply 'balls of electricity'. They do possess some electromagnetic characteristics, but also others that are exotic and extraordinary. They seem to hover on the very edge of normal physical reality. While eyewitnesses were tracking the course of one light over Hessdalen, for instance, the radar signal blipped on and off rapidly, although to the naked eye the light seemed to be continuous. Some reports exist of lightballs that can be seen from certain angles but not from others. In a report of one of the Pennine lights, the witness, a farmer, watched an orange light hovering over a stream and felt that it was somehow not occupying three dimensional space correctly. The countless reports of the shapes and behaviour of light phenomena point to something beyond our present understanding of physics.

There are even more weird aspects. It is quite common in an area where there is an intense outbreak of lights for various psychic effects, such as poltergeists, to appear. This aspect is virtually unresearched. But perhaps the most telling, and most resisted, quality of the lights is that some of them seem to display intelligence. They often seem inquisitive in a playful sort of way. They will approach people and move round them. Witnesses often feel the phenomenon is somehow watching them. Two geologists who chased two lights across Mitchell Flat near Marfa, Texas, felt that the luminous balls were playing tag with them. Biologist Frank Salisbury noted in his study of the Uintah events that 'many witnesses reported the feeling that the UFOs seemed to *react* to their actions or even their thoughts. . . . Reactions to thoughts would be difficult to prove. . . . Nevertheless, there are many cases in which some action taken by the observer . . . resulted in rapid departure of the UFO. This seems to be a clearly discernable pattern'.[52] Members of the Hessdalen team told Devereux they were convinced that a certain percentage of the lights they had seen were able to respond to thoughts, whispered comments between team members, or slight actions (such as lifting a camera). In precisely the same manner, Dr Harley Rutledge, who led a university team to study a 'flap' at Piedmont, Missouri, in the 1970s, felt that a certain percentage of the lights they saw, and frequently photographed, reacted to him and his team members. 'A relationship, a cognisance' was set up between the observers and the lights, Rutledge felt. 'A game was played.' It was an aspect that 'perturbed' him and he had 'thought about it every day' since.[53] Police sergeant Tony Dodd, who has seen many lights on the moors around Grassington in Yorkshire, told Devereux that he and some of his colleagues had noted that the lights would come towards their police cars if they switched on their flashing roof beacons. Such anecdotes are legion.

If we are not prepared to accept that the lights harbour tiny, telepathic extraterrestrial pilots, or are drones piloted telepathically from some remote mother ship, we have to start thinking that the phenomena themselves are intelligent or at least sensitive to consciousness. Perhaps we are looking at a type of energy that forms a direct interface with the Earth field, the *chi* of the planet, as much a part of the field of consciousness as it is part of electromagnetic fields.

In the context of the idea being explored in this book, it would seem certain that an important part of research would be to locate such lights and attempt interaction with them. As we have noted, they can be seen by multiple witnesses, they can be photographed, and they can leave physical traces. For these reasons they are accessible to the 'big science' approach in the way the other areas of research suggested on earlier pages are not, as yet. For what would be a pittance in normal scientific funding terms, it should be eminently possible to establish to the satisfaction of mainstream thought that these lights do indeed exist.

But mainstream science says the lights do not exist – so why waste money on useless research? At the same time, ufologists argue amongst themselves whether 'UFOs' are simply the product of psychosocial effects or come from outer space, while in the actual places where light phenomena regularly occur, local people are too embarrassed to talk about them to outsiders, treat it all as something that should be kept secret, or think nothing of them. So between the scientists, the ufologists and the local people, these most remarkable and unexpected manifestations of our planet shimmer and gleam away almost unnoticed.

'*THIS IMPERISHABLE TABLET*'

We may have to await better days for this phenomenon, perhaps an actual expression of the Earth field itself, to be properly studied by mainstream science, but the question is: do we have the time to wait?

If we are to put a halt to the destruction of our planet, we – the present generation – need to find out soon whether communication between human and planetary consciousness is truly a possibility. If contact can be made, and if it can be a conscious, interactive contact, we shall have to learn how to interpret the information that Earth itself may give us. Above all, we may learn to respect our planet once more.

Even if mainstream science will not co-operate, we must urgently attempt to create a new shamanism. This is not just wishful thinking. At the time of writing, the Dragon Project Trust and a small group of researchers covering many areas of expertise, are already starting work on a research scheme that is based on traditional methods used by ancient peoples but filtered through the understanding and language of disciplines such as geophysics, psychology, biology and quantum physics. In a sense this is in keeping with AE's dream that the Earth's memory, 'the imperishable tablet', should become the subject of a 'training in seership' which would lead to 'a revolution in human knowledge'. The new shamanism will be one that can speak to our age; the knowledge itself, the wisdom, is perennial.

Quite simply, we literally have to sit down and talk once more with this immense being, Earth, whom we have almost forgotten how to recognize. The conversation will be about old times, and where we go from here.

REFERENCES

CHAPTER ONE

1. Puharich, Andrija, *Beyond Telepathy*, Doubleday, 1962. See Chapter 5, 'The Memory Capacity of Objects'.
2. Hughes, J. Donald, *American Indian Ecology*, Texas Western Press, 1983.
3. Quoted from Steiner, Stan, *The Vanishing White Man*, Harper and Row, 1976.
4. Quoted from de Wit, Dorothy, ed. *The Talking Stone*, Greenwillow Books, 1979.
5. Watson, Lyall, *Lightning Bird*, Hodder and Stoughton, 1982.
6. Hughes, J. Donald, *op. cit.*
7. Quoted from Rothenberg, Jerome, ed. *Shaking the Pumpkin*, Doubleday, 1972.
8. McKenna, Terence. Quoted from lecture 'Vision Quest through Sacred Plants' presented at the International Transpersonal Conference, October 15, 1988, Santa Rosa, California.
9. Thomas, Lewis, 'Debating the Unknowable: When the Scientific Method Won't Work'. *Proceedings of the Conference 'Is the Earth a Living Organism?'* (August 1–6, 1985) held at the University of Massachusetts, Amherst. Published by the National Audubon Society Expedition Institute, Sharon, Connecticut, 1985.
10. Levy-Bruhl, Lucien, *Primitive Mentality*, Macmillan, New York, 1923.
11. Jung, Carl. Commentary on 'The Secret of the Golden Flower' in *The Collected Works*, Vol. 13, Bollingen Series XX, Pantheon Books, 1962.
12. Quoted from Opler, Morris, 'Myths and Tales of the Jicarilla Apache Indians', 1938. *Memoirs of the American Folklore Society*, Vol. 31.
13. Metzner, Ralph. Quoted from lecture 'Shamanism Before and Beyond History', presented at the Ojai Foundation, California, October 4–5, 1988.
14. Lawrence, D.H., *Studies in Classical American Literature*, Thomas Seltzer, 1923.
15. Eliade, Mircea, *Myths, Dreams and Mysteries*, Harper and Brothers, 1960.
16. McKenna, Terence, *The Invisible Landscape*, Seabury Press, 1975.
17. McKenna, Terence. Quoted from lecture 'Vision Quest through Sacred Plants', *op. cit.*
18. Duerr, Hans Peter, *Dreamtime*, Blackwell, 1985.

19. Quoted from Breeden, Stanley, 'The First Australians', *National Geographic*, February 1988.
20. *ibid.*
21. Quoted from Eliade, Mircea, *Australian Religions: An Introduction*, Cornell University Press, 1973.
22. *ibid.*
23. Chatwin, Bruce, *The Songlines*, Penguin Books, New York, 1987.
24. Van der Post, Laurens, *The Heart of the Hunter*, William Morrow, 1961.
25. *ibid.*
26. *Techqua Ikachi* (Land and Life), 1978. No. 13, Hotevilla, Arizona.
27. Whorf, Benjamin Lee, *Language, Thought and Reality*, MIT Press, 1956.
28. Hughes, J. Donald, *op. cit.*
29. Cochrane, Hugh, *Gateway to Oblivion*, W.H. Allen, 1981.
30. Price, Joan, 'The Earth Is Alive and Running Out of Breath' in *ReVision*, Winter/Spring 1987.
31. Quoted from Hobson, Geary, ed. *The Remembered Earth*, University of New Mexico Press, 1981.
32. Quoted from Hughes, J. Donald, *op. cit.*
33. Van der Post, Laurens, *op. cit.*
34. Hughes, J. Donald, *op. cit.*
35. *ibid.*
36. Zak, Nancy, 'Sacred and Legendary Women of Native America: Their Relationship to the Earth Mother' in *Proceedings of the Conference 'Is the Earth a Living Organism?'*, *op. cit.*
37. Walker, Barbara, *The Women's Encyclopedia of Myths and Secrets*, Harper and Row, 1983.
38. Stone, Merlin, *When God was a Woman*, Harvest Brace and Jovanovich, 1976.
39. Gimbutas, Marija. Quoted from lecture 'Ancient Goddesses – Faces of the Feminine', presented November 8, 1985, at the Ojai Foundation, California.
40. *ibid.*
41. Gimbutas, Marija, 'The Earth Fertility Goddess of Old Europe', *Dialogues D'Histoire Ancienne*, No. 13, 1987.
42. *ibid.*
43. Dames, Michael, *The Silbury Treasure: The Great Goddess Rediscovered*, Thames and Hudson, 1976.
44. Gimbutas, Marija, 'The Gift of the Goddess Returning', presented May 1985 at the Ojai Foundation, California.
45. Gimbutas, Marija, personal communication, January 1989.
46. Levy, Gertrude Rachel, *The Gate of Horn*, Faber and Faber, 1948.

47. Eliade, Mircea, *Myths, Dreams and Mysteries, op. cit.*
48. Gimbutas, Marija, 'The Earth Fertility Goddess of Old Europe', *op. cit.*
49. Gimbutas, Marija, 'The Three Waves of the Kurgan People into Old Europe, 4500–2500 B.C.', *Archives Suisse D'Anthropologies Generale,* Vol. 43, No. 2, 1979.
50. *ibid.*
51. *ibid.*
52. Eisler, Riane, *The Chalice and The Blade,* Harper and Row, 1987.
53. Walker, Barbara, *op. cit.*
54. Gadon, Eleanor, 'Sacred Places of India'. Lecture presented at the 'Spirit of Place' Symposium, University of California, Davis, September 8–11, 1988.
55. Bateson, Gregory, *Mind and Nature,* Dutton, 1979.
56. Mookerjee, Ajit, *Kali,* Destiny Books, 1988.
57. *ibid.*
58. *ibid.*
59. Lorca, Federico Garcia, 'The Duende: Theory and Divertissement' in *Poet in New York,* Grove Press, 1955.
60. Quoted from Kopp, J.A., 'The Present Status of Scientific Research on Soil Radiations', *Transactions of the Swiss Society of Science,* 1970.
61. Eitel, Rev. E.J., *Feng Shui,* Cokaygne Press, 1973.
62. Stone, Merlin, *op. cit.*
63. Reymond, E.A.E., *The Mythical Origin of the Egyptian Temple,* 1969. Manchester University Press, Barnes & Noble, New York.
64. *ibid.*
65. *ibid.*
66. *ibid.*
67. *ibid.*
68. *ibid.*
69. *ibid.*
70. Grossinger, Richard, ed. 'Alchemy: pre-Egyptian Legacy, Millennial Promise' in the *Alchemical Tradition in the Late Twentieth Century,* North Atlantic Books, 1983.
71. Gimbutas, Marija, personal communication, February 1989.
72. Quoted in Grossinger, *op. cit.*
73. Grossinger, *ibid.*
74. Sperling, Harry, and Simon, Maurice, translators, *The Zohar,* Tol'Doth, Vol. 2, Soncino Press, 1984.
75. Quoted in Eliade, Mircea, *Cosmos and History,* Garland Publishing, 1985.
76. Walker, Barbara, *op. cit.*

77. Matt, Daniel. Quoted from lecture 'The Shekinah' presented at 'The Goddess and the Living Earth' Conference, April 1988, California Institute of Integral Studies, San Francisco.

78. Berman, Morris, *The Re-enchantment of the World*, Bantam Books, 1984.

79. Hertz, Dr J.H., ed. Exodus III, 5, Quoted in *The Pentateuch and Haftorahs*, Soncino Press, 1971.

80. Also known as the Mount of Myrrh or the Mount of Awe of God, the same place where Abraham prepared to sacrifice his son Isaac.

81. Weissman, Rabbi Moshe, 'Vayaitzay' in *The Midrash Says*, Benei Yakov Publications, 1980. According to the oral tradition of the Torah, Jacob actually went to sleep on 12 stones as a pillow, each stone crying out, 'I want the tzaddik (holy man) to rest his head on me.' During the night all the small stones merged into a single large stone.

82. Hertz, Dr J.H., *op. cit.* Genesis XXVIII, 17.

83. Kirk, G.S. and Raven, J.E., Theogony, 116 in *The Presocratic Philosophers*, Cambridge University Press, 1960.

84. Evelyn-White, Hugh G., translator, *Homeric Hymns*, The Loeb Classical Library, 1914.

85. Eisler, *op. cit.*

86. Kirk, G.S. and Raven, J.E., *op. cit.*

87. Precope, John, *Hippocrates on Diet and Hygiene*, Zeno, 1952.

88. Kirk, G.S. and Raven, J.E. *op. cit.*

89. Plato, *Timaeus* 30D. Quoted from Hughes, J. Donald, 'Man and Gaia, A Classical View', *The Ecologist*, Vol. 13, No. 2/3, 1983.

90. Plato, *Philebus* 29A–30A. Quoted from Hughes, J. Donald, *ibid.*

91. Plato, *Laws.* Quoted from Hughes, J. Donald, 'History of the Spirit of Place in the West'; lecture presented at 'The Spirit of Place' Symposium, *op. cit.*

92. *Republic* 414E. Quoted from Hughes, J. Donald, 'Mother Gaia, An Ancient View of Earth', *Omnibus* (London), No. 8, November 1984.

93. Hughes, J. Donald, 'History of the Spirit of Place in the West', *op. cit.*

94. Hughes, J. Donald, 'Mother Gaia, An Ancient View of Earth'. *op. cit.*

95. Walker, Barbara, *op. cit.*

96. Rose, H.J., *Religion in Greece and Rome*, Harper & Brothers, 1959.

97. *ibid.*

98. *ibid.*

99. LaChapelle, Dolores, 'Sacred Land, Sacred Sex' in Tobias, M., ed., *Deep Ecology*, Avant Books, 1984.

100. Talland, George, *Deranged Memory*, Academic Press, 1965.

101. Plutarch, *On the Decline of Oracles*, 419B–420A, Loeb Classical Library, V. 5, Heinemann, 1936.

CHAPTER TWO

1. See Evans, Arthur, *The God of Ecstacy. Sex Roles and the madness of Dionysos*, St. Martin's Press, 1988; Pagels, Elaine, *The Gnostic Gospels*, Vintage, 1981; Mylonos, George E., *Eleusis and the Eleusian Mysteries*, Princeton University, 1961, appendix; Cumont, Franz, *The Oriental Religions in Roman Paganism*, Dover, 1956.

2. Augustine, *Concerning the City of God against the Pagans*, transl. Henry Bettenson, ed. David Knowles, Penguin Books, New York, 1981.

3. *ibid.*; Fox, Matthew, O.P., 'Creation-Centered Spirituality from Hildegard of Bingen to Julian of Norwich. 300 Years of an Ecological Spirituality in the West', in *Cry of the Environment*, ed. Joranson and Bukigan, Bear and Co, 1984; Gilson, Etienne, *History of Christian Philosophy in the Middle Ages*, Random House, 1955.

4. *Phoenix Fire Mysteries. An East-West Dialogue on Death and Rebirth...* (Compiled and ed.) Head, Joseph, and Cranston, S.L., Crown, 1977.

5. Grinsell, Leslie V., *Folklore of Prehistoric Sites in Britain*, David & Charles, 1976; Michell, John, *The View Over Atlantis*, Sago Press, 1969; Thomas, Keith, *Religion and the Decline of Magic*, Charles Scribner's Sons, 1971.

6. Grinsell, *op. cit.*

7. Examples can be found as late as the nineteenth century (and probably into the present century). See Duerr, Hans Peter, *Dreamtime*, Blackwell, 1985; Bord, Janet and Colin, *Earth Rites. Fertility Practices in Pre-Industrial Britain*, Granada, 1982; Grinsell, *op. cit.*; Borlase, William, *Antiquities, Historical and Monumental, of the County of Cornwall*, London, 1769.

8. *Meditations with Hildegard of Bingen*, transl. by Uhlein, Gabriele, OSF, Bear and Co., 1983.

9. Hildegardis: *Scivias* quoted in Fox, Matthew, *op. cit.*

10. Duerr, *op. cit.*

11. Quoted in Boorstin, Daniel J., *The Discoverers*, Vintage, 1985.

12. Evans, Joan, *Magical Jewels of the Middle Ages and the Renaissance, Particularly in England* (Oxford, 1922), Dover edition, 1976.

13. Assorted sources have been helpful, for example: Sodoul, Jacques, *Alchemists and Gold*, transl. by Sieveking, Olga, G.P. Putnam's Sons, 1972: Cockren, A., *Alchemy Rediscovered and Restored*, Mokelumne Hill, California, Health Research, reprinted 1963; Burland, C.A., *The Arts of the Alchemists*, Weidenfeld & Nicolson, 1967; Klossowski de Rola, Stanislas, *Alchemy the Secret Art*, Bounty Books, 1973; Sherwood Taylor, F., *The Alchemists*, Collier, 1962; Burkhardt, Titus, *Science of The Cosmos*,

Science of the Soul, Penguin Books, 1971; Reed, John, *Through Alchemy to Chemistry, A Procession of Ideas and Personalities*, Harper & Row, 1963; Eliade, Mircea, *The Forge and the Crucible*, transl. by Corrin, Stephen, Harper & Row, 1962; Berman, Morris, *The Re-enchantment of the World*, Cornell University Press, 1981; Debus, Allen G., *The English Paracelsians*, Oldbourne Book Co. Ltd., 1965. See also Debus, *The Chemical Dream of the Renaissance*, W. Heffer and Sons Ltd., Cambridge, 1968; Ashmole, Elias, ed. *Theatrum Chemicum Britannicum . . .* (1652), ed. Debus, Allen G., reprint Johnson Reprint Corp., 1967; Merchant, Carolyn, *The Death of Nature. Women, Ecology and the Scientific Revolution*, Harper & Row, 1980.

14. Economou, George, *The Goddess Natura in Medieval Literature*, Harvard University Press, 1972.

15. I am greatly indebted to Ms Anne Brannen both for drawing my attention to this text and for her interpretation of it. The work is found in *Middle English Literature*, ed. Dunn, Charles W., and Byrnes, Edward T., Harcourt Brace Jovanovich Inc., 1973.

16. Bord, Janet and Colin, *op. cit.*

17. Branston, Brian, *The Lost Gods of England*, Oxford Unversity Press, New York, 1974.

18. Warner, Rev. Richard, *Antiquitates Culinariae or Curious Tracts Relating to the Culinary Affairs of the Old English*, London, 1791. See also Bord, Janet and Colin, *op. cit.*

19. Bord, Janet and Colin, *op. cit.*; Branston, *op. cit.*

20. Rice Jr., Eugene, F., *The Foundations of Early Modern Europe*, Norton & Co., 1970.

21. See Merchant, *op. cit.*; Burtt, Edwin Arthur, *The Metaphysical Foundation of Modern Physical Science*, Doubleday Anchor Books, 1954; Dijksterhuis, E.J., *The Mechanization of the World Picture*, transl. by Dikshoorn, C., Clarendon Press, 1961.

22. My descriptions of the turmoil in the English countryside and the various marginal classes owes much to Hill, Christopher, *The World Turned Upside Down. Radical Ideas during the English Revolution*, Viking Press, 1972. Also Burg, B.R., *Sodomy and the Perception of Evil: English Sea Rovers in the Seventeenth Century Caribbean*, New York University Press, 1983. I am grateful to Mr Sean McShee for this reference.

23. Hill, *op. cit.*; Merchant, *op. cit.*

24. *ibid.*; Rosen, George, M.D., *The History of Miners' Diseases. A Medical and Social Interpretation*, Schuman's, 1943.

25. My discussion of coal mining activity draws upon J.U. Nef's classic, *The Rise of the British Coal Industry*, 2 Vols, London, 1932. See also Rosen, *op. cit.*

26. Nef, *op. cit.*; Rosen, *op. cit.*

27. See Nef, *op. cit.*, and Rosen, *op. cit.*

28. Eliade, *op. cit.*

29. Bord, Janet and Colin, *op. cit.*

30. Berman, *op. cit.*; Rosen, *op. cit.*

31. Hill, *op. cit.*

32. Quoted in Merchant, *op. cit.*

33. Agricola, Georg, *de re Metallica*, Dover edition, 1950.

34. Rice, *op. cit.*; Merchant, *op. cit.*

35. Mintz, Samuel, *Sweetness and Power, The Place of Sugar in Modern History*, Penguin, New York, 1986.

36. Merchant, New York, *op. cit.*; Hill, *op. cit.*

37. Hill, *op. cit.*

38. Bord, Janet and Colin, *op. cit.*

39. Debus, *Chemical Dream, op. cit.*; Thomas, *op. cit.*; Hill, *op. cit.*

40. Hill, *op. cit.*; Bailey, Margaret, *Milton and Jakob Boehme, A Study of German Mysticism in Seventeenth Century England*, Oxford University Press, New York, 1914; Thomas, *op. cit.*

41. Rattansi, P.M., 'Paracelsus and the Puritan Revolution', *Ambix* 11, 1963.

42. Kubrin in his 'Newton's Inside Out! Magic, Class Struggle, and the Rise of Mechanisms in the West', in Woolf, Harry, ed. *The Analytic Spirit, Essays on the History of Science in Honor of Henry Guerlac*, Cornell University Press, 1981, has a fuller discussion of why this overlap existed. See also Hudson, Winthrop S., 'Mystical Religion in the Puritan Commonwealth', *Journal of Religion* 28, 1948. The quotation from Vaughan is from (Vaugha) N., (Thoma) S., *Aula Lucis, or the House of Light*, London, 1652. The claim for an earlier appreciation of 'dialectical' logic has been met with scepticism on the part of some scholars, but has been suggested by a number of Marxists and ex-Marxists. See, for example, Needham, Joseph, and Ling, Wang, *Science and Civilization in China*, Cambridge, 1956; Hill, Christopher, *op. cit.*; and Kubrin, 'How Sir Isaac Newton Helped Restore Law 'n' Order to the West', (privately distributed), a copy of which has been placed at the Library of Congress. Also, Morton, A.L., *The Everlasting Gospel. Study in the Sources of William Blake*, Lawrence and Wishart, 1958; Merchant, *op. cit.* See also Mao Tse Tung, 'On Contradiction', *Selected Readings from the Works of Mao Tse Tung*, Peking, 1967.

43. Hill, *op. cit.*

44. This phrase was used by Prof. Allison Coudert. See Hill, *op. cit.*

45. Bord, Janet and Colin, *op. cit.*

46. 'Earth Mother, Worship of', New Catholic Encyclopedia, Vol. 5, McGraw-Hill, 1967–79; Evans, Arthur, *op. cit.*; Duerr, *op. cit.*

47. Evans, *op. cit.*

48. Shapiro, Barbara, *John Wilkins 1614–1672, An Intellectual Biography*, University of California Press, 1969; Wilkins, John, *Vindicaiae Academiarum. . . .* Oxford, 1654; Rattansi, *op. cit.*; Berman, *op. cit.*; Lenoble, Robert, *Mersenne ou la naissance du mechanisme*, Librairie Philosophique, J. Vrin, 1943; Rattner Gelbart, Nina, The Intellectual Development of Walter Charleton, *Ambix* 18, 1971; Merchant, *op. cit.*

49. *The Crisis in Europe 1560–1660*, ed. Aston, Trevor, Routledge & Kegan Paul, 1965.

50. Keill, John, *An Introduction to Natural Philosophy*, Oxford, 1740.

51. Sprat, Thomas, *History of the Royal Society of London for the Improvement of Natural Knowledge* (London, 1667), reprint, ed. Cope, Jackson I., and Jones, Harold, W., University of Washington, 1958.

52. For the Civil War period, see Trevor Davies, R., *Four Centuries of Witch Beliefs. With Special Reference to the Great Rebellion*, Methuen, 1972.

53. For aristocratic witches and seven kings who practised the 'old religion', see Ericson, Eric, *The World, the Flesh, the Devil. A Biographical Dictionary of Witches*, Mayflower Books, 1981; see also Burke, Peter, *Popular Culture in Early Modern Europe*, T. Smith, 1978.

54. Burke, *op. cit.*; Ginzburg, Carlo, *The Night Battles, Witchcraft & Agrarian Cults in the Sixteenth & Seventeenth Centuries*, Penguin Books, 1985; Sjoo, Monica, and Mor, Barbara, *The Great Cosmic Mother. Rediscovering the Religion of the Earth*, Harper & Row, 1987.

55. As a number of historians have noted, asylums for the insane began only in the eighteenth century.

56. Berry, Wendell, *The Unsettling of America, Culture and Agriculture*, Avon Books, 1978.

57. *ibid.*

58. Burke, *op. cit.*; compare Duerr, *op. cit.* p. 60.

59. Compare Burke's comment that some Protestants were against the very idea of a festival (*op. cit.*).

60. *ibid.* Compare More, Henry, *Enthusiasmus Triumphatus; or a Brief Discourse of the Nature, Kinds, and Cure of Enthusiasm* (London 1656), reprint William Andrews Clarke, Los Angeles, 1966.

61. *ibid.*

62. *ibid.*; Beloff, Max, *Public Order and Popular Disturbances, 1660–1714*, Oxford, 1938.

63. Burke, *op. cit.*

64. Shaw, W.A., *A History of the English Church during the Civil War and Under the Commonwealth 1640–1660*, Vol. 1, Longman, Green and Co., 1900.

65. Michell, John, *The Old Stones at Land's End, An Enquiry into the Mysteries of the Megalithic Science*, Pentacle Books, 1979, citing Borlase. Also, private communication from John Michell. Other stones met violent ends in the seventeenth century. See, for example, Grinsell, *op. cit.*

66. Stukely, William, M.D., *Abury, A Temple of the British Druids. . . .*, London, 1743.

67. The best biography of Newton is Westfall, Richard S., *Never at Rest. A Biography of Isaac Newton*, Cambridge University Press, 1980. On his attraction and repulsion to Cartesianism, see especially Koyre, Alexandre, *Newtonian Studies*, Chapman and Hall, 1965.

68. This is found in his Questiones quaedam Philosophiae, Cambridge University Library, Ms. Add 3996, fol. 85–135. A discussion of the notebook is found in Westfall, Richard S., 'The Foundations of Newton's Philosophy of Nature', *British Journal for the History of Science* 1, 1962; Hall, A.R., Sir Isaac Newton's Notebook, 1661–65, *Cambridge Historical Journal* 9, 1948. The notebook itself has recently been published, with extensive commentary, as *Certain Philosophical Questions. Newton's Trinity Notebook*, ed. McGuire, J.E., and Tamny, Martin, Cambridge University Press, 1983.

69. Newton, Isaac, *de Gravitatione* in Boas Hall, Marie, and Hall, A.R., ed. *Unpublished Scientific Papers of Isaac Newton*, Cambridge University Press, 1962.

70. Newton's biological notions are discussed by Henry Guerlac in 'Theological Voluntarism and Biological Analogies in Newton's Physical Thought', *Journal of the History of Ideas* 44, 1983. The discussion of Newton's alchemy draws upon Westfall's biography, *op. cit.*; Teeter Dobbs, Betty Jo, *The Foundations of Newton's Alchemy, or, The Hunting of the Green Lyon*, Cambridge, 1975; and Rattansi, P.M., 'Newton's Alchemical Studies', in *Science, Medicine and Society in the Renaissance. Essays to Honor Walter Pagel*, ed. Debus, Allen G., New York, 1972, Vol. 2. *The Vegetation of Metals* is found in Bundy Ms 16.

71. This distinction, although sometimes using different terminology, was a central concern for Newton throughout his career.

72. Bundy Ms 16. See also *The Correspondence of Isaac Newton*, ed. Turnbull, H.W. *et al.*, Cambridge University Press, 1959, Vol. I. Henry More singled out the need of the stars for nourishment, which Newton also asserted, as a Paracelsian doctrine. (More, *op. cit.*)

73. Westfall, *op. cit.*

74. *ibid.*

75. Quoted in *ibid.* p. 371. Compare p. 363.

76. *ibid.*

77. Cambridge University Library, Ms. 3970, fols, 619^r–620^v.

78. Such hints are found throughout the Queries to the *Opticks* and in the famous General Scholium to the *Principia*, as well as in scattered places in the unpublished manuscripts.

79. The discussion of Newton's changed notion of the qualities of matter draws upon McGuire, J.E., 'The Origin of Newton's Doctrine of Essential Qualities', *Centaurus* 12, 1968.

80. Hooke's cosmogony in relation to Newton is the subject of Kubrin, David, "'Such an Impertinently Litigious Lady', Hooke's 'Great Pretending' vs. Newton's *Principia*, & Newton's and Halley's Theory of Comets," to be published in *On the Shoulders of Giants*, ed. Thrower, Norman, University of California Press, 1990.

81. Kubrin has treated Newton's hidden cosmogony in his 'Newton and the Cyclical Cosmos: Providence and the Mechanical Philosophy', *Journal of the History of Ideas* 28, 1967, and in his Cornell dissertation, 'Providence and the Mechanical Philosophy. The Creation and Dissolution of the World in Newtonian Thought. A Study of the Relations of Science and Religion in Seventeenth Century England', Ithaca, 1968. See Newton, *Opticks or A Treatise of the Reflections, Refractions, Inflections & Colours of Light*, Dover, 1952.

82. The discussion of Toland draws upon Jacob, Margaret C., 'John Toland and the Newtonian Ideology', *Journal of the Warburg and Courtauld Institutes* 22, 1969.

83. Bord, Janet and Colin, *op. cit.* See also Hall, Thomas, *Funebria Florae, The Downfall of May Games: Wherein Is Set forth the Rudeness, Prophaneness, Stealing, Drinking, Fighting, Dancing, Whoring, Misrule, Misspence of Precious Time. . . .*, London, 1661.

84. Westfall, *Never at Rest, op. cit.*

85. *ibid.* Letters passed between Locke and Newton, after Boyle's death, regarding the portion each man had of Boyle's secret alchemical recipes; see Newton's *Correspondence*.

86. Duerr, *op. cit.*

CHAPTER THREE

1. Playfair, Guy Lyon, and Hill, Scott, *The Cycles of Heaven* (1978), Avon edition, 1979.

2. Tompkins, Peter, and Bird, Christopher, *The Secret Life of Plants* (1973, 1974), Penguin edition, 1975.

3. Frankel, Richard, B., 'Magnetic Guidance of Organisms', *Ann. Rev. Biophys. Bioeng*, 1984.
4. Gauquelin, Michel, *The Cosmic Clocks* (1967), Granada edition, 1973.
5. Baker, Robin, ed. *The Mystery of Migration*, Macdonald Futura, 1980.
6. Becker, Robert O., and Selden, Gary, *The Body Electric*, William Morrow, 1985.
7. Bird, Christopher, *Divining* (1979), Macdonald and Jane's edition, 1980.
8. Beal, James B., 'The New Biotechnology', *Frontiers of Consciousness* (John White, ed.), Avon, 1974.
9. Shallis, Michael, *The Electric Shock Book*, Souvenir Press, 1988.
10. Becker and Selden, 1985, *op. cit.*
11. Playfair and Hill, 1978, *op. cit.*
12. Cade, C. Maxwell, and Coxhead, Nona, *The Awakened Mind* (1979), Element edition, 1987.
13. Becker and Selden, 1985, *op. cit.*
14. Watson, Lyall, *Earthworks*, Hodder and Stoughton, 1986.
15. Sheldrake, Rupert, *The Presence of the Past*, Collins, 1988.
16. Becker and Selden, 1985, *op. cit.*
17. Watson, Lyall, *Supernature* (1973), Coronet edition, 1974.
18. Sheldrake, 1988, *op. cit.*
19. Sheldrake, 1988, *op. cit.*
20. Including, amongst several others:
    Schaut, G.B., and Persinger, M.A., 'Global Geomagnetic Activity During Spontaneous Paranormal Experiences: A Replication', *Perceptual and Motor Skills*, 61, 1985;
    Persinger, M.A., 'Geomagnetic Factors in Subjective Telepathic, Precognitive and Postmortem Experiences', *Journal* of the American Society of Psychic Research, 82, July 1988.
21. Persinger, M.A., 'Spontaneous Telepathic Experience from "Phantasms of the Living" and Low Global Geomagnetic Activity', *Journal* of the ASPR, 81, January 1987.
22. Persinger, M.A., 'Subjective Telepathic Experiences, Geomagnetic Activity and the ELF Hypotheses', *PSI Research*, June 1985.
23. Teyler, T.J., and DiScenna, P., 'The Topological Anatomy of the Hippocampus: a Clue to its Function', *Brain Research Bulletin*, Vol. 12, 1984.
24. Persinger, June 1985, *op. cit.*
25. Puharich, Andrija, *Beyond Telepathy* (1962), Picador edition, 1973.
26. Watson, Lyall, 1973, *op. cit.*
27. Becker and Selden, 1985, *op. cit.*

CHAPTER FOUR

1. Swentzell, Rina, 'An Understated Sacredness', *MASS*, University of New Mexico.
2. Crow, W.B., *A History of Magic, Witchcraft and Occultism*, Aquarian Press, 1968.
3. Pennick, Nigel, and Devereux, Paul, *Lines on the Landscape*, Hale, 1989.
4. Renfrew, Colin, *Before Civilization*, Cape, 1973.
5. Thom, A., *Megalithic Sites in Britain*, OUP, 1967.
6. Argüelles, José, *The Mayan Factor*, Bear, 1987.
7. Michell, John, *Megalithomania*, Thames and Hudson, 1982.
8. Critchlow, Keith, *Time Stands Still*, Gordon Fraser, 1979.
9. Glover, John, 'Paths of Shadow and Light', *The Ley Hunter*, 84, Winter 1979.
10. Brennan, Martin, *The Stars and the Stones*, Thames and Hudson, 1983.
11. Krupp, E.C., *Echoes of the Ancient Skies*, Harper and Row, 1983.
12. *ibid.*
13. Glover, John, in *The Ley Hunter*, 94, Autumn, 1982.
14. Woodley, Helen, 'Where Stones Touch the Sky', *Meyn Mamvro*, 4.
15. *Field Monuments in the National Park*, Brecon Beacons National Park Committee, 1983.
16. Burl, Aubrey, *Stone Circles of the British Isles*, Yale, 1976.
17. Pennick and Devereux, 1989, *op. cit.*
18. Kincaid, Chris, ed. *Chaco Roads Project, Phase I*, U.S. Bureau of Land Management, Albuquerque, 1983.
19. Discussed in depth in *Lines on the Landscape*, 1989, *op. cit.*
20. Méreaux, Pierre, and the KADATH team, *Carnac – une porte vers l'inconnu*, Laffont, 1981.
21. Michell, John, *The View Over Atlantis*, Sago Press, 1969.
22. Devereux, Paul, *Earth Lights*, Turnstone, 1982.
23. Pryce, William, *Mineralogia Cornubriensis*, 1778.
24. Persinger, Michael, and Lafrenière, Gyslaine, *Space-Time Transients and Unusual Events*, Nelson Hall, 1977. (And many papers by Persinger in *Perceptual and Motor Skills.*)
25. Devereux, 1982, *op. cit.*
26. Devereux, P., McCartney, P., Robins, D., 'Bringing UFOs Down to Earth', *New Scientist*, September 1, 1983.
27. Derr, J.S., and Persinger, M.A., 'Luminous Phenomena and Earthquakes in Southern Washington', *Experientia*, 42, 1986.
28. Devereux, Paul, *Earth Lights Revelation*, Blandford, 1989. (This contains an extensive and up-to-date bibliography on the subject, and fully

recounts the nature of the phenomenon, and all or most of the key research projects that have so far gone into the study of the lights.)

29. Devereux, Paul, *Places of Power*, Blandford (in press).
30. *ibid.*
31. Robins, Don, *Circles of Silence*, Souvenir, 1985.
32. The Dragon Project Trust, Box 5, Brecon, Powys, Wales, U.K.
33. Hitching, Francis, *Earth Magic*, Cassell, 1976.
34. Brooker, Charles, 'Magnetism and the Standing Stones', *New Scientist*, January 13, 1983.
35. In a series of articles by Keith Stevenson (pen name 'Llowarch') in *The Cambrian News*.
36. Devereux, *Places of Power*, *op. cit.*
37. Méreaux, Pierre, 1981, *op. cit.*
38. *Living with Radiation*, NRPB, 1981 edition.
39. Robins, Don, 'The Dragon Project and the Talking Stones', *New Scientist*, October 21, 1982.
40. Michie, U. McL., and Cooper, D.C., *Uranium in the Old Red Sandstone of Orkney*, HMSO, 1979.
41. Lemesurier, Peter, *The Great Pyramid Decoded*, Compton Press, 1977.
42. More complete facts and figures are given in *Places of Power*, *op. cit.*
43. Pepper, Elizabeth, and Wilcock, John, *Magical and Mystical Sites* (1976), BCA edition, 1977.
44. Barnatt, John, personal comment (full account in *Places of Power*).
45. Larkman, Brian, personal comment (full account in *Places of Power*).
46. May, Jo, personal comment (full account in *Places of Power*).
47. 'Radon Mines', *Newsnight*, CNN, November 22, 1987.
48. Dem, Marc, *Megaliths et Routes Secretes de l'Uranium*, Michel, 1977.
49. Merz, Blanche, *Points of Cosmic Energy* (1983, 1985), C.W. Daniel edition, 1987.
50. Niehardt, John G., *Black Elk Speaks* (1932, 1959), Pocket Books edition, 1972.
51. Luce, Cynthia Newby, 'Brazilian Spooklights', *Fortean Times*, 49, 1987, and in personal communication to Andy Roberts (editor, *UFO Brigantia*), February 1988, shown to Devereux.

CHAPTER FIVE

1. Sayers, Michael, in interview with Paul Devereux, New York, 1988.
2. Russell, G.W. ('AE'), 'At the Dawn of the Kaliyuga', *The Irish Theosophist*, October 1893.

3. —, 'The Awakening of the Fires', *The Irish Theosophist*, January/February 1897.
4. Shepard, Leslie, in the Introduction to the University Books (1965) edition of *The Candle of Vision*.
5. Russell, G.W. ('AE'), *Song and its Fountains* (1932), in the Colin Smythe edition *The Descent of the Gods – The Mystical Writings of G.W. Russell – AE* (Raghavan and Nandini Iyer, eds.), 1988.
6. Russell, G.W. ('AE'), *The Candle of Vision* (1918), Colin Smythe edition, 1988.
7. *ibid.*
8. *ibid.*
9. *ibid.*
10. *ibid.*
11. *Song and its Fountains.*
12. *The Candle of Vision.*
13. Wentz, W.Y. Evans, *The Fairy Faith in Celtic Countries* (1911), Colin Smythe edition, 1977.
14. *The Candle of Vision.*
15. Strieber, Whitley, *Communion*, Century Hutchinson, 1987.
16. Quoted by Neville Braybrooke in 'The Vision of Teilhard de Chardin' in *Teilhard de Chardin: Pilgrim of the Future*, ed. N. Braybrooke (1964), Libra edition, 1965.
17. *ibid.*
18. *ibid.*
19. Teilhard de Chardin, Pierre, *The Phenomenon of Man* (1955), Collins edition, 1959.
20. —, *Human Energy* (1962), Collins edition, 1969.
21. —, Lecture at French Embassy in Peking, 1945, quoted in *The Future of Man* (1959), Fontana.
22. *ibid.*
23. *ibid.*
24. *The Phenomenon of Man.*
25. Teilhard de Chardin, Pierre, in *Revue des Questions Scientifiques*, January 1947 (reprinted in *The Future of Man*).
26. *Human Energy.*
27. *ibid.*
28. Teilhard de Chardin, Pierre, 1947, reprinted in *The Future of Man.*
29. Huxley, Julian, in his 1958 introduction to *The Phenomenon of Man.*
30. *The Phenomenon of Man.*
31. Russell, Peter, *The Awakening Earth*, RKP, 1982.
32. Lovelock, J.E., 'The Independent Practice of Science', *CoEvolution*

Quarterly, Vol. 25, 1980.

33. *Time*, January 2, 1989.

34. Lovelock, J.E., 'Stand Up For Gaia'. (Transcript from the Schumacher Lectures 1988). *Resurgence*, No. 132, 1988.

35. *ibid.*

36. Lovelock, J.E., *The Ages of Gaia*, W.W. Norton & Company, 1988.

37. Lovelock, J.E., 'The Evolving Gaia Hypothesis', in *Proceedings of the Conference 'Is the Earth a Living Organism?'* (August 1–6, 1985) held at the University of Massachusetts, Amherst. Published by the National Audubon Expedition Institute, Sharon, Connecticut, 1985.

38. Lovelock, J.E., 'Gaia as seen through the atmosphere', *Atmospheric Environment*, 6, 1972.

39. Lovelock, J.E., *Gaia: A New Look at Life on Earth*, Oxford University Press, 1979.

40. *ibid.*

41. *ibid.*

42. Lovelock, J.E., 1988; panel discussion in *GAIA, the Thesis, the Mechanisms and the Implications*, eds. Bunyard, P., and Goldsmith, E. Proceedings of the First Annual Camelford Conference on the Implications of the Gaia Hypothesis, Wadebridge Ecological Centre, Worthyvale Manor, Camelford, Cornwall.

43. Lovelock, J.E., *The Ages of Gaia, op. cit.*

44. *ibid.*

45. *ibid.*

46. Hutton, J., 1788, 'Theory of the Earth; or an investigation of the laws observable in the composition, dissolution, and restoration of land upon the globe.' *Royal Society of Edinburgh, Tr.*, 1. Quoted in Lovelock, J.E., 1988, 'The Gaia Hypothesis' in *GAIA, the Thesis, the Mechanisms and the Implications, op. cit.*

47. Lovelock, J.E., *The Ages of Gaia, op. cit.*

48. Lovelock, J.E., 'Geophysiology, the Science of Gaia,' presented at the *American Geophysical Union Chapman Conference on the Gaia Hypothesis*, San Diego, California, March 1988.

49. Lovelock, J.E., 'New Views of the Earth', New Dimensions Foundation radio interview, November 10, 1988, San Francisco, California.

50. Lovelock, J.E., *The Ages of Gaia, op. cit.*

51. Doolittle, W.F., 'Is Nature Really Motherly?', *CoEvolution Quarterly*, Vol. 29, 1981.

52. Dawkins, R., *The Extended Phenotype*, Freeman, 1982.

53. Lovelock, J.E., *The Ages of Gaia, op. cit.*

54. *ibid.*

55. Lovelock, J.E., 1988, panel discussion in *GAIA, the Thesis, the Mechanisms and the Implications, op. cit.*

56. Lovelock, J.E., *The Ages of Gaia, op. cit.* In *New Scientist,* December 18, 1986, Lovelock remarked that 'Michael Whitfield, Andrew Watson and I proposed that the puzzling constancy of the Earth's temperature since life began, despite a 25 per cent increase in the output of the Sun, was attributable to the ability of living organisms to regulate the amount of carbon dioxide in the air. As the Sun warmed up, so organisms drained carbon dioxide from the air with an ever increasing efficiency, so that this gas is about a thousand times less abundant than it was at the beginning of life'.

57. Lemonick, M., 'Feeling the Heat', *Time,* January 2, 1989.

58. In 1961 Steele worked as a laboratory assistant on an atmospheric geochemistry project at Scripps Institute of Oceanography in California, birthplace of the greenhouse warming theory. He was monitoring the increase of carbon dioxide in the air. He told a visiting reporter about the trend of global warming and the possibility of the polar ice caps melting. His superiors were angry because he had alarmed the reporter. They asked him not to say anything else about it. Times have changed.

59. Lovelock, J.E., *The Ages of Gaia, op. cit.*

60. Lovelock, J.E., 'Stand Up for Gaia', *op. cit.*

61. Lovelock, J.E., 'New Views of the Earth', *op. cit.*

62. Lovelock, J.E., 'Stand Up for Gaia', *op. cit.*

63. Lovelock, J.E., *The Ages of Gaia, op. cit.*

64. Lovelock, J.E., 'New Views of the Earth', *op. cit.*

65. Margulis, L., response to Ford Doolittle's article 'Is Nature Really Motherly?', *CoEvolution Quarterly,* Vol. 29, 1981.

66. Boston, P., 'Gaia: A New Look at Global Ecology and Evolution', presented at the American Geophysical Union Chapman Conference on the Gaia Hypothesis, San Diego, California, March 1988.

67. Swimme, B., *The Universe is a Green Dragon,* Bear & Co., 1984. Quoted in Thomas Berry's paper, 'Human Presence to the Earth', in *Proceedings of the Conference 'Is the Earth a Living Organism?', op. cit.*

68. Swan, J., 'Sacred Places', *Shaman's Drum,* Winter 1986.

69. Lovelock, J.E., *The Ages of Gaia, op. cit.*

70. Lovelock, J.E., 'New Views of the Earth', *op. cit.*

71. Lovelock, J.E., *The Ages of Gaia, op. cit.* In the same work he stated that: 'True knowledge can never be gained by attributing "purpose" to phenomena. But equally strongly, I deny the notion that systems are never more than the sum of their parts.'

72. Lovelock, J.E., *The Ages of Gaia, op. cit.*

73. Lovelock, J.E., 'New Views of the Earth', *op. cit.*
74. Lovelock, J.E., *Gaia: A New Look at Life on Earth*, *op. cit.*
75. Bateson, G., 1972, 'Pathologies of Epistemology', *Steps To An Ecology Of Mind*, Ballantine Books, 1974.
76. Bateson, G., 1972, 'Form, Substance and Difference', *Steps To An Ecology Of Mind*, *op. cit.*
77. Dynamic system memory is illuminated by what general systems theorist Eric Jantsch called a 'holistic system memory which appears already at the level of chemical reaction systems. The system "remembers" the initial conditions which made a particular development possible, the beginnings of each new structure in its evolution not in separable details, but in a sequence of holistic autopoietic regimes'. *The Self-organizing Universe*, Pergammon Press, 1980.
78. Lovelock, J.E., *The Ages of Gaia*, *op. cit.*
79. *ibid.*
80. *ibid.*
81. *ibid.*
82. Lovelock, J.E., *Gaia: A New Look at Life on Earth*, *op. cit.*
83. *ibid.*
84. Bateson, G., 'Form, Substance and Difference'. *op. cit.* Quoted by Lovelock in *The Ages of Gaia*.

CHAPTER SIX

1. Russell, Peter, *The Awakening Earth*, RKP, 1982.
2. Leary, Timothy, *Psychedelic Prayers*, Poets Press, 1966.
3. Pagels, Heinz R., *The Cosmic Code* (1982), Bantam edition, 1983.
4. Smith, C.W., 'High-Sensitivity Biosensors and Weak Environmental Stimuli', *International Industrial Biotechnology*, April/May 1986.
5. Watson, Lyall, *Supernature* (1973), Coronet edition, 1974.
6. Lieber, Arnold, *The Lunar Effect* (1978), Corgi edition, 1979.
7. Skinner, Stephen, *The Living Earth Manual of Feng Shui*, RKP, 1982.
8. Anderson, H.E., and Reid, B.L., 'Vicinal, Long Range and Extremely Long Range Effects on Growth of Sodium Chloride Crystals from Aqueous Solutions Containing Protein', *Applied Physics Communications*, 4 (2–3), 1984.
9. Johnson, Raynor, C., *The Light and the Gate*, Hodder and Stoughton, 1964.
10. Bentov, Itzhak, *Stalking the Wild Pendulum* (1977), Bantam edition, 1979.
11. Fraser, J.T., *Time – The Familiar Stranger*, Tempus, 1987.

12. Becker, Robert O., and Selden, Gary, *The Body Electric*, William Morrow, 1985.
13. See Mircea Eliade's *Shamanism* (1951, 1964), for example.
14. Watson, Lyall, *Earthworks*, Hodder and Stoughton, 1986.
15. Gauquelin, Michel, *The Cosmic Clocks* (1967), Granada edition, 1973.
16. Watson, Lyall, 1986, *op. cit.*
17. Benveniste, J., *et al*, 'Human Basophil Degranulation Triggered by Very Dilute Antiserum Against IgE', *Nature*, June 30, 1988.
18. Maddox, J., 'When to Believe the Unbelievable', *ibid.*
19. Shallis, Michael, *The Electric Shock Book*, Souvenir Press, 1988.
20. Smith, C.W., 'Water – Friend or Foe?', *Laboratory Practice*, October 1985.
21. Wolf, Fred Alan, *Mind and the New Physics* (1984), Heinemann edition, 1985.
22. Watson, Lyall, 1986, *op. cit.*
23. Snider, Jerry, and Daab, Richard, 'The Advocacy of Marcel Vogel', *Magical Blend.*
24. Bird, Chris, 'Latest from the Front', American Society of Dowsers' *Journal*, Winter 1988.
25. Skinner, Stephen, 1982, *op. cit.*
26. Cooper, J.C., *An Illustrated Encyclopaedia of Traditional Symbols*, Thames and Hudson, 1978.
27. Branigan, K., ed. *The Atlas of Archaeology*, Macdonald, 1982.
28. Hersh, James, 'Ancient Celtic Incubation', *Sundance Community Dream Journal*, Winter 1979.
29. Leroy-Gourham, Arlette, 'The Flowers Found with Shanidar IV, a Neanderthal Burial in Iraq', *Science*, November 7, 1975.
30. Dr Paul Mankowicz via personal communication from Professor Bethe Hagens.
31. Jeff Gaines quoted by T. McKenna in *ReVision*, Spring 1988.
32. Kalweit, Holger, *Dreamtime and Inner Space*, Shambhala, 1988.
33. *ibid.*
34. Villoldo, Alberto, and Krippner, Stanley, *Healing States*, Simon and Schuster, 1987.
35. McKenna, Terence, 'Hallucinogenic Mushrooms and Evolution', *ReVision*, Vol. 10, No. 4. Spring 1988.
36. Kalweit, Holger, 1988, *op. cit.*
37. Paul Devereux's *Places of Power* (Blandford, London; in press) gives full details of those that have so far been identified.
38. See further discussion of this in *Places of Power, op. cit.*
39. Cooper, J.C., 1978, *op. cit.*
40. McClure, Kevin, *The Evidence for Visions of the Virgin Mary*, Aquarian

Press, 1983.

41. Devereux, Paul, *Earth Lights Revelation*, Blandford, 1989.

42. Hitching, Francis, *The World Atlas of Mysteries*, Collins, 1978.

43. Persinger, Michael, and Lafrenière, Gyslaine, *Space-time Transients and Unusual Events*, Nelson-Hall, 1977. (Also many papers from the 1970s to the present by Persinger, and Persinger and associates, particularly in *Perceptual and Motor Skills*).

44. Derr, J.S., and Persinger, M.A., 'Luminous Phenomena and Earthquakes in Southern Washington', *Experienta*, 42, 1986.

45. Persinger, M.A., and Derr, J.S., 'Relations Between UFO Reports Within the Uinta Basin and Local Seismicity', *Perceptual and Motor Skills*, 60, 1985.

46. Mattsson, Dan, 'UFOs in Time and Space', AFU *Newsletter*, 27, 1985.

47. Mattsson, Dan, and Persinger, M.A., 'Positive Correlations Between Numbers of UFO Reports and Earthquake Activity in Sweden', *Perceptual and Motor Skills*, 63, 1986.

48. *Earth Lights Revelation, op. cit.*

49. Persinger, M.A., 'Clinical Consequences of Close Proximity to UFO-Related Luminosities', *Perceptual and Motor Skills*, 56, 1983.

50. Brady, Brian T., and Rowell, Glen A., 'The Laboratory Investigation of the Electrodynamics of Rock Fracture', *Nature*, May 29, 1986.

51. *Places of Power, op. cit.*

52. Salisbury, Frank, B., *The Utah UFO Display*, Devin Adair, 1974.

53. Rutledge, Harley, *Project Identification*, Prentice Hall, 1981.

ACKNOWLEDGEMENTS

Paul Devereux

First and foremost I wish to thank contributing authors John Steele and David Kubrin. John wrote Chapter 1 and the James Lovelock material in Chapter 5. John and I had many pleasant and productive exchanges of views during his time with the Dragon Project (see Chapter 4), and during the earlier stages of preparation for this book. David has kindly contributed Chapter 2, developed specially from his own doctorate research. I have written the rest of the work, and while I feel John and David will be largely in sympathy with it, they must not necessarily be held responsible for all the ideas and views I have expressed – and that qualification naturally applies also to those whose material I have quoted and referred to.

I thank Colin Smythe for giving me permission to quote extensively from the works of G.W. Russell (AE). Thanks too to Robin Williamson (formerly of the Incredible String Band) for allowing me to quote from one of his songs. Other quotations I have used in this book are within the usual permissible extents and are all duly credited, but I nevertheless wish to extend my appreciation to all those concerned.

For help with items of information and research sources I thank Chris Ashton, John Barnatt, Paul Bennett, David Clarke, Michael de Styrcea, Cosimo and Ann Favaloro, Bethe Hagens, Rodney Hale, David Ironside, Brian Larkman, Jo May, Paul McCartney, Nigel Pennick, Michael Persinger, Trish Pfeiffer, Bevan Reid, Andy Roberts, Bill Rudersdorf, George Sandwith, Michael Sayers, Michael Shallis, Jeanne Sheridan, Keith Stevenson, Caroline Wise, and the numerous volunteer fieldworkers on the Dragon Project. Many other people have contributed insights and information over the years, which inevitably find their way into works with a scope such as this present book displays. My gratitude to them all.

Albert Li and my son Solomon helped greatly with the mysteries of computer modem interaction across the globe. Thanks to them and also to PeaceNet (USA) and GreenNet (UK) for providing global electronic communication facilities. My thanks also to our agent Jonathan Tootell.

Finally, I owe a debt of gratitude to my wife Charla for being the catalyst who caused me to get this project rolling at last, and for being such a support throughout the project.

John Steele

I would like to express my grateful appreciation to Marija Gimbutas, Chris and Leila Castle, Donald Hughes, Jim Swan, Terence McKenna, Rupert

Sheldrake, Joan Price, Ami Markel, Michael Poe, Dave Ironside, Richard Bird and other friends too numerous to mention. Special thanks to Dr and Mrs Burns Steele, Gigi Coyle and Albert Li.

David Kubrin
I would like to acknowledge the help of the following: Anne Brannen, Barbara Clow (of Bear and Co., publishers), Carolyn Merchant, John Michell, Arthur Evans, Starhawk, Rose May Dance, and Riva Enteen.

INDEX